WE'RE
ON

WE'RE ON

A

JUNE JORDAN

Reader

EDITED BY CHRISTOPH KELLER & JAN HELLER LEVI
Introduction by Rachel Eliza Griffiths

10 9 8 7 6 5 4 3 2 1

Alice James Books are published by Alice James Poetry Cooperative, Inc., an affiliate of the University of Maine at Farmington.

Alice James Books
114 Prescott Street
Farmington, ME 04938
www.alicejamesbooks.org

Library of Congress Cataloging-in-Publication Data

Names: Jordan, June, 1936-2002, author. | Keller, Christoph, 1963- editor. |
    Levi, Jan Heller, editor. | Griffiths, Rachel Eliza, writer of
    introduction.
Title: We're on : a June Jordan reader / edited by Christoph Keller & Jan
    Heller Levi ; introduction by Rachel Eliza Griffiths.
Other titles: We are on
Description: Farmington, ME : Alice James Books, [2017]
Identifiers: LCCN 2017015981 (print) | LCCN 2017028264 (ebook) | ISBN
    9781938584459 (eBook) | ISBN 9781938584350 (paperback)
Subjects: | BISAC: LITERARY COLLECTIONS / American / General. | POETRY /
    American / African American.
Classification: LCC PS3560.O73 (ebook) | LCC PS3560.O73 A6 2017 (print) | DDC
    818/.5409--dc23
LC record available at https://lccn.loc.gov/2017015981

Alice James Books gratefully acknowledges support from individual donors, private foundations, the University of Maine at Farmington, the National Endowment for the Arts, and the Amazon Literary Partnership.

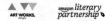

WORKS BY JUNE JORDAN (A PARTIAL LIST)

POETRY

Who Look at Me (1969)
Some Changes (1967, 1971)
New Days: Poems of Exile and Return (1974)
Things that I Do in the Dark: New and Selected Poems (1977)
Passion: New Poems 1977-1980 (1980)
Living Room: New Poems (1985)
Lyrical Campaigns: Selected Poems (1989)
Naming Our Destiny: New and Selected Poems (1989)
Haruko/Love Poems: New and Selected Love Poems (1993)
Kissing God Goodbye: Poems 1991-1997 (1997)
Directed by Desire: The Collected Poems of June Jordan,
    edited by Jan Heller Levi and Sara Miles (2005)

ESSAYS

Civil Wars: Observations from the Front Lines of America (1981)
On Call: Political Essays (1985)
Moving Towards Home: Selected Political Essays (1989)
*Technical Difficulties: African-American Notes on the State of the
    Union* (1992)
Affirmative Acts: Political Essays (1998)
Some of Us Did Not Die: New and Selected Essays (2002)
Life as Activism: June Jordan's Writings from The Progressive, edited
    by Stacy Russo (2014)

YOUNG ADULT NOVEL

His Own Where (1971)

PLAYS/LIBRETTI

The Issue (The Arrow That Flies By Day) (1981)
Bang Bang Über Alles (1986)
All These Blessings (1989)
I Was Looking at the Ceiling and Then I Saw the Sky (1995)

TEACHING
June Jordan's Poetry for the People: A Revolutionary Blueprint (1995)

MEMOIR
Soldier: A Poet's Childhood (2000)

ANTHOLOGIES
soulscript, Afro-American Poetry (1970)
The Voice of the Children, with Terri Bush (1970)

CHILDREN'S BOOKS
Fannie Lou Hamer (1972)
Dry Victories (1972)
New Life: New Room, illustrated by Ray Cruz (1975)
Kimako's Story, illustrated by Kay Burford (1981)

My life seems to be an increasing revelation of the intimate face of universal struggle. You begin with your family and the kids on the block, and next you open your eyes to what you call your people and that leads you into land reform into Black English into Angola leads you back to your own bed where you lie by yourself, wondering if you deserve to be peaceful, or trusted or desired or left to the freedom of your own unfaltering heart. And the scale shrinks to the side of a skull: your own interior cage.

And then if you're lucky, and I have been lucky, everything comes back to you. And then you know why one of the freedom fighters in the sixties, a young Black woman interviewed shortly after she was beaten up for riding near the front of an interstate bus—you know why she said, "We are all so very happy."

It's because it's on. All of us and me by myself: we're on.

—June Jordan, 1981

PRAISE FOR *WE'RE ON: A JUNE JORDAN READER*

"I can think of no writer more committed to making space for our voices in the world, and I can say without doubt my life in poetry—all it has been, all I dream it to be—would be impossible without June Jordan making that space. And I know I am one of many. We're like a big choir, singing because June Jordan showed us how." —Ross Gay

"Here she is in her many facets: a great American woman of letters, a Renaissance woman/ writer/ poet/ prophet/ intellectual/ satirist/ linguist/ storyteller/ teacher / absolutely free spirit, here to say 'I am black alive and looking back at you,' here 'to start the song//to stop the scream,' pursuing the dream 'into pride and poems,' as much in love with the force and sass and slide of language as with truth and justice—June Jordan will be staying alive far into everyone's future." —Alicia Ostriker

"When I'm asked if I think poetry can really do something, really matter, I think of June Jordan. When I'm asked if poetry can truly change things, change a person, I think of June Jordan. And now, when someone is on the brink of giving up on poetry because they think language has no power anymore, no guts anymore, I will give them this brilliant new June Jordan Reader and they will, no doubt, find their faith and courage again." —Ada Límon

"June Jordan's transformative work challenges us, still, to examine the complexities of individual oppression—politicizing our human experiences in a way that mothers revolutionaries into existence. Jordan's ferocious critique of power and politeness manifested into a refusal to sanitize the world's atrocities; a timeless phenomenon we must continue today in the fight for visibility and survival." —Rachel McKibbens

"June Jordan is our consummate word warrior. Her versatility and veracity has enthralled generations with the genius and generosity of her literary lion's he(art) With Jordan the personal is the political and the political has never been more beautiful and prescient as these precarious times. Jordan's poetry and prose claimed Black lives mattered before it became destiny and determination for a generation. Whether she's writing about Phillis Wheatley,

Palestine, Kimako or DeLiza—or waxing poetic about her rights, June Jordan's soulscript is as necessary and nourishing as bread, water, and breathing. Her own where is where it has always been—among the people." —Tony Medina

"*We're On: A June Jordan Reader* brings us up close to this indispensable writer who,with the fearlessness of her words and physical presence was indefatigable in defying the diction and actions of the powerful. This anthology of Jordan's collected writings could not have arrived at a better moment. It is timely reminder of how fiercely she believed that we are always the people we are waiting for." —Wesley Brown

"Political, personal, funny and tragic—June Jordan's voice is individual, indomitable. This book is a gift that can power a revolution-- open, read, change the world. If you are looking for a gateway poet, a way to turn people onto the art, June Jordan is your go to. Simply the fiercest poet around."—Bob Holman

"This collection might be instead a meeting at a motel in a dowdy part of town where a cocktail party is being held in the June Jordan Cerebral Ultimatum Suite. Emma Goldman and Sojourner Truth show up together, arm in arm. Joe Hill, replete with firing squad wounds is right behind them carrying a jug of moonshine. Emily Dickinson, Phillis Wheatley, and Homer himself come together singing rounds of verse. It is meant to be and is a celebration of the victory of the heart and mind over dollars and blindness. Read this book; read it five times and a seed will be planted that will grow into elegant revolution." —Walter Mosley

"June Jordan's intelligent passion and fierce spirit of resistance, more needful now than ever, speak through this gorgeous collection. Christoph Keller and Jan Heller Levi have chosen work that reveals Jordan's range and depth, and their incisive comments provide valuable context. There is fresh news here, not only for Jordan's newest readers but also for those of us privileged to have heard the wild honey of her musical, prophetic voice." —Joan Larkin

"Times in which we can access our own outrage but cannot find our way into speech or poems, I think I miss June Jordan most of all. How exquisite her ability to—urge and need to—write out of a crisis at hand. How much it helped us. How I miss her voice, her vision, her revolutionary love. How fortunate we are to have these beloved poems and essays." —Donna Masini

PREVIOUS PRAISE FOR JUNE JORDAN:

"In political journalism that cuts like razors, in essays that blast the darkness of confusion with relentless light; in poetry that looks as closely into lilac buds as into death's mouth.... she has comforted, explained, described, wrestled with, taught and made us laugh out loud before we wept... I am talking about a span of forty years of tireless activism coupled with and fueled by flawless art." —Toni Morrison

"June Jordan's work, at this point and for many years now, is perfect. ... She manages to tap that place where race and sexuality, class and justice, gender and memory come together. She doesn't go with the cutting-edge idea but reaches for that difficult terrain where others may fear to tread." —Margaret Randall, *American Book Review* (1993)

"Jordan's resistance to the limiting expectations of others marks [*Directed by Desire: The Collected Poems of June Jordan*.] So does her curiosity about how to define herself in a divided world. She pressed for answers with a dizzying array of political and personal passions—as a woman toward other women, often other black women, other poets, men, women and children facing political, sexual and psychological adversity in the face of power." —*San Francisco Chronicle*

"Jordan was a populist who engaged in a wondrous and troubling struggle with the world and herself. At times, she was a mother without a husband, or a poet without a publisher, but she could never be accused of being a woman without a vision. Her reflections on Dr. King's legacy mirror her own: 'How could anyone quarrel with the monumental evidence of his colossal courage?' Jordan's days were spent in constant revelation. Read her words, risk your own unveiling." —*The Village Voice*

"She is among the bravest of us, the most outraged. She feels for us all. She is the universal poet." —Alice Walker

"June Jordan's poems and essays are survival methods, love notes, smoke signals, and courageous testimony." —Aja Monet, from her essay "June Jordan: I Am Trying to Find My Way Home" (2016)

"[Jordan's] lifelong devotion to justice, equality and radical democracy seemed to revolve around the pleasure she felt in hurling beautiful words at a world full of racism, poverty, homophobia and inane politicians determined to present this awful state of affairs. There was always joy in her rage." —Angela Davis

CONTENTS

4

"IF IT'S WRONG IN STANDARD ENGLISH IT'S PROBABLY RIGHT IN BLACK ENGLISH, OR, AT LEAST, YOU'RE HOT"
JORDAN ON THE POLITICS OF LANGUAGE (1972-1985)

5

"THEY MINING THE RIVERS / WE MAKING LOVE REAL"
FROM *NEW DAYS: POEMS OF EXILE AND RETURN* (1974)

6

"JEWELS OF OUR SOUL"
JORDAN ON COUNTEE CULLEN'S ANTHOLOGY, *CAROLING DUSK*, RICHARD WRIGHT, ZORA NEALE HURSTON, LANGSTON HUGHES & PHILLIS WHEATLEY (1974-1985)

7

"I MUST BECOME A MENACE TO MY ENEMIES"
FROM *THINGS THAT I DO IN THE DARK: NEW AND SELECTED POEMS* (1977)

8

"THIS IS MY PERSPECTIVE, AND THIS IS MY FAITH"
JORDAN ON HER LIFE AND WORK (1977-2000)

9

"SO HOT SO HOT SO HOT SO WHAT / SO HOT SO WHAT SO HOT SO HOT"
COLLABORATIONS: THEATER, MUSIC, TEACHING, POETRY (1981-1996)

10

"WE ARE THE ONES WE HAVE BEEN WAITING FOR"
FROM *PASSION: NEW POEMS 1977-1980* (1980)
& FROM *CIVIL WARS: OBSERVATIONS FROM THE FRONT LINES OF AMERICA* (1981)

11

"I NEED TO TALK ABOUT LIVING ROOM / BECAUSE I NEED TO TALK ABOUT HOME"
FROM *ON CALL: POLITICAL ESSAYS* (1985) & FROM *LIVING ROOM: NEW POEMS* (1985)

12

"EVERY NIGHT THE WATERS OF THE WORLD"
FROM *NAMING OUR DESTINY: NEW AND SELECTED POEMS 1985-1989* (1989)

13

"MISBEGOTTEN AMERICAN DREAMS HAVE MAIMED US ALL"
FROM *TECHNICAL DIFFICULTIES: AFRICAN-AMERICAN NOTES ON THE STATE OF THE UNION* (1992)

14

"LET ME BE VERY / VERY / VERY / VERY / VERY / SPECIFIC"
FROM *HARUKO / LOVE POEMS: NEW AND SELECTED LOVE POEMS* (1993), FROM *KISSING GOD GOODBYE: POEMS 1991-1997* (1997) & FROM *AFFIRMATIVE ACTS: POLITICAL ESSAYS* (1998)

15

"I GUESS IT WAS MY DESTINY TO LIVE SO LONG"
FROM HER LAST POEMS (1997-2001) IN *DIRECTED BY DESIRE: THE COLLECTED POEMS OF JUNE JORDAN* (2005) & FROM *SOME OF US DID NOT NOT DIE: NEW AND SELECTED ESSAYS* (2002)

INTRODUCTION

Rachel Eliza Griffiths

"Sometimes I am the terrorist I must disarm." - June Jordan

*

In June Jordan's work one is anointed in perpetual discovery. More than double-consciousness there is a plural consciousness. The muse, the seer, the sacred feminine, the lover, the activist, the essayist, the mother, the daughter, the soldier, the poet, the advocate, the trickster, the educator, the survivor—all surge in an American lyric no other poet has ever sung as clearly and phenomenally.

Her literary charisma, beauty, humor, intelligence, and power reveal and indict us again and again. Through the testament of her drums, flowers, thunderstorms, wildfires, and the fall-out shelters of her words, Jordan commanded language in a way that has earned her, rightly, a reputation as one of America's greatest literary warriors - an inimitable force.

Even now, Jordan introduces herself to us directly:

"I am black alive and looking back at you."

The writings and witness of June Jordan are inalienable to the American psyche as well as the greater, universal humanity through which we try to create and develop a narrative of hope. She helps us discover what our humanity is worth, what it will cost us—even our lives— should we continue to oppress, capture, and murder our own civilization.

*

Yesterday America chose Donald Trump as her 45th president.

His voice, pinched with privilege and worse, has followed me these last months. His voice is a voice that insists on building walls and deporting millions of immigrants, insists that Mexicans are rapists, insists that the people of color at his campaign rallies deserved violence and insults, insists that women are "nasty" objects and "disgusting" animals (dogs and pigs), or that women can mostly be valued and defined by the quality and pedigree of their looks and genitalia. His voice is a voice that flogs and neglects Black life. In an effort to win Black support, Trump pitched his questions at us like good ole boy rope: "What the hell do you have to lose?" His voice whines (and wins!), and he insists, righteously, to America that we—Americans *everywhere*—respect and *like* him, that we *want* him, that he, as our president, will be able to bring America's heart back to her deep, flowing wounds and *bind* those wounds.

And is it not true? Are the wounds not also segregated and select?

The American people chose him because they loved that his voice was the voice they have been missing for so long. They chose his voice because it is the voice that they themselves dare neither share nor name. In their fear and rage of lost power and supremacy, both racially and culturally, they cast their votes, millions and millions of their voices raised in their amplified lust for America's return to 'Greatness' —a word and idea that has always been brutally transparent from the first moment it was uttered and manipulated into useful propaganda. Through their votes, Americans articulated their national mourning of power and a peculiar identity of whiteness that had been challenged and subverted far too long.

This morning I wake, hearing June's voice in my head. *A kind of listening I have never experienced before wakes inside my life.*

With my brothers and sisters I wept and raged, coated in a wonderment of reality so bleak and dark I could not fathom recognizing sunlight itself were it to cross and greet me on my path.

I return to the electrifying kingdom of Jordan's prophetic works. In thirst I read passages from her essays aloud. She whispers flames into my ears.

Here is her knowing voice from "Poem about My Rights":

> I am the history of rape
> I am the history of the rejection of who I am
> I am the history of the terrorized incarceration of
> my self
> I am the history of battery assault and limitless
> armies against whatever I want to do with my mind
> and my body and my soul and
> whether it's about walking out at night
> or whether it's about the love that I feel or
> whether it's about the sanctity of my vagina or
> the sanctity of my national boundaries
> or the sanctity of my leaders or the sanctity
> of each and every desire
> that I know from my personal and idiosyncratic
> and indisputably single and singular heart

*

We are seeing now what always was. We are seeing what June Jordan sensed as bloodroot, as blues, as brutality, as revolution, as reckoning.

Like Langston Hughes, Richard Wright, James Baldwin, Audre Lorde, Adrienne Rich, Lucille Clifton, Toni Morrison, Wole Soyinka, Chinua Achebe, Czeslaw Milosz, Federico García Lorca, Octavio Paz, Mahmoud Darwish, and so many other poets and writers to whom we return in these times (and always), June Jordan offers language through which we are able to celebrate and confront the constellation of human experience and its breathtaking flares of both wounds and joys.

Jordan's scathing truths inflict good scars, a scarring that signifies new skin, new language, and new insight. This morning's roll call screams in my head and I have no answers for my spiritual tribunal of poets. I have no more questions about American freedom or the corrosive democracy that turns and turns upon itself and its people, even as the country promises prosperity, security, equality, and yes, *happiness*.

We are dreaming under America's ambush.

But it is June Jordan's seeing, inflected with rage and vulnerability, that cuts across this American body that has always existed, disfigured in both its devastation and its glory.

Jordan's writing reminds me of the terrible and beautiful vocation that is the poet's task. And to be specific, I claim the value, meaning, imagination, and vision of the Black poet's eyes. There is a word amongst a fiery thicket of letters burning behind my eyes.

June's word: *Persistence.*

From Jordan's *soulscript* (1970), the poet focuses on the merit and significance of Black poets within the context of American Arts and Letters. About Black poetry, Jordan writes:

"These poems tell that spirit and that survival, even as they spell black dreams."

In another direct observation of the relationship of Black poetry and the American canon of poetry, which is ever a political one, Jordan notes:

"A discouraging number of published critics pretend that the litera-
ture, the poetry, of black artists buckles like some inferior stuff when
measured by the usual criteria. That is a patronizing, absolute mis-
take."

And, in Jordan's "The Difficult Miracle of Black Poetry in America or
Something Like a Sonnet for Phillis Wheatley" (1985) she writes:

> "This is the difficult miracle of Black poetry in America: that we
> persist, published or not, and loved or unloved: we persist."

Would June Jordan yell and whoop (then return militantly and exul-
tantly to the page!) if she could see the indisputable shift, the color
correction and queering, of what American poetry now looks like in
this country?

Tracing the lineage of the Harlem Renaissance, Black Arts Movement,
Last Poets, Dark Room Collective, Callaloo, Cave Canem, CantoMundo,
Kundiman, Kimbilio—would she demand more?

Her eyes stare out from the photographs I've placed above my writing
desk. She is smiling or not in some of these images. But she is always
looking.

*

There is little I can write to introduce June Jordan to a reader. She
speaks for herself and her voice, her knowing, has been here long be-
fore she actually arrived.

This voice arrived here in the ancestors, blues and spirituals, funk
music, crops, visual arts, fashion, cities, sports, recipes, and lives that
lived, worked, and dreamt of June Jordan.

You. We. Our. Us.

*

An arrangement of Jordan's language, titles to be shared, screamed, celebrated, memorized, and sung:

Who would paint a people black or white?; honey people murder mercy U.S.A.; They mining the rivers/we making love real; I must become a menace to my enemies; This is my perspective, and this is my faith; we are the ones we have been waiting for; I need to talk about the living room/because I need to talk about home; Misbegotten American dreams have maimed us all; Let me be very/very/very/very/very/ specific

We are looking directly at a woman, into her raw and radiant eyes, who is as real in speech as we have ever seen.

*

Some poets have the impulse to strip the political chords from a poem, amputating the message from the marrow. Some poets frown at the blood that appears despite their precise scrubbing. They believe they should sacrifice their flaws and unsightly birthmarks in the name of pristine poems.

This was not June Jordan's impulse.

Hers, I believe, was to reinforce the sacred and funky, the systemic flow of life in a body being both experiential and episodic.

*

She would not maim or police her tongue. She would not mutilate her intelligence or identity in order to survive within the America that promised to love and to protect her and her family.

Daughter of West Indian immigrants, Jordan was always aware of the tenuous and shallow promises of the American dream, which has always been (sus)stained by the blood of black and brown bodies. She rejected the offering of a specific democracy that had little interest (because there was and is no perceived profit) in a full and total citizenship for those black and brown bodies and their needs.

Jordan's life and works announce an articulation of *embodiment*, an argument for the contradictory pulse and impulse of the heart, and the troubling—through action, both intimate and public—of justice, equality, beauty, reform, and freedom on a universal scale.

Humanity is the only ovation we must always stand for.

*

"What would happen if one woman told the truth about her life?
The world would split open."
                                                    —Muriel Rukeyser

*

In her debut collection, *Who Look at Me* (1969), Jordan's evocative voice revises, exhumes, and arms the "Other" with a voice and narrative of American history.

Her words are as blistering, intimate, and immediate now as they were when she crafted so much of this work. Think of her time and her crowning. *Who Look at Me* arrives just a year after the assassination of Martin Luther King, Jr. Just four years before that Malcolm X was assassinated, and prior to both, Medgar Evers. In December of that same year, 1969, that *Who Look at Me* is published, Black Panther Party activist Fred Hampton is assassinated while sleeping next to his eight-and-a-half month pregnant fiancée in his apartment on Monroe Street in Chicago.

Unlike the style or voice of anyone else writing at that time, Jordan's distinct tongue speaks to us and has not stopped speaking.

It is the insistent dignity of a kindred voice that also speaks, grieves, plots, explodes, and prophesizes in Langston Hughes's "I, Too America", Paul Lawrence Dunbar's "We Wear the Mask", Gwendolyn Brooks's "We Real Cool", and that appears in the works of Wheatley, Whitman, Dickinson, Hurston, Baldwin, Ellison, Wright, Morrison, Fanon, Cesaire, and many others.

The narrative of native sons and daughters arrived from Jordan's "otherwhere" in *Who Look At Me*:

> I am stranded in a hungerland
> of great prosperity
>
> *
>
> shelter happens seldomly and
> like an accident
> it stops
>
> *
>
> No doubt
> the jail is white where I am born
> but black will bail me out
>
> *
>
> We have lived as careful
> as a church and prayer
> in public
>
> *
>
> we reveal
>
> *
>
> a complicated past
> of tinderbox and ruin
> where we carried water
> for the crops

we come from otherwhere
victim to a rabid cruel cargo crime

to separate and rip apart
the trusting members of one heart

my family

I looked for you
I looked for you

And in a later passage, Jordan's argument razes, through a plural chorus of voices (as in so many Greek tragedies), those American mythologies of freedom and equality to the ground.

Brandishing intellect and wound, turning over the American body, her words cut the body down from the rope, the tree. Holding this body within her gaze and wisdom, she holds firmly to its weakening pulse with clarity and tenderness.

Jordan offers to tell us another narrative, a story of American Genesis:

In part we grew
by looking back at you

that white terrain
impossible for black America to thrive
that hostile soil to mazelike toil
backbreaking people into pain

we grew by work by waiting
to be seen
black face black body and black mind
beyond obliterating
homicide of daily insult daily death

the pistol slur the throbbing redneck war
with breath

In part we grew
with heroes who could halt a slaveship
lead the crew

*

Jordan's words are salves, swords, bread, oxygen.

June Jordan is for you. Or is she against you?

Americans are still waiting for a salvation to show up that was never worked for collectively and mutually, never earned. American salvation arrived at the toll of murdered and oppressed native and indigenous nations. It grew from the cuffed hands and hopes of those who were hauled here as cargo. Its dream and pride was birthed by those who arrived, fleeing other threats of persecution. The birth of America included nearly everyone—peoples and races from all over the world.

Those who settled here seeking freedom achieved it, or its illusion, by the oppression, enslavement, and sanctioned massacres of people (and women) who were perceived as less deserving, less able to define and understand (for themselves) the actual manifestation and pursuit of that freedom.

It remains one of this country's inflexible ironies: a troubling that begs examination and deconstruction.

But our healing is *all* of us. Without each of us working for human dignity and rights, we will remain impoverished in creation, spirit, and prosperity as a human nation.

*

June Jordan was born in 1936. Here are her presidents, the presidents we share during her lifetime, and my presidents thus far:

Franklin D. Roosevelt : Harry S. Truman : Dwight D. Eisenhower : John F. Kennedy : Lyndon B. Johnson : Richard Nixon : Gerald Ford: Jimmy Carter : Ronald Reagan : George H.W. Bush : Bill Clinton : George W. Bush : Barack Obama : Donald Trump :

*

Jordan taught her students to question and to listen and to work. She mothered her own son as well as countless other brown and black babies. For many, she is a literary midwife and mother. From Jordan's work you can trace her literary blood and its fruit in many, many directions.

Jordan believed in dialogues, collaborations, and community. And, she spoke out whether it required her anger or her passion or both.

June told her only son never to run on the street.

She had to teach her son that his black body, in any movement at any age, would elicit suspicion or worse. *She had to teach her son not to run.* And, it is that counsel—the doubling of meaning and definition —that also lives in the writings of the poets who love and uphold common principles of social justice in her name.

Her writing requires us to remember our humanity, to recognize it in ourselves and other beings wherever we go, and to resist all forces and agendas that exclude any person or people from full humanity. We are agents of oppression—*terrorists*—if we do not listen, or worse, do nothing.

Let me be clear: the seismic shock being experienced in our nation right now regarding the election of our 45th president is indicative of what Jordan would have recognized immediately about America.

But she was bigger than that. She would have reminded us about ourselves.

She would have counseled us to remember where we come from. She would have reminded us that our future is incubated in both the past and the present. Our future cannot exist, or change, without what is immediately eye-level and what has come before in the narrative. She would have interrogated any fixed and authoritative narrative. Perhaps she would have then cited Chimamanda Ngozi Adichie's warning and explanation of "the danger of a single story."

Then she would have blown our heads off—split them wide open with the corroded axe of our own grief and rage—with a poem.

Of Nightsong and Flight

There are things lovely and dangerous still

the rain
when the heat of an evening
sweetens the darkness with mist

and the eyes cannot see what the memory will
of new pain

when the headlights deceive
like the windows wild birds believe to be air
and bash bodies and wings
on the glass

when the headlights show space
but the house and the room and the bed and your face
are still there

while I am mistaken

and try to drive by

the actual kiss
of the world everywhere

*

From Jordan's introduction to *June Jordan's Poetry for the People: A Revolutionary Blueprint* with editor Lauren Muller and the Blueprint Collective (1995), Jordan (excerpted here) writes:

> Poetry is a political action undertaken for the sake of information, the faith, the exorcism, and the lyrical invention, that telling the truth makes possible. Poetry means taking control of the language of your life. Good poems can interdict a suicide, rescue a love affair, and build a revolution in which speaking and listening to somebody becomes the first and last purpose to every social encounter.
>
> I would hope that folks throughout the U.S.A. would consider the creation of poems as a foundation for true community: a fearless democratic society.

*

When America has chosen, *elected*, a celebrity, as its president, to speak and lead on our behalf, as our domestic and global representative, it is no wonder our children are unable to discern what is not reality, what is not entertainment. Will we too be transformed into celebrity citizens? Will we embrace and applaud this theater?

America, who has incarcerated millions of the black male population over decades, since its earliest beginnings, wonders *why* so many of its citizens, consciously or not, find themselves conned or entrapped, whether by education or class, rigged medias, paranoia, supremacy or law, in living prisons.

With the fantasy that mass technology and unabated fear and isolation has provided this country, arming us with escape routes, immediate gratification, hyper-individualism, and avoidance, it is no surprise that our children, mostly white male youth, walk into ordinary sets of life—movie theaters, clubs, churches, schools, and even their own homes—and transform those spaces into bloody, surreal sets of inestimable violence and loss that is cinematographic and incomprehensible in its vision.

What are we able to offer our wounds? Better yet, what can we possibly offer to ourselves as true healing?

*

Jordan's writings offer all of herself to us.

Therefore we are also challenged to make offerings ourselves. We are called—Jordan's immeasurable voice raised in solidarity and conspiracy—to give of ourselves with the understanding of our flaws and a resolution to reinforce change through action.

Those flaws and impediments, Jordan reminds us, are as much a part of the struggle as the victory. And, in this country, we must redefine our notion of victory, which too often concerns power and modes of economic triumph that are gained at the expense of black and brown peoples.

Frequently I have been told that Jordan was a difficult, prickly person, but I believe that's the point. She was also loving, giving and gracious. She was both patient and impatient! She was complicated.

She challenged her fellow poets, brothers and sisters, American citizens through her outrage, her bi-sexuality, and her imagination, which also served her activism. In her work, she conveyed the rigorous practice and gestation of the struggle.

Jordan knew this struggle intimately. The ample body of her work springs from her refusal to unsee herself or reduce black life to tropes or silhouettes. Jordan shone the hot lamp of her intellect and her love upon Black life. Black love.

We need her as much as America needs to look at itself.

We need her grace and anger each time black and brown peoples are asked (or forced) to witness the dehumanizing, desensitized viral broadcast of a murdered black body, or ignore the cruelly surreal, reality-television event and insult of it.

We will always need June Jordan each and every time we are asked to teach, educate, and explain privilege to those in possession of it.

We will always need June Jordan whenever we demand better from this country.

*

What does it mean - to be on?

*

In "I Must Become a Menace to My Enemies" the rhythm and enjambment employed convey Jordan's clear declaration of action and visibility:

> I will no longer lightly walk behind
> a one of you who fear me:
>   Be afraid.
> I plan to give you reasons for your jumpy fits
> and facial tics
> I will not walk politely on the pavements anymore

and this dedicated in particular
to those who hear my footsteps
or the insubstantial rattling of my grocery
cart
then turn around
see me
and hurry on
away from this impressive terror I must be:

Later, in the third section of the poem, listen to what she does with
sound, repetition, reiteration through imagery, and enjambment:

And if I
if I ever let love go
because the hatred and the whisperings
become a phantom dictate I o-
bey in lieu of impulse and realities
(the blossoming flamingoes of my
                    wild mimosa trees)
then let love freeze me out.

I must become
I must become a menace to my enemies.

*

"Perhaps for some of you here today, I am the face of one of your fears.
Because I am woman, because I am Black, because I am lesbian, be-
cause I am myself—a Black woman warrior poet doing my work—come
to ask you, are you doing yours?"

—Audre Lorde

*

Dear June -

Donald Trump is not my President.
To whom does he Belong?
When America is Great again will that mean I am
to be
a Slave? Ain't I a Woman? Woke? Why Did the Women
Vote for -

     Is he Theirs?

*

Hearing over and over again that Jordan's personality was 'difficult' I am reminded of the Angry-Black-Woman syndrome that only recently has been countered with the celebratory, aggressive movement of 'Black Girl Magic.'

The language employed to describe and define our first Black First Lady of the United States, Michelle Obama, was lurid. Despite her intelligence, beauty, warmth, kindness, and eloquence, some people in this country could not resist their familiar language. She was written about and rendered visually as militant, as primate, or worse.

It is no surprise that those in power interrupt and overpower voices of women of color with charges of chronic anger and undesirability when we express a natural response—anger and self-protection—to lies and ignorance. Jordan's fury was backed with action, perseverance, and education of the finest caliber.

Light and lightning struck (and strike) at the darkest tongue of America's silence.

June Jordan charged toward it.

Her anger gave us permission as poets, writers, and artists. Her anger sent me (and still does) to the poems, writings, and activism of Audre Lorde, Lucille Clifton, Lorraine Hansberry, Adrienne Rich, Denise Levertov, Muriel Rukeyser, Rita Dove, Fanny Lou Hamer, Ida B. Wells, Sojourner Truth, Harriet Tubman, Harriet Jacobs, Ann Petry, Shirley Chisholm, Sonia Sanchez, Nikky Finney, Toni Cade Bambara, Toni Morrison, Maya Angelou, Angela Davis, Ntozake Shange, Nikki Giovanni, Adrienne Kennedy, Gayle Jones, Gloria Naylor, Octavia Butler, Gwendolyn Brooks, Toi Derricotte, bell hooks, Farah Jasmine Griffin, Trudier Harris, Patricia Smith, Valerie Boyd, Paule Marshall, Jamaica Kincaid, Patricia Hill Collins, Terry McMillan, Wanda Coleman, Jayne Cortez, Suzan-Lori Parks, Claudia Rankine, Edwidge Danticat, Roxane Gay, Buchi Emecheta, Chimamanda Ngozi Adichie, and so many, many others.

Jordan was an agent, a maverick, a siren who wailed and warned us with her pen and—to conjure Alice Walker's call to arms—*furious dancing.* Jordan's authority did not exclude imagination or uncomfortable questioning. Never imperial, though national and universal, she would not give up her anger.

Jordan wrote explicitly about her own feminist identity. Here is an excerpt from "Where Is the Love?" (1978), which was first given as a paper at a seminar entitled "Feminism and the Black Woman Writer," that shares Jordan's uncanny criticism (and call for revision) of definitions:

> I am a feminist, and what that means to me is much the same as the
> meaning of the fact that I am Black: it means that I must undertake
> to love myself and to respect myself as though my very life depends
> upon self-love and self-respect. It means that I must everlastingly

seek to cleanse myself of the hatred and the contempt that sur-
rounds and permeates my identity, as a woman, and as a Black
human being, in this particular world of ours. It means that the
achievement of self-love and self-respect will require inordinate,
hourly vigilance, and that I am entering my soul into a struggle that
will most certainly transform the experience of all peoples of the
earth, as no other movement can, in fact, hope to claim: because
the movement into self-love, self-respect, and self-determination is
the movement now galvanizing the true, the unarguable majority of
human beings everywhere.

*

To write or think near Jordan's center you must think of the entire
world. This is what June Jordan does, expanding and constricting her
vision and revolutionary seeing at once. And so it is no surprise but a
fortune that we have been endowed with Jordan's poetry, essays, lec-
tures, plays, architectural blueprints, etc.

Upon the page and in the world, June Jordan fleshed a city.

*

One of the most important movements taking place now is self-care
and self-love of Black spirit and body.

Jordan devoted significant attention to this subject in her work. Erot-
ic, smart, vibrant and sensual, Jordan uplifted Black beauty and desire
into a guiding constellation in the cosmos of Black life.

There, excellence and love persist as sacred, nuanced, and indisput-
ably necessary firmaments to Black experience. Love is the talisman
and the letter that batters those narratives of brutality and loathing,

which were taught and reinforced through violence and disenfranchisement.

Her love has charged each of us with agency, accountability, criticism, and insisted that we look at ourselves. She charges us, again and again, to ask ourselves to whom we give our love. Also, we must look even more clearly at those we have denied (and still deny) our love, and whom we have rejected or defined as not deserving any love at all.

It is love that will unlearn and repair those terrible educations and sanctioned genocides and suicides.

Here, I do not mean a passive creature. I mean Love.

And, in the common spirit that poets during the Black Arts Movement, such as Sonia Sanchez, Etheridge Knight, Henry Dumas, Jayne Cortez, Haki R. Madhubuti, Ishmael Reed, Mari Evans, Maulana Ron Karenga, Larry Neal, Quincy Troupe, Amiri Baraka, and others demanded, Jordan also worked, on her own terms, to announce the afro-futuristic heralds of Black Pride and Power.

In "The Difficult Miracle of Black Poetry in America or Something Like a Sonnet for Phillis Wheatley," Jordan writes of both astonishment and persistence. These spaces double and exert themselves for Jordan and her meditation upon the audacity of her existence and Wheatley's own claiming of poetry—a Black poetry—of Wheatley herself.

At the close of this extraordinary argument and love letter, Jordan writes:

> And because Black people in North America persist in an irony profound, Black poetry persists in this way:
>
>
> > Like the trees of winter and
> > like the snow which has no power

makes very little sound
but comes and collects itself
edible light on the black trees
The tall black trees of winter
lifting up a poetry of snow
so that we may be astounded
by the poems of Black
trees inside a cold environment

*

BLACK LIVES MATTER.

*

I was twenty-four years old when June Jordan died in Berkeley, California in 2002. During those years, frequently hospitalized for dissociative and mental health ruptures, I wrote poetry and dreamt secretly, frustrated by my inability, then, to heal myself from depression and aggravated sexual traumas. Simply, I mostly wanted to die. I intended to heal myself by myself. Suicide could not be discounted in such a narrow arsenal. The only heart that flickered in me those years responded to reading, writing, and art. In that glimmering, I read everything I could. I wrote my thoughts and fears and desires into lyrics, paintings, and stories. I needed to accept that I belonged to something bigger and more loving than myself. I would transform my ache into a language I knew had been spoken and constructed to heal me. With this truth laid bare in me I would move forward in my life, claiming poet and artist as my true names, as an actual body where I might live and love others (and myself) back. This, I knew, meant that my life would be more fulfilling and dangerous than the half-lit life I had tried to live, believing it was a life.

In 2004, I enrolled in Sarah Lawrence College's MFA program as a fiction writer because Alice Walker, Muriel Rukeyser, Grace Paley, Adrienne Rich, and other great warriors I admired had spent time there.

I found my way towards Jordan through reading Alice Walker. I realized had I read Jordan earlier I would not have been so affected, so joined and sustained by her inherent and abundant excellence. I would not have possessed the vocabulary, as a poet or a reader, to appreciate Jordan's mastery on the page as a maestro poet. I would not have fully grasped the tension of her lyric, or of the spoken-ness of Black language, the blues and bruises and control she used.

One of my favorite poems of Jordan's is "I guess it was my destiny to live so long" and here is an excerpt from it:

> Don't chase me down
> down
> down
> death chasing me
> death's way
>
> And I'm not done
> I'm not about to blues my dues or beg
>
> I am about to teach myself
> to fly slip slide flip run
> fast as I need to
> on one leg

This poem, for me, amplifies the courage and audacity that also appears in Lucille Clifton's poem "won't you celebrate with me".

Jordan rejected a death that prohibited her from her dignity; her defiance arrives by the ownership and authorship of her own death, which itself is always begat by Life. And in the midst of that dialogue there is a space shaped for transformation and celebration. This power resonates for me with what Clifton also shares in her poem, "something has tried to kill me/and has failed."

The things that have tried to kill Jordan have not killed her spirit or her mind. Her life resurrects itself in the language, whenever any of us speak her words into the air she no longer breathes.

Her too soon death at age 65 from aggressive cancer is only a footnote to what she was able to give and share with us through her writing.

In such a brief time Jordan provided us with a dazzling and formidable blueprint of the work at hand.

And, she *loved* us.

*

June -

America Was Lynched By the American Dream Yesterday. Today America is licking her own corpse.

June -

Freedom was repealed. Fear mongering won the electoral vote and maybe the popular vote too.

June -

If democracy cannot dismantle the master's house, nothing can.

*

BLACK LOVE MATTERS.

*

Come to these pages. Stand up for your invitation. Your birthright.

Here, we are not Waiting we are Working. We are The Ones. We are loving and raging and asking for what we know is justice. We are asking and taking it. We are sharing and grieving and giving it back as hard as we can.

There is Nothing Left to Wait For.

Years ago, Jordan knew this and cast her vote.

She spelled a prodigious stream of syllables that crossed poetry, prose, essays, criticism, children's books, plays, libretti, pamphlets, speeches, interviews, dialogues, and more.

Deeply, I kneel and drink.

Thank you, sister, for the cup you shaped and shared with your own hands.

Under the dark and broken eaves of injustice and ignorant supremacies, we must welcome each other into the living room and begin to imagine what will be required of each of us to name this dream, American Dream, our Home. Where, an imperfect democracy, and both its violators and violated begin to look into each other's eyes instead of at a flag we do not, in reality, honor or share despite what we say.

What exactly are we *doing*? For exactly whom and what do we *work*? Do we believe in the value of our labor or our dreams? And why is there something these days that feels so utterly *empty* in the privilege of the dream and the privilege of labor?

America voted to scrape away whatever had tried to seed new roots of freedom and equal rights. There will be more scraping, in the old regime's fever to 'Make America Great Again'. Well-tended lists and records of persons-non-grata, intellectuals and dissenters, as well as innocent citizens will become targets because of their faith, sexual orientation, intelligence, truth-telling, and whistle-blowing. The American people have been promised that any voices that oppose and resist this toxic revision will be monitored, imprisoned, deported, and forced to relinquish their citizenship. Whether through legislation or the bold, criminal attacks (which are as recent as the country was first birthed) of hatred, Americans everywhere are bracing themselves as children look to us for their social education.

And so, it is students who are chalking their college and university campuses with hate speech. It is children in schools who are tagging their water fountains with 'Whites Only' signs. It leers at us in the spray-painted wall drawings of swastikas. It is children who are sexually assaulting and grabbing other children and young girls in the name and victory of the newly elected president. It is the parents of those children who are flying Neo-Nazi flags from their porches and homes. It is those parents and their relatives who are enacting surrogate lynchings by hanging chairs or effigies from the trees in front of their own homes. It is the surge of target practice and gun sales. It is yet another student who grabs a woman's hijab, choking her with it. It is the flyers and pamphlets being openly distributed by the Ku Klux Klan. It is the mass-resurrection of the words 'nigger' and 'faggot' (and worse) that are plainly spoken and graffiti-ed in public spaces, including churches, restaurants, and schools. It is what parents share, in the bigoted, homophobic, Anti-Semitic, Islamophobic, misogynistic, xenophobic, and racist sanctuary, of their own homes, at their dinner tables that is then carried, lovingly and carefully, by their children into the classroom.

June Jordan's writing continues to probe America's most brutal socket, the birthmark of the body where no new skin, no new muscle, no soul can grow despite dire need.

And the need, now and only now, requires an uncomfortable therapy and rehabilitation, which consists of tense conversations and acknowledgement coupled with action and love, that will take the country further than it has ever gone.

Now and only now.

*

James Baldwin wrote, "Your crown has been bought and paid for. All you must do is put it on."

June Jordan's words are crowns, hard won garlands of suffering, clarity, and joy.

When I teach Jordan's writing, when I place my own black body on a New York street in the company of other bodies protesting the murder of my brothers and sisters, I know I am wearing a truth that is more valuable, greater than any single story, greater than the fear that sometimes makes me feel like lying down in my own blood, which is the blood of justice and survival.

Take June Jordan's life from these pages into our community. Share them. Begin here on the page next to her where she gave it and gave it and gave it.

Your voice, your struggle, your privilege, your neglect, your vote, your joy, your oceans and farms and mountains, your emancipation, your death, your family, your honor, your music, your memory, your grief, your devotion, your silence, your greed, your birth and blood matter.

Hold high her words. These are our stars, advocates, beloveds, and descendants. Don't go away from our life in despair.

We're On.

Rachel Eliza Griffiths
November 9, 2016

THE HOPED-FOR APOCALYPSE: JUNE JORDAN, AGENT OF CHANGE

Editors' Introduction

"A Black woman who would be an agent for change, an active member of the hoped-for apocalypse," with Aretha Franklin singing "A Change Is Gonna Come" in her ear—that's how she described herself. And that's the difficult miracle of June Jordan, visionary-progressive-revolutionary poet/essayist/activist/teacher who committed herself to work—literary and political—that is never done. She was writing out of the moment to change that moment. They say political writing ages quickly, yet that greatest plunderer of political everyday life, Shakespeare, keeps holding our interest. It was Shakespeare, along with the Bible and the poetry of Paul Laurence Dunbar, that Jordan knew first, as a toddler almost, her mother's milk still in her, her father's unrelenting ambition shaping her into both a soldier and a poet.

The "crumbling of morale, the assassination of leaders, the systematic disintegration of our meager gains from that era have left us, today, with apparently small belief, no summoning voice, and ever yet worsening needs": the "today" of her essay "Angola: A Victory and a Promise" was 1976, and the era she was referring to was, of course, that of the Civil Rights, which, to put it simply, is the extension of the Civil War, which, to put it bluntly, is not over.

In 2017, as this *Reader* goes to press, and fifteen years after Jordan's death, the needs are still worsening, the voice still not summoned. For eight years, the Republican opposition has rejected everything the first nonwhite, biracial, African-American president in history has put forward, because *he*, the first nonwhite, biracial, African-American president in history, put it forward. Over the last two decades, the face of Jim Crow has become the prison system, fed—literally—with funds that used to go to education. The police are as brutal and lethal as ever, still getting away with murder. Racism is on the rise, again. 2016 is a strong contender to go down in history as the most divisive—let's called it the ugliest—election year in the history of this country. The question asked after the 2014 and 2015 murders of Michael Brown, Eric Garner, Tamir Rice, Freddie Gray, and too many others—do Black lives matter?—has not been answered with enough clarity. Or has it been answered by the Republican nominee for president, who shamelessly, gleefully, narcissistically rides on a wave of unabashed racism and hatred for everything not white, male, and able-bodied? Or by Michigan's governor who didn't think the people of Flint, mostly Black and poor, deserved healthy water? Or by 2016 being as lethal as 2015?

In 2002, at age sixty-five, the voice of June Jordan, descendant of both Phillis Wheatley and Walt Whitman, fell silent. What would she say today? She still says it: her political writing doesn't age.

In her last essays, she wrote about the Aryan Nations "hunting for Jews," about the stolen election of 2000, about terrorism—that of others as well as our own: "Is there an honorable means to pursue and capture the perpetrators of that atrocity without ourselves becoming terrorists?" she asked in *Some of Us Did Not Die*, written after the 9/11 atrocities. The answer she found is in one of the most brutally honest lines ever written: "Sometimes I am the terrorist I must disarm."

In that book she also wrote:

> As of September 11, 2001, the world we thought we knew went down.
> And how shall we rebuild?
> And should we reconstruct, or should we dare ourselves into an unforeseen millennial recovery, a millennial upholding of our best ambitions, a millennial declaration of a slow kiss dedication to equality and justice?

Of course, that didn't happen. Our official answer was violence. More war. And more violence.

Jordan's way to disarm herself and others was always to have a good, as-impartial-as-it-gets, painfully honest look at herself. This helped her look at others with the same honesty: *Who Look at Me* was the title of her first book. Look close: "I am black alive and looking back at you." No one who really looks can deny anyone else's life; to not look is what makes you a terrorist.

Jordan looked and looked and looked.

In the years since her death, the divide among Americans—the divides of race, gender, politics, income growing ever wider—has deepened to the point that civil discourse is barely possible, and the tearing up of the social contract can be heard louder and louder. Facts don't count anymore; what counts is the loudest, shrillest distortion. For many, in their angry despair, hatred and murder seem to be the answer.

"And what shall we do, we who did not die?" she asks in her last book, *Some of Us Did Not Die*, published months after her death on June 14, 2002.

The answer is simple: do what June Jordan would have done.

Be on.

Make the brave, good news.

Never turn from freedom, equality and justice, art, faith, and love.

Most of all love.

***

Here's a healthy sampling of June Jordan's fighting and loving words, of the daily hell she delivered to those in power, of the fearless voice she gave to those who went unheard, of the tender declarations she whispered to her lovers. Here are a lot of her greatest hits and some of her lost treasures.

June Jordan—Alice Walker called her "the universal poet"—was the most published African-American writer of her time, with an equally wide range of genres. Here are her poems, everything from free verse to sonnets and tankas; here are her essays, keynote addresses, columns, reviews, journalism, polemics, pamphlets, prefaces; children's books; a young adult novel; stage works; libretti; memoir; writings about, and for, teaching.

Toni Morrison called her "our premiere black woman essayist"; as E. Ethelbert Miller put it, she wrote about everything that mattered: urban planning, land reform, civil rights, Black English, the politics of sexuality, South Africa, Lebanon, Nicaragua, supremacist policies, theft of American democracy, race and gender inequality, Mike Tyson, Anita Hill, Bill Clinton, affirmative action, disability rights, education, growing up Black in America, love, hatred, child abuse, rape, riots, police brutality, the American dream, breast cancer, Martin Luther King, Jr., Jesse Jackson, Nelson Mandela, her mother's death, the silences of friendship, Walt Whitman, Phillis Wheatley.

A subgenre of sorts are her many collaborations, with architect R. Buckminster Fuller; the Teachers & Writers Collaborative; with singer/composer Bernice Johnson Reagon and Sweet Honey in The Rock; with writers/activists Angela Davis, Alice Walker, and Ntozake Shange; with poet/activist Sara Miles; with filmmaker Pratibha Parmar, composer/pianist Adrienne Torf; and with composer John Adams and director Peter Sellars.

For this *Reader*, we faced the challenge of too much brilliance. We know your favorite poem or essay may not be included: that's the teasing nature of any reader. Fortunately, her collected poems, *Directed by Desire*, is in print, as are her selected essays, *Some of Us Did Not Die*, her columns for *The Progressive* in *Life as Activism*, her revolutionary blueprint for teaching and reaching out, *Poetry for the People*, and more. Search any important American poetry anthology, and she's there (and if she's not there, it's not an important anthology). Search "June Jordan" + [ANYTHING THAT MATTERS], and you'll find her. That's the goal of this *Reader*: to inspire you to keep reading.

"I'm centered, but I'm not finished," Jordan told interviewer Karla Hammond in 1978. "I'm coming into my life as an explorer, making discoveries and trying to pay attention so that when I have to make these changes or when changes are necessary, I'll be able to consider them. Much of what I'm saying now to you, for example, in three months I may feel differently about; but that wouldn't disturb me at all. If you're alive and you're not changing, you're blocked. Change is threatening, uncomfortable."

Centered, not finished, able to make changes: that is how we approached choosing, and placing, texts from the vast body of Jordan's writings. During the long and beautiful process of doing that, we, the editors, became the explorers of Jordan's work. We came to the conclusion that the organizing principle of *We're On: A June Jordan Reader* should be both chronological and thematic. The chronological elements show what happened when, the thematic ones how it was all connected.

Section 4, "If it's wrong in Standard English it's probably right in Black English, or, at least, you're hot," for instance, groups three of her landmark essays on the politics of language, which she wrote in the course of a dozen years. Others, like Section 10, "*we are the ones we have been waiting for*," combine texts from poetry and essay collections (in this case from *Passion* and *Civil Wars*): for Jordan, form was complementary, not exclusively reserved for one subject or the other, a way of conversation within her work. She was all about dialogue, about community; hence Section 9, "so hot so hot so hot so what / so hot so what so hot so hot," about collaborations. There are also sections with examples from just one work, offering platforms for unguided explorations: for instance, Section 2, "Who would paint a people black or white?," with the entire text of *Who Look at Me*, or Section 7, "I must become a menace to my enemies," with selections from her first New & Selected Poems, *Things that I Do in the Dark*.

Any book, but maybe especially a reader, covering so much ground, choosing from the many things she did in the dark and in broad daylight, needs help. Our gratitude, particularly, to Sara Miles for being such a sensitive, illuminating, and prompt responder to everything we shared with her; to Carey Salerno and Alyssa Neptune, our devoted editor and managing editor at Alice James Books, for their never-ending enthusiasm and patient support of this huge and not-always-easy project, in short for being one-of-a-kind Jordan-ites; to Anne Marie Macari, for her support of this project in every way; to Marilyn Morgan of the Schlesinger Library, for being curator and archivist extraordinaire in her devotion and dedication, and for answering with with superhuman speed and competence all sorts of obscure questions, and to all the staff at the Schlesinger, for keeping up the good work of taking care of the June Jordan archives; to the late Adrienne Rich, for being the first to offer material, her dialogue poem with June, when we first put out the call for participation from Jordan's friends and associates; and to her son, Pablo Conrad, for granting permission for its use; to Julia Masnik and Gloria Loomis of the Watkins/Loomis Agency, and Sam Stoloff and Frances Goldin of the Frances Goldin Agency for all their help and support; to Karla Hammond for so generously letting us use her insightful interview with June; to Pratibha Parmar, for helping us in the acquisition of "Other Kinds of Dreams" and providing us with material for the headnote; to Janet Neary, Nijah Cunningham, Rachel Eliza Griffiths for her June-channeling spirit: to Janet Neary and Nijah Cunningham for valuable conversations and their cheerleading for this book.

We are also very grateful to *all* those whose writings and works on Jordan, her life, and her times, which we consulted, and want to mention, particularly, Cheryl Clarke, for her *After Mecca: Women Poets and the Black Arts Movement* (2005), Valerie Kinloch, for her *June Jordan: Her Life and Letters* (2006), and her and Margret Grebowicz's *Still Seeking an Attitude: Critical Reflections on the Work of June Jordan* (2005); Cheryl J. Fish, for her research into "Skyrise for Harlem," which unearthed the real contribution of Jordan to this project (see "Place, Emotion, and Environmental Justice in Harlem: June Jordan and Buckminster Fuller's 1965 'Architextual' Collaboration" (*Discourse* vol. 29, 2007)); and Peter Erickson, for his thoughtful interview, "After Identity," with Jordan in *Transition* no. 63, 1994].

And finally, we are grateful to all those, named and unnamed, who knew and loved June, and all those who continue to carry her work forward.

Christoph Keller with Jan Heller Levi

***

I met June only twice, once in our home in New York in 2001, then in hers in Berkeley in 2002, less than three weeks before she died. Jan and I then lived in a tiny[1] studio apartment in the West Village. June was in town to give a keynote address at Barnard, the college she'd dropped out of to embark on her brilliant career—to become that agent of change, that leader of the hoped-for apocalypse—that so brilliantly included teaching.

---

[1] Never—never!—use the word "tiny" in a poem, June told Jan and the other poets in her workshop at the Poetry Society of America. But this isn't a poem, and I have used it once, because in the context of New York City real estate, she might have made an exception. (After we moved out, we learned our landlord had divided the tiny studio with a partition and advertised and rented it as a 1BR.) Jan confesses in advance that she uses the word "tiny" several times in her introduction.

It was on November 11, 2001, two months to the day after 9/11. The city was still in shock, the fire beneath the rubble of the Twin Towers still burning (it smoldered for a hundred days), the smell of burnt bodies still in the air. We sat at our small, round, oak dinner table, which doubled as my desk, and had salmon, bagels, yogurt. June's breast cancer—she'd been diagnosed in early 1992—had come back with a vengeance, and, after her return to Berkeley, she faced her fourth chemotherapy. But she was strong. She didn't just *look* strong—she was electrified, optimistic, curious about everything.

And she was in cheerful "hoped-for apocalyptic" fighting mode, her discourse unfettered. Did we notice that hundreds of thousands were now without jobs since 9/11 but that none of them were from the FBI, which, despite all its funds, had fucked up royally? How about using California's model during the oil crises—curb consumerism statewide by 10%—instead of going shopping mindlessly, as "Bush II" had urged the nation to do? Curb consumerism by 10% *nationwide. 20%!* We wouldn't need Afghanistan's oil. Or Alaska's. June, on. Always filled with questions—and answers. And the facts to support them. Problems *and* solutions. And why wasn't the CIA, despite all *its* funds, able to avert the second attack? How long does it take a U.S. military plane to get to Lower Manhattan? What about the attack on the Pentagon? That one happened AN HOUR—by now she was speaking in caps—after the first attack, AND THE PLANES CAN BE IN THE AIR WITHIN TWO MINUTES! WHY DIDN'T ANY OF *THOSE* PEOPLE GET FIRED?

She gave us a preview of what she'd say later that day at Barnard's Center for Research on Women, where she was invited to speak on the occasion of the Center's 30th anniversary celebration: *Some of us are not dead so what do we do with that?* Modified, that became the title of her last book, *Some of Us Did Not Die*, a few new —her last—essays, and many selected. As she told us, and as she later told the Barnard audience, she'd heard an Auschwitz survivor, Elly Gross, on the radio, saying, "I guess it was my destiny to live."

The second time I saw her was only half a year later in Berkeley, in May 2002. There was no mistaking that it would be the last time. The chemo hadn't worked; June was dying. This was the fight our soldier would lose. We came to say goodbye. It was a mild, sunny spring afternoon. We sat with her devoted friend Adrienne Torf, drinking coffee and beer in the half-shade of the backyard of June's house and waited for her to summon the strength to come out and see us. We heard her coughing. There was a note on her bedroom door saying that NO ONE—AND BY NO ONE I MEAN NO ONE—KNOCK ON THIS DOOR. "Oh, June! There she is!" I exclaimed when I caught a glimpse of her inside the house. She'd managed to get to the kitchen but no further. Adrienne and Jan jumped up to help, as I waved from my wheelchair. June was wearing a baseball cap with the words I WRITE FOR FOOD on it—she had always done that, I was to discover later—but now she was also wearing the cap to hide her loss of hair. Still, June at sixty-five looked like fifty, youthful and bright.

Adrienne helped her down the steps into the backyard. June greeted Jan and me with a kiss. She was, gaunt, hurting, exhausted, but, the minute she was seated, became alive, electrified, quick-witted, curious about the world, our work. More beer? Was the sun bothering me? Was I comfortable? When she learned that we were planning to see Gary Snyder read that night at a Berkeley bookstore, she grabbed the phone and called the bookstore, telling them that her friends, "two distinguished writers" she deemed us, were coming, and asked if they would make sure they'd reserve good seats. She ended the call and then turned to Jan: "Gary Snyder?" she asked. "What's the deal with him—*rock, rock, stone, stone*?" And laughed her inimitable, unforgettable, mischievous, infectious, conspiratorial laugh. And she asked us to help keep her work alive. Jan, with Sara Miles, was already her literary executor; June gave me the assignment to publish what I could of hers in German—maybe a book, but at least in magazines.

Jan was losing an old friend; and I had just won a new one, one I knew I could from now on only meet in memory and in her vast, powerful work. Two-and-a-half weeks later, in Switzerland, on June 14, 2002, we got the call we knew was coming: June had died. There were a few crows on the lawn. That entire summer we saw June's spirit in those beautiful, black birds.

The German language is more generous with those creatures:

they're called *Rabenkrähe*, a composite blending of the similar birds raven and crow into one mythic yet real creature, the *ravencrow*. The bird—raven and crow—stands for vision, for intuition and intelligence, for foresight: these birds can learn how to speak, which made them the ideal augural birds for the Romans. They're closely associated with battlefields, with warriors (yes, they're scavengers too). They are guardians, keeping us safe (still successfully protecting the Tower of London). They're beautiful, curious, strong, indomitable. They're magical. The raven is also the Native American bearer of secrets—and exposer of uncomfortable truths.

There should be more of them.

So many more.

Christoph Keller

***

I saw her first in action at the Fort Greene branch of the Brooklyn Public Library, in the early summer of 1977. Passing the library on my way home, I spotted the flyer. Those were the days my poet-feminist friends and I were reading *American Poetry Review*, *The Nation*, *The Village Voice*, *The Soho Weekly News*, *WIN Magazine*, *Ms. Magazine*, *Off Our Backs*, *Chrysalis*, *Conditions*, *Women's Review of Books*, *Heresies*, *13th Moon*. We'd find her poems in those pages, and in her most recent collection, *Things that I Do in the Dark*. She captured life as we lived it: fervent, frenetic, hopeful, outraged. Crazy, righteous, angry, but full of delicious tenderness. She could make us laugh and cry at the same time; she could say what we wanted to say, or what we didn't dare to say. And she made this look easy, though we knew it wasn't, with titles like "After Reading the Number One American Intellectual Best Seller, *Future Shock*, All about Change Is Where We're At" or lines like this:

momma momma
teach me how to kiss
the king within the kingdom

teach me how to t.c.b/to make do
and be
like you
teach me to survive my
momma
teach me how to hold a new life
momma
help me
turn the face of history
to your face.

That Saturday, I raced home to grab my camera. (That was the first summer after college, and I was thinking about becoming a photographer.) By the time I got back to the Clinton Hill Public Library, June Jordan was already reading. Her audience was mostly children, sitting on folding chairs, listening with unusual eagerness and respect. I was surprised by how tiny she was. She still had her Afro though, which made her seem bigger; as did her respectful attention to the children she was reading to and speaking with. From the back of the room, I took some shots of her; I now wish I'd become a photographer and had archived them. I remember I was too afraid to go up to talk to her afterwards, much less ask her to sign my copy of *Things that I Do in the Dark.*

Every time I saw her after that, and in all the time I knew her, I was always surprised by how small she was, almost elfin. But she was *big.*

I met her closer up in a workshop at the Poetry Society of America in the fall of 1985. The Poetry Society offices are in the National Arts Club building, a beautiful but not ostentatious town house on Gramercy Park. I've been to the National Arts Club since that workshop, and was astonished to see how opulently it's decorated—all those jaw-dropping stained-glass panels and skylights, crystal chandeliers, sumptuous, velvet arm chairs and plush settees, lavish, gilded mirrors, and gleaming, marbled statuettes of Greek Gods like Hermes and Eros and attendees, amid all this, striking their poses of eroticized power. It's the kind of unbelievably plush décor—somewhere between a palace and a bordello—that good-intentioned robber barons seemed so drawn to in their time. (In fact, the town house had originally been the home of Governor Samuel Tilden, trusted lawyer of the railroad magnates, also the founder of the New York Public Library.) But the rooms of the National Arts Club that I remember going to in 1985 were the modest but warm offices of the Poetry Society of America housed within, and its intimate, wood-paneled library where a dozen or so of us gathered every Saturday around a large, mahogany table. June Jordan gave us her guidelines for critiquing a poem; she said first we would read it aloud, then we would consider the following: I still have the notes from that day, or some of them, in my journal, scrawled in my loopy handwriting:

- intensity
- poetry as a way of truth-telling
- maximum impact with minimum amount of words
- is the poem completely given? (but not to sound like you're in a hurry)
- is it coherent? (have you followed your images to where they lead?)
- what is the purpose of the poem? (if the poem's purpose can't be identified, then it's not a good poem)
- craft:
    - rhythm, alliteration, assonance, consonance, syllable clusters, horizontal or vertical sound patterns
    - use the forms of the verbs "to be" or "to have" almost never—if you use them, you must be able to defend them
    - passive voice—never!—unless that's a method you have decided
    - upon to communicate something specific
    - no! to the words empty, tiny, children
    - is the diction colloquial/formal? is the diction chosen maintained? if it is not stayed with consistently, does that enhance or detract?
    - re: punctuation and all that—don't write with punctuation.
    - Poetry is words. if you don't say it you don't need it

re: line breaks — must come at a unit of meaning. In other
    words,
"and" and "of" are possible, but not "the" because "the" is not a
unit of meaning.

IS THE POEM BEAUTIFUL

MEMORABLE

SURPRISING

And so, with these guidelines in mind, we read our different truths to one another. Sometimes we cheered one another on, and sometimes we lashed out. I remember one of us reading a poem about her uncle raping her in her backyard, and a poet on the other side of the table who blurted out, *At least you had a backyard!*

We were all a little scared. June knew that, and she knew we were all trying our best not to be. After all, she, whom we all admired for her strength, had dedicated her 1980 book of poetry, *Passion*, to "everybody scared as I used to be." We started talking about a powerful image in the poem, a marigold crushed in the little girl's hand. I said it made me think of the terrible beauty of the mushroom cloud, its awful, awe-ful blossoming. I was talking about form separated from meaning, I said. But June could not even begin to entertain that notion and said so. People could be beautiful. Anything that did damage to them could not be beautiful. She wrote a poem later that chastised me for what she saw as my separation of action and consequence, for making an "excuse" for violence. But we became friends.

"Talking back to power" has become a cliché, but because it so aptly describes June Jordan, I want to think that the first time it was said it must have been said about her. Never has so much indignation at the status quo been delivered—in poetry, in essays, speeches, in her marvelous conversation—with such linguistic excellence, virtuosity, range, bravado. She was ever a David against a humongous Goliath, but she knew exactly how and where to aim her shots. Here, as in so much of her work, she's like another fighting poet who could dance like a butterfly and sting like a bee. Asked what is the shortest two-line poem, Muhammad Ali replied proudly, "Sure, I wrote it," and he quoted it:

Me
We

Just think of her name: **June**, the first full month of summer, sweet pea, and peonies, all kinds of roses, jasmine, and honeysuckle; **Jordan** crossing the river to freedom.

If you were blessed to know her in any way—as a teacher, as a speaker at a rally or demonstration, as a reader of her poems in a small public library, or as a listener to her in a radio interview, or working with her in some planned or spontaneous political demonstration to protest one of the multimillion injustices in our screwed-up world, or just sitting around a table, gabbing and gossiping—you will always hear her. Her voice (and laughter) will always be in your head.

As the napalm dropped on Vietnam, Cambodia, and Laos,

as the asbestos-filled World Trade Center rose in Lower Manhattan,

as Reagan launched Star Wars (movie-style, but not the movie),

as Nelson Mandela served his life sentence in South Africa,

as Israel invaded Lebanon,

as women in the U.S. fought and lost the fight for equal rights,

as crack and cops wacked young black men

—every time we thought it couldn't get any worse, and then it did—

my generation was fortunate: we could always turn to June Jordan to cut through the crap, to lay it out straight, to act on her words.

With this *Reader* we have tried to give June Jordan to the next generations, to make them as fortunate as we are.

Jan Heller Levi

1

"NO ONE WILL MOVE ANYWHERE BUT UP"

JORDAN ON SPACE, ARCHITECTURE, COMMUNITY, & DESIGN FOR HUMANS
(1964-1971)

[June Jordan knew a thing or two about urban housing. She spent her earliest years in the just-inaugurated Harlem River Houses. "In New York City there were very few places anybody not 'white' could live"; it was a "necessity and a safe harbor for Black families." Among low-rise redbrick buildings and wide pathways, lawns, and maple trees, with the "man-made valley of light to one side and the slow flowing of the river on the other," as Jordan wrote in her memoir, *Soldier* (2000), she felt very happy. All that was to change when her family moved to a fixer-upper in Bedford-Stuyvesant when she was five. There, on Hancock Street, she became aware of the roughness of city life. Later, at Barnard College, she studied with Herbert Gans, a leading sociologist in urban planning. When she and Michael Meyer married, the couple lived in the projects of Long Island City. There, in 1958, their son

Christopher was born.

Raising a young boy deepened Jordan's fascination with land use, architecture and design, and its impact on people. On early walks with her son, she took him to the East River to experience the sense of horizon. When a friend suggested she spend a summer in Greece, Jordan began studying photographs of the country. "I began to think about what I was seeing, what I was learning to see," she wrote in *Civil Wars* (1981). At the Donnell Library, she pored over pictures of Japanese gardens and Bauhaus chairs and common objects made with care and beauty. "The picture of a spoon, of an elegant, spare utensil as common in its purpose as a spoon, and as lovely and singular in its form as sculpture, utterly transformed my ideas about the possibilities of design in relation to human existence."]

FROM "LETTER TO R. BUCKMINSTER FULLER"

(1964)

[In July 1964, a white police officer in Harlem shot and killed Black youngster Jimmy Powell. Riots erupted in Harlem. *Esquire Magazine* commissioned Jordan to write about the riots. But rather than describe the police brutality and the violence she had witnessed and experienced, she proposed a collaboration with visionary architect, innovator, and inventor R. Buckminster Fuller, whose work she had discovered at the Donnell Library. Together, they developed a radical architectural plan. It would go to the roots of the problem and make riots obsolete. (Jordan was actively tackling point four of the Black Panthers' Ten-Point Program for self-determination: "decent housing, fit for shelter of human beings.") And since "urban renewal" more often than not meant "Negro removal," their plan made sure that wouldn't happen. A new Harlem would—literally—be built above the old. When construction was completed, residents would just move up into their new apartments.

Today the architectural renderings for "Skyline for Harlem" may look dystopian; concave cylinders jutting into the sky remind us more of the towers of nuclear plants than the desirable tall-storied, light-flooded high-rises with community gardens that the collaborators envisioned, an ecological oasis for living and growing with organic connections to the landscape, the rivers, and the rest of New York City. But Jordan and Fuller were working at the time of the 1964 World's Fair, where Americans were being enticed by visions of a Brutalist future. It goes without saying, for example, that Walt Disney and General Electric's Carousel of Progress, with robot-powered "actors" playing the roles of fathers, mothers, and children in the bourgeois homes of tomorrow, were all white.

In the fall of 1964, as they were beginning their work, Jordan wrote to Fuller. She published the letter in *Civil Wars* in 1981. Here is an excerpt.]

Dear Mr. Fuller,

I hope you are very well. [....]

Recently I was able to get away to the country for several days. As the plane tilted into the hills of Laconia, New Hampshire, I could see no one, but there was no tangible obstacle to the imagining of how this land, these contours of growth and rise and seasonal definition could nurture and extend human life. There was no obvious site that might be cleared for housing. No particular grove nor patch visually loomed as more habitable, more humanly yielding than another. And yet, I surmised no menace of elements inimical to life in that topography. It seemed that any stretch, that every slope, provided living possibilities. With just a tent and a few matches, just the minimum of provisions could convert a randomly selected green space into human shelter. Perhaps one explanation of this easy confidence is that such land clearly suggests the activities required for construction of efficient shelter, and, further, these requirements imply necessary labor both feasible and quickly rewarding for human beings to accomplish.

By contrast, any view of Harlem will likely indicate the presence of human life—people whose surroundings suggest that survival is a mysterious and even pointless phenomenon. On the streets of Harlem, sources of sustenance are difficult to discover and, indeed, sources of power for control and change *are* remote. Nor is labor available—labor that directly affects, in manifold ways, the manners of existence. Keeping warm is a matter of locating the absentee landlord rather than an independent expedition to gather wood for a fire. This relates to our design for participation by Harlem residents in the birth of their new reality. I would think that this new reality of Harlem should immediately reassure its residents that control of the quality of survival is possible and that every life is valuable. Hospital zones where strict control is exercised over noise, dirt, and traffic serve as examples of peculiar exception to city habits of chaotic indifference to environmental functions on behalf of human life. I am much heartened by your insistence on the invention of a physical device rather than efforts of social reform. I also believe that the architecture of experience deeply determines an incalculable number and variety of habits—i.e., the nature of quotidian existence.

... The map you kindly gave me indicates Mt. Morris Park and Morningside Park in Harlem. Mt. Morris Park *is* just a rock. Morningside Park does not function as a pleasurable means of escape from entirely man-made environments. These two might well be replaced by park-playgrounds such as I have seen designed in the studio of your friend, Isamu Noguchi.

I plan to explore the New Jersey coastline just below the George Washington Bridge to see if another bridge might be justified between New Jersey and New York at a level invading Harlem. From the Lincoln Tunnel to the George Washington Bridge is quite a leap. Similarly, might there be a possible unification through design of the convergencies of the 8th Ave. Subway, the IRT Subway, and the N.Y. Central Railroad on 125th Street?

I notice on the map that, from W. 125th St. to W. 155th St., the land body of Manhattan is progressively squeezed as the Harlem/East River swerves westward. And, as you see, the sense of green space as a center of island life ends once you stand north of W. 110th St., with the termination of Central Park. While Riverside Drive affords some park area to the west of Harlem, there is no corresponding usage of the eastern shore.

Now, this last year, N.Y.C.'s Planning Commissioner, William F. R. Ballard, has attempted to proceed toward two aims original with his tenure of office. One is the construction of waterfront housing and the use of waterways for daily transit. His second aim is the procurement of a feasible, master plan for New York City. Apparently, N.Y.C. has had nothing that even resembles a master plan since 1811!

I wonder if our plan for Harlem could provide for access to shoreline and thus to natural fluency that would devolve from dwelling places alternating with circles of outdoor safety along the water's edge. This would mean domestication of the littoral, but not the occlusion of the autonomous energies of the river. Would you think it worthwhile to connect interior green space with peripheral rivers?

And interconnection—an arterial system of green spaces leading to water; an arterial system psychologically operative from any position in Harlem. For example, a concentric design with the perimeter touching water east and west. Interior orbitry would spot open spaces—plazas, playgrounds, campus, parks.

Given our goal of a pacific, life-expanding design for a human community, we might revise street patterning so that the present patterns of confrontation by parallel lines would never be repeated. The existing monotony limits pleasures of perspectives. Rigidly flat land is ruled by rectilinear form. The crisscrossing pattern too often becomes a psychological crucifixion; an emergence from an alleyway into a danger zone vulnerable to enemies approaching in at least two directions that converge at the target who is the pedestrian poised on a corner.

I suppose I am appealing for as many curvilinear features of street patterning as possible. This bias seeks to overcome physical patterns of inevitability; the sense of inexorable routes, the impossibility of differentiated approach, of surprise. All of these undesirable effects now result from the gridiron layout of city blocks.

I remember the comparison you drew between the two professions of architecture and medicine. If the physician had continued healing practices determined by the criteria of tradition and expectation, his practice might well have lost its justification, namely, the patient.

I would wish us to indicate the determining relationship between architectonic reality and physical well-being. I hope that we may implicitly instruct the reader in the comprehensive impact of every Where, of any *place*. This requires development of an idea or theory of place in terms of human being; of space designed as the volumetric expression of successful existence between earth and sky; of space cherishing as it amplifies the experience of being alive, the capability of endless beginnings, and the entrusted liberty of motion; of particular space that is open-receptive and communicant yet sheltering particular life.

FROM "SKYRISE FOR HARLEM"

(1965)

[At the same time that Amiri Baraka (then LeRoi Jones) was moving to Harlem, and founding the Black Arts Repertory Theater, Jordan was proposing her and Fuller's radical, revitalizing architectural innovation for that community. *Esquire* published their project in its April 1965 issue. The collaborators called it "Skyrise for Harlem." The editors of the magazine, however, re-titled the article "Instant Slum Clearance," and credited Jordan as only the writer, not the co-creator, of the visionary plan. As late as 2008, when the Whitney Museum mounted an R. Buckminster Fuller retrospective and displayed drawings for the project, Jordan's role was not included in the museum signage or materials. Scholar and writer, Cheryl J. Fish, alerted the Whitney curators to their mistake (Fish is the author of "Place, Emotion, and Environmental Justice in Harlem: June Jordan and Buckminster Fuller's 1965 'Architextual' Collaboration," published in *Discourse*, vol. 29, 2007, and Jordan's name was reinstated three weeks before the show closed. Here are excerpts from "Skyrise for Harlem."]

Harlem is life dying inside a closet, an excrescence beginning where a green park ends, a self-perpetuating disintegration of walls, ceilings, doorways, lives. It is also, of course, a political embarrassment for which no political solution is adequate. A housing project planted in the middle of a slum is not an answer. [...]

Redevelopment generally means the *removal* of slum residents while land is cleared for new buildings and new purposes. In fact, "redevelopment" is frequently a pretext for the permanent expulsion of Negro populations. Fuller's design permits all residents to remain on site while new and vastly improved dwelling facilities rise directly above the old. No one will move anywhere but up. New Harlem will be supported by columns driven into the backyards of the slum, and once the elevated replacement is complete and inhabited, the lower depths will be cleared for roadways and park space. The design will obliterate a valley of shadows: Skyrise for Harlem means literal elevation of Harlem to the level of Morningside Heights. Partial renovation is not enough. Piecemeal healing provides temporary relief at best and may create as many problems as it cures. A half century of despair requires exorcism. [...]

An aerial view of New Harlem will disclose a radical landscape: vast, cleared ranges of space with fifteen peaks rising into the sky. These fifteen widely separated conical structures will house a half million people. A cross section of these structures resembles abstract, stylized Christmas trees evenly broadening toward their base with central, supporting trunks. Each tree town is one hundred circular decks high. The lowest level begins ten stories aboveground, above dust level and major cloverleaf-highway systems.

Fuller's circular decked towards are fireproof (concrete and steel cables) and may be delivered in large sections by helicopter. A central supporting mast also functions as the distributing tube for power, light, heat and disposal facilities independent of municipal utilities. The mast is compressional while the decks hang inside a tensional web (i.e., steel supporting cables). Open space between decks avoids a sense of impenetrable mass. From the masthead, lenses capture the light and heat of the sun.

Circling the central mast is a parking system of ramps that never cross. The huge interior space next permits a circling of shops, supermarkets, game rooms and workshops on every deck, plus, on some levels, a cross view of four hundred feet. The penultimate circling of the central mast contains dwelling units which provide an average of 1200 square feet per family as against an average of 720 in today's public housing. This 1200 square feet does not include the parking space given each family nor the balconies which constitute the perimeter of these great wheels of life. Every room has a view. From these hanging gardens, both rivers will be visible.

[...] Protective watersheds will enclose the sky of Harlem like overlapping umbrellas. Rain may cascade visibly from these watersheds to be piped into New York reservoirs. The watersheds float on the strength of transparent truss systems.

Rather than the commonly known sidewalk, there will be wide walkways entirely separate from the cloverleaf ribbonry that will divide the high-speed through traffic from local traffic. Normal grid layout of city blocks will not stifle the reconstructed Harlem. Roughly, eight square city blocks will equal one of the new towering trees of life. [...]

Skyrise for Harlem creates cultural centers decked into the sky: cultural centers offering practice studios for musicians, concert halls, theaters, workshops, forums for symposia, dancing pavilions, and athletic fields as well as pathways for strolling under trees. Contemporary sculpture will enrich the open spaces of elevated Harlem. [...]

Where we are physically is enmeshed with our deepest consciousness of self. There is no evading architecture, no meaningful denial of our position. You can build to defend the endurance of man, to protect his existence, to illuminate it. But you cannot build for these purposes merely in spasmodic response to past and present crises, for then crisis, like the poor, will be with us always. If man is to have not only a future but a destiny, it must be consciously and deliberately designed.

"NOWADAYS THE HEROES GO OUT LOOKING FOR THE CRADLE IN THE COLD..."
(1969)

[The day after the first moon landing on July 21, *The New York Times* asked Jordan (as well as Jesse Jackson, Pablo Casals, Kenneth B. Clark, Rene Dubos, Saul Alinsky, Isaac Stern, Charles Evers, Reinhold Niebuhr, Paul Goodman, Lewis Mumford, Ella Winter, Vladimir Nabokov, R. Buckminster Fuller, and others) for reactions. The following text is Jordan's response. See also "Nowadays the Heroes" (p. 93-94), in which Jordan casts this text as a poem.]

Nowadays the heroes go out looking for the cradle in the cold. They explore a cemetery for beginnings. And irony can kill. The children panic at the research in the glowing graveyard. (What about humanity in heat; the arms that kept the sleep alive?)

That moon, the moon, is the silver myth of a golden America. Money is the sun that makes us shine. Look for the life that reflects more than a conscience losing human value. (Can anybody sell this idea?) Look for the life, the godly gossip soon enough disclosing laughter and the belly of real joy.

Real seems to be the problem: How to push explosions into love, into soil that will not sully and destroy: love yielding only to more of the same. Or how to budget hunger into the columns of rumor and mistake. Well, it is here. The possibility is here. Not there. Next to me. And I am next to you.

I wait to celebrate a discovery program that will develop that alarming, maybe wonderful fact. It means that we are very near, you know, unknown, and dollar bills don't help. Not even twenty-four billion, for example.

So the President declares a holiday. The country glorifies its landing outside the whole scene, outside the extraordinary, common kiss among peoples. Nobody boggles at the mystery we, man and woman, used to offer the world.

How about a holy day, instead, a day when we concentrate on the chill and sweat worshipping of humankind, in mercy fathom? I mean, brothers and sisters, have you ever heard of children—bankrupt, screaming—on the moon?

FROM *HIS OWN WHERE*

(1971)

[Jordan's popular young adult novel carries over her ideas about architecture and design for "human beings" into the flesh and blood characters of Angela and Buddy, two teenagers in Harlem struggling for love and dignity. *His Own Where* is an urban love story, a kind of Black Romeo and Juliet, but with a happy ending. It is also the first young adult novel written entirely in Black English. "If it don't sound like something that come out somebody mouth then it don't sound right. If it don't sound right then it ain't hardly right. Period," Jordan wrote later in defense of the beauty and power of that language. In this excerpt, from the beginning of the book, Buddy and Angela take on the design of street crossings as a political issue and, later, come upon a spot they can imagine as a new kind of home.]

◆◆◆

ONE

First time they come, he simply say, "Come on." He tell her they are going not too far away. She go along not worrying about the heelstrap pinching at her skin, but worrying about the conversation. Long walks take some talking. Otherwise it be embarrassing just side by side embarrassing.

Buddy stay quiet, walking pretty fast, but every step right next to her. They trip together like a natural sliding down the street.

Block after block after block begin to bother her. Nothing familiar is left. The neighborhood is changing. Strangers watch them from the windows.

Angela looking at Buddy, look at his shoes and wish for summertime and beaches when his body, ankle, toes will shock the ocean, yelling loud and laughing hard and wasting no sand.

Buddy think about time and the slowspeed of her eyes that leave him hungry, nervous, big and quick. Slide by the closedup drugstore, cross under the train, run the redlight, circle past two women leaning on two wire carts, and reach the avenue of showrooms. Green, blue, yellow, orange cars driving through, cars at the curb, cars behind the glass, cars where houses used to stand, cars where people standing now, and tree to tree electric lights.

"Play the radio?"

Buddy turn it with his thumb. The plastic handle strings around his wrist.

> No moon no more
> No moon no more
> I want to see what I seen before.

> Please no surprise
> Please no surprise
> I just want to see your lovin eyes.

Holding her hand in his is large and hers almost loose inside it. She feel visitor-stiff, but the music make a difference, and his hand.

Cars make Buddy mad. Right now his father lying in the hospital from what they call A Accident. And was no accident about it, Buddy realize. The street set up that way so cars can clip the people easy kill them even. Easy.

"What you say?" she ask him.

"Damn," he answer her. "Another one. Another corner. Street-crossing-time again."

"You crazy, Buddy? What you mean?"

"I hate them. Corners. They really be a dumb way try to split the people from the cars. Don't even work. Look how a car come up and almost kill my father, minding his own business, on the corner. Corners good for nothing." Buddy frown so bad that Angela start laughing. Buddy swing around her waist.

"Show you what I mean."

He jump back behind her. Walk forward like a flatfoot counting steps: Left-foot-right-foot-left-foot-one-two.

"Here come the corner!"

Down. Buddy buckle at the knee for *down.* When he really reach the corner then he drop to one knee. Seem like a commando on the corner. Wild looking left then right. Arms like a rifle in rotation: Covering the danger east and west. Buddy standing on his two feet urgent. Put his face an inch from her: "Watch now. Here. It's here." He roll the radio dial to loud yell over it. "Not clear! Not clear at the crossing. On your mark," (whispering in her ear) "get set." Buddy stop. "Green. Where's the green? You seen it, Angela?" He fold his arms and spread his legs and hold everything right there. "Well my Lookout Man is out to lunch." Buddy sitting on the curb, to wait.

Angela feel a question, but the radio so loud she would have to scream. With him, she rather not be screaming.

Angela not laughing and no smile. Buddy sitting on the curb and she beside him, so he roll the dial to soft.

"You see them signs. The curb-your-dog signs. But the people be like slaves. Don't need no signs. Just do it. Curb-the-People. Step right up, then down, then up. Then out. Into it. Into the traffic, baby.

You be crucify like Jesus at the crossing. Traffic like a 4-way nail the joker on his feet. It be strictly D.O.A. for corners. Danger on Arrival. D.O.A. Even dogs can smell that danger, smell it just as good as looking at the lights. You tired?"

"No," She is. But nothing they can do about that. No bench. No sidewalk, walkway tables, benches. Only fences fixed out front.

"Buddy, this no place to stop."

Rises from the curb, his arm around her, moving on together, slower walking easy on the edge. The sidewalk is a concrete edge.

[...]

They notice the one-by-one increasing trees. She watch Buddy how he walk ahead of her, how he seems a bit ahead of her. They come to a silent place. The only sounds, the engine highway sounds.

They climb up sidesoil to a fence that stretches high above their heads and out beyond armstretching.

Angela be blinded by the light wiggles blinding in the silent water fills her eyes. They say nothing, just look and feel full. It be like a big open box, sides of sloping stone, moss covered rainy dark and, behind them, a little to the left, there be a small brick tower room, a locked-up house where no one ever live.

Buddy say, "This is the reservoir." Angela be thinking water and, over by the furthest rim of it, they see the roof of streets and houses that they know. Nobody close to them. Buddy and Angela begin to make believe about the house next to the reservoir. They see how they would open it up, how they would live inside, what they would do with only the birds, the water, and the skylight fallen blinding into it.

"What they saving the water for? Who suppose to use it."

"Saving it for birds. This a bathroom for the birds."

They laugh about the pretty water bathroom for the birds.

"Be nice if we can swim here."

"They not hardly let you swim in it. Unless you be a bird."

Go over to the doorsill of the house, sit down for talking.

"Why you bring me here?"

"You don't like it?"

"So quiet. I don't know."

"How come you always want some sound?"

"Real quiet bother me. But then again, when I go to like the supermarket they be playing loony tunes and you be looking at a can of soup, or pork chops, but you have to hear dah-dah-blah- blah and violins and mustard and potatoes dah-dah-blah-blah-violins, it can make you feel really weird."

"So what you want to hear with mustard and potatoes?"

"Well, could be somebody like that kind of music, but I don't. I rather be hearing other things. Like if you play the radio and we decide what we want to hear I mean at this very moment."

"What you want?"

"You talk to me, Buddy. Tell me what you thinking."

"WHO WOULD PAINT A PEOPLE BLACK OR WHITE?"

WHO LOOK AT ME (1969) & *SOULSCRIPT* (1970)

[By 1967, Jordan was teaching in the SEEK (Search for Education, Elevation, and Knowledge) program at City College, through which "disadvantaged" students took classes that would prepare them for the further rigors of college academic life. At City, Jordan was among an amazing group of writers teaching in the program, including Toni Cade Bambara, Adrienne Rich, Audre Lorde, David Henderson, and Raymond Patterson. Jordan also became one of the guiding spirits of the newly founded Teachers & Writers Collaborative, a group including Rosellen Brown, Victor Hernández Cruz, Kenneth Koch, Herbert Kohl, Phillip Lopate, Grace Paley, Muriel Rukeyser, Anne Sexton, and Robert Silvers, which brought equally inspiring poetry workshops to young people in New York City. Jordan was a dedicated, imaginative teacher. It was upsetting to her to learn that many of the African-American children she worked with knew so little about the histo-

ry and cultural contributions of their people. She made it her business
to do something about that.]

WHO LOOK AT ME

(1969)

[Jordan's *Who Look at Me* is a primer in Black identity, an illustra-
tion of Black history, a very short version of *Invisible Man*, a searing
meditation on race, identity, and the American character, and a lyric
tour de force in which Jordan's long, sequenced poem serves as kind
of "soundtrack" for twenty-seven full-color reproductions of paint-
ings chronicling Black life in America, most of them the work of Af-
rican-American artists. The art works came from a vast collection of
illustrations acquired by writer and editor Milton Meltzer, who was
originally working on the project with Langston Hughes. When Hughes
died, Jordan took on the project, honored to carry on his work. She
composed the work, coordinating her text with the images, while she
was in Atlanta, attending Martin Luther King, Jr.'s funeral. *Who Look
at Me*—Jordan's poem in conversation with the paintings, including
works by Charles Alston, John Wilson, Colleen Browning, and Romare
Bearden—is a lost American treasure. It stands beside Jacob Law-
rence's 1941 combination of text and image, *The Migration Series*, as
an essential document of 20th century Black experience and expres-
sion. We still have the great poem reprinted here. The full book, long
out of print, calls out to be republished; we hope it will be, soon.]

WHO LOOK AT ME

For Christopher my son

Who would paint a people
black or white?

*

For my own I have held
where nothing showed me how
where finally I left alone
to trace another destination

*

A white stare splits the air
by blindness on the subway
in department stores
The Elevator
                    (that unswerving ride
where man ignores the brother
by his side)

A white stare splits obliterates
the nerve-wrung wrist from work
the breaking ankle or
the turning glory
of a spine

*

Is that how we look to you
a partial nothing clearly real?

who see a solid clarity
of feature
size and shape of some
one head
an unmistaken nose

the fact of afternoon
as darkening
his candle eyes

Older men with swollen neck

(when they finally sit down

who will stand up
for them?)

I cannot remember nor imagine pretty
people treat me
like a doublejointed stick

WHO LOOK AT ME
WHO SEE

the tempering sweetness
of a little girl who wears
her first pair of earrings
and a red dress

the grace of a boy removing
a white mask he makes beautiful

Iron grille across the glass
and frames of motion closed or
charred or closed

The axe lies on the ground
She listening to his coming sound

him
just touching his feet
powerful and wary

anonymous and normal
parents and their offspring
posed in formal

*

I am

impossible to explain

remote from old and new interpretations
and yet
not exactly

*

look at the stranger as

he lies more gray than black
on that colorquilt
that
(everyone will say)
seems bright beside him

look
black sailors on the light
green sea the sky keeps blue
the wind blows high
and hard at night
for anyhow anywhere new

*

Who see starvation at the table
lines of men no work to do
my mother ironing a shirt?

Who see a frozen skin the midnight
of the winter and the hallway cold
to kill you like the dirt?

where kids buy soda pop
in shoeshine parlors
barber shops so they can hear
some laughing

Who look at me?

Who see the children
on their street the torn down door the wall

complete an early losing
                        games of ball
the search to find
a fatherhood a mothering of mind
a multimillion multicolored mirror
of an honest humankind?

                              *

look close
and see me black man mouth
for breathing (North and South)
A MAN

I am black alive and looking back at you.

                              *

see me brown girl throat
that throbs from servitude

see me hearing fragile
leap
and lead a black boy
reckless to succeed
to wrap my pride
around tomorrow and to go
there
without fearing

see me darkly covered ribs
around my heart across my skull
thin skin protects the part
that dulls from longing

                              *

Who see the block we face
the thousand miles of solid alabaster space
inscribed keep off keep out don't touch
and Wait Some More for Half as Much?

                              *

To begin is no more agony
than opening your hand

*

sometimes you have to dance
like spelling
the word joyless

*

Describe me broken mast
adrift but strong
regardless what may
come along

*

What do you suppose he hears
every evening?

*

I am stranded in a hungerland
of great prosperity

*

shelter happens seldomly and
like an accident
it stops

*

No doubt
the jail is white where I am born
but black will bail me out

*

We have lived as careful
as a church and prayer
in public

*

we reveal

a complicated past
of tinderbox and ruin
where we carried water
for the crops

we come from otherwhere

victim to a rabid cruel cargo crime

to separate and rip apart
the trusting members of one heart

my family

I looked for you
I looked for you

*

(slavery:) the insolence

*

came to frontiers
of paralyze highways
freedom strictly underground

came here to hatred hope labor love
and lynchlength rope

came a family to a family

*

I found my father
silently despite the grieving
fury of his life

Afternoons he wore his hat
and held a walking stick

I found my mother
her geography
becomes our home

*

so little safety

almost nowhere like the place
that childhood plans
in a pounding happy space
between deliberate brown and clapping
hands
that preached a reaping to the wildly
    sleeping earth
brown hands that worked for rain a fire inside
    and food to eat
from birth brown hands
    to hold

                    *

New energies of darkness we
disturbed a continent
like seeds

and life grows slowly
so we grew

We became a burly womb
an evening harvest kept by prayers
a hallelujah little room

We grew despite the crazy killing scorn
that broke the brightness to be born

In part we grew
by looking back at you

that white terrain
impossible for black America to thrive
that hostile soil to mazelike toil
backbreaking people into pain

we grew by work by waiting
to be seen

black face black body and black mind
beyond obliterating
homicide of daily insult daily death
the pistol slur the throbbing redneck war
with breath

In part we grew
with heroes who could halt a slaveship
lead the crew
like Cinqué (son
of a Mendi African Chief) he
led in 1839
the Amistad Revolt
from slavehood forced
a victory he
killed the captain killed the cook
took charge
a mutiny for manhood
people
called him killer but
some
the Abolitionists
looked back at robbery
of person
murdering of spirit
slavery requires
and one
John Quincy Adams (seventy-three)
defended Cinqué who
by highest court decree
in 1841 stood free
and freely he returned
to Africa
victorious

In part we grew

grandmother husband son
together when the laborblinding day was done

In part we grew
as we were meant to grow
ourselves
with kings and queens no white man knew

we grew by sitting on a stolen chair
by windows and a dream
by setting up a separate sail
to carry life
to start the song

to stop the scream

*

These times begin the ending of all lies
the fantasies of seasons start and stop
the circle leads to no surprise
for death does not bewilder
only life can kill can mystify can start
and stop like flowers ripening a funeral
like (people) holding hands across the knife
that cuts the casket to an extraordinary size

*

Tell the whiplash helmets GO!
and take away
that cream and orange Chevrolet
stripped to inside steel and parked
forever on one wheel

Set the wild dogs chewing up
that pitiful capitulation
plastic flower plastic draperies
to dust the dirt

Break the clothesline
Topple down the clotheslinepole

O My Lives Among The Wounded Buildings
should be dressed in trees and grass

*

we will no longer wait for want for watch
for what we will

*

We make a music marries room to room.

*

listen to that new girl
tears her party dress to sweep
the sidewalk as the elderly slow
preacher nears the mailbox in a black suit
emptyhanded

*

Although the world
forgets me
I will say yes
AND NO

*

NO
to a carnival run by freaks
who take a life
and tie it terrible
behind my back

No One Exists As Number Two
If you deny it you should try
being someone number two

*

I want to hear something other than a single
ringing on the concrete

*

I grieve the sorrow roar the sorrow sob

of many more left hand or right
black children and white
men the mountaintop the mob
I grieve the sorrow roar the sorrow sob
the fractured staring at the night

Sometimes America the shamescape
knock-rock territory losing shape
the Southern earth like blood
rolls valleys cold gigantic
weeping willow flood
that lunatic that lovely land
that graveyard growing
trees remark where men
another black man
died he died again
he died

*

I trust you will remember how we tried to love
above the pocket deadly need to please
and how so many of us died there
on our knees.

*

Who see the roof and corners of my pride
to be (as you are) free?

WHO LOOK AT ME?

FROM *SOULSCRIPT*

(1970)

[A year after *Who Look at Me* (1969), Jordan published an outstanding anthology of African-American poetry for young people, *soulscript*. (The same year, she co-edited with Terri Bush *The Voice of the Children*, a selection of poems by the young Black and Puerto Rican teenagers in their creative writing workshop in Brooklyn.) *Soulscript* is a love letter to Black literary art in America and a polemic on how it has been condescended to by the white establishment. As she was to do all her life, Jordan included the young in the world of poetry. She also included some poems by her students. Here's Jordan's introduction to *soulscript*.]

Coast to coast, on subways, in bedrooms, in kitchens, in weekend workshops, at parties—almost anywhere except the classroom, as a matter of fact—Afro-Americans are writing poetry. It's happening now, and it's wonderful, fine, and limitless, like love—that love the sisters and the brothers exchange inside the family living here. And when American classrooms switch from confrontation to communion, black poetry will happen in the schools as well.

Poetry tells the feeling.

A poem tells the relationship.

By picturing a street for freedom, or by rhyming *whitestare* with *nightmare*, or by laying down lines the way a man runs crazy, poetry reveals the various feelings of relationship. People live a poem every minute they spend in the world. Reaction, memory, and dream: these are the springs of poetry. And a four-year-old flows among them as fully as any adult.

Since poetry turns the individual drama of being human into words, it is an art open to all vocabulary made personal. Poetry changes life into a written drama where words set the stage and where words then act as the characters on that stage.

Soulscript presents the poetry of Afro-Americans.

Over the past several years, Afro-America has flourished as a national community concerned to express its own situation and its own response. The concern to choose, find, and create relationship leads naturally into poems. Here, in this anthology, the reader will follow along where Afro-American concern for a vocabulary-made-personal leads. Governed by a beautiful, proud spirit, the Afro-American grows from the experience of brave, continuing survival despite the force of deadly circumstance. These poems tell that spirit and that survival, even as they spell black dreams.

Language is something common, something always shared—like air. The human voice depends on air. Poetry depends on language. But voice transforms the air into a spoken personality. And poetry transforms a language into voice. Poems are voiceprints of language, or if you prefer, *soulscript*. In part, the problems of poetry-writing stem from the nature of its material: language as everybody's identical tool.

The craft of poetry is an everlasting challenge to the language blur of individuality.

This struggle to determine and then preserve a particular, human voice is closely related to the historic struggling of black life in America.

Slavery meant that certain men comfortably destroyed other, real people as individuals. Enslaved, black men and women were forced into the status merely of machines making money for the "master." Literally lashed into a role rejecting particular, human life, the cultivation of *own voice* became a workaday occupation, an unrelenting protest, and an ultimate social triumph. After slavery, the Afro-American fought to stay alive in a land amused by stereotypes hostile to the integrity of his person.

Just as Malcolm Little redefined his self into Malcolm X, Afro-America, for its integrity and survival, pursues this history into pride and poem. We must redefine the words, the names, of our universe and the values attached to every written tag—such as *white*, *black*, *darkness*, *light*, *good*, and *evil*. And indeed, from San Francisco to Brooklyn, from Watts to Fort Greene, we are working into poetry the future of our love.

In all forms of personally crafted language, there is an exceptional, lengthy tradition of black American literature. From the time of Frederick Douglass down through Eldridge Cleaver, Afro-American leaders of first rank have been distinguished by extraordinary,

unique word-power. If we will remember the relations between poet-
ry and language, there is scarcely reason for surprise at the wealth
of outstanding poets among black people. Even less surprising is the
frequency of black political figures who are also poets. For example:
Julian Bond, LeRoi Jones, Julius Lester. And yet, the youngest reader
may be shocked to consider that, until quite recently, most black
literature remained unpublished. This neglect was hardly accidental.
Literature, the crafting of language by special, human experience,
acts as witness. Great literature acts as an unforgettable, completely
convincing witness. Poetry raises the human voice from the flat, fa-
miliar symbols on a paper page. Great poetry compels an answering;
the raised voice creates communion. Until recently, the Afro-Amer-
ican witness suffered an alien censorship. And even as slaves were
not allowed to congregate alone, to create communion of their own,
poetry has been recognized as dangerous by the enemies of free men
everywhere. Consequently, the typical textbook offers the poetry of
Carl Sandburg, Hart Crane, Amy Lowell, and e. e. cummings (white
American poets), protected from competition from Jean Toomer, Mar-
garet Walker, Countee Cullen, and Robert Hayden.

(Who?)

However, the weight of alien censorship is lifting.

James Weldon Johnson's line

"O Black and Unknown Bards"

no longer predicts the public career of written Black Art.

Yet the weight lifts slowly, and as it does, still another barrier to
normal recognition meets the Afro-American. A discouraging number
of published critics pretend that the literature, the poetry, of black
artists buckles like some inferior stuff when measured by the usual
critieria. That is a patronizing, absolute mistake. To be consistent,
such critics would have to deny the artistic validity of world litera-
ture characterized by social conscience and the perilous heroism of
rebellion. W. B. Yeats, Stephen Vincent Benét, and Federico García
Lorca are simply a few whose political commitment would compro-
mise the admiration they now command as poets. In *soulscript*, the

poetry of Afro-America appears as it was written: in tears, in rage, in hope, in sonnet, in blank/free verse, in overwhelming rhetorical scream. These poems redeem a hostile vocabulary; they witness, they create communion, and they contribute beauty to the long evening of their origins.

To emphasize the living purpose of black poetry, I have chosen the poems primarily of people who could read them aloud next week. Privileged as the editor, my difficulty has been to delimit rather than to secure. Given the time and volume, these poems would appear as the fractional part of an entire literature that they really are. More than one poet, for instance Jay Wright and Calvin Hernton, would have much heavier representation but distance, changing address, and like complications of have prevented the inclusion of many poems here. *Soulscript* opens with the poetry written by black children ranging in age from twelve to eighteen. These young poets, more or less accidentally known by me, should powerfully suggest the fabulous efflorescence of black literary art that we, Afro-American and white, can enjoy and honor with our lives.

In faith,
June Meyer Jordan

"HONEY PEOPLE MURDER MERCY U.S.A."

SOME CHANGES (1967, 1971)

[Fueled by rage at the assassination of Malcolm X and the continued racism in America on all levels, the Black Arts Movement emerged, in the mid-1960s—a fiery expression of Black pride, Black literature, and Black revolutionary activity. By the turn of the decade, many of the women associated with, or inspired by the movement, had become uncomfortable with the misogyny, sexism, and homophobia so problematically entrenched in it. In 1970, the publication of Toni Morrison's *The Bluest Eye*, Alice Walker's *The Third Life of Grange Copeland*, and Toni Cade Bambara's anthology, *The Black Women,* were incontrovertible proof that the perspective of Black women was essential, and not just as "an / in and out/ rightside up /action-image / of her man" as Don L. Lee (later Haki R. Madhubuti) put it in "BLACKWOMAN." With the publication of her first full-length collection of poems, Some Changes, Jordan was recognized as a voice to be reckoned with, "officially" joining the ranks of notable Black women writers of the time, among them Gwendolyn Brooks, Nikki Giovanni, Audre Lorde, Barbara Smith,

Sonia Sanchez, and Gayl Jones.

A Black male poet closely connected with the Black Arts Movement got the message. Julius Lester, recently taking the helm of a newly established and ultimately short-lived Black Poets Series at Dutton, had immediately lined up Stanley Crouch's *Ain't No Ambulances For No Nigguhs Tonight* and Larry Neal's *Hoodoo Hollerin' Bebop Ghosts* for publication. But he chose Jordan's *Some Changes* to kick off the series (an earlier version published in 1967 had not received critical notice). In his introduction, Lester wrote: "June Jordan is a black poet. A black woman poet. That's a devastating combination. To be black and to be a woman. To be a double-outsider, to be twice-oppressed, to be more than invisible. June Jordan is a black woman poet. Think about that. A Black woman poet. That's triple vision."

Here is a selection of Jordan's achievement in *Some Changes*—poems that are beautifully crafted and syncopated conversations in the here and now, presenting both Black men and woman as complex, admirable characters forging a destiny in a sometimes beautiful, sometimes devastating world. These poems are footloose, furious, lyrical, ironic, tender, revelatory.]

◆◆◆

THE WEDDING

Tyrone married her this afternoon
not smiling as he took the aisle
and her slightly rough hand.
Dizzella listened to the minister
staring at his wrist and twice
forgetting her name:
Do you promise to obey?
Will you honor humility and love
as poor as you are?
Tyrone stood small but next
to her person
trembling. Tyrone stood

straight and bony
black alone with one key
in his pocket.
By marrying today
they made themselves a man
and woman
answered friends or unknown
curious about the Cadillacs
displayed in front of Beaulah Baptist.
Beaulah Baptist
life in general
indifferent
barely known
nor caring to consider
the earlywed Tyrone
and his Dizzella
brave enough
but only two.

◆◆◆

THE RECEPTION

Doretha wore the short blue lace last night
and William watched her drinking so she fight
with him in flying collar slim-jim orange
tie and alligator belt below the navel pants uptight

"I flirt. You hear me? Yes I flirt.
Been on my pretty knees all week
to clean the rich white downtown dirt
the greedy garbage money reek.

I flirt. Damned right. You look at me."
But William watched her carefully
his mustache shaky she could see

him jealous, "which is how he always be

at parties." Clementine and Wilhelmina
looked at trouble in the light blue lace
and held to George while Roosevelt Senior
circled by the yella high and bitterly light blue face

he liked because she worked
the crowded room like clay like molding men
from dust to muscle jerked
and arms and shoulders moving when

she moved. The Lord Almighty Seagrams bless
Doretha in her short blue dress
and Roosevelt waiting for his chance:
a true gut-funky blues to make her really dance.

◆◆◆

NOWADAYS THE HEROES

Nowadays the heroes go out looking
for the cradle in the cold
explore
a cemetery for beginnings
(irony can kill
                the children panic at
the research in the glowing graveyard
what
what about
the sleep alive?)
                Look.
Look for the life
Look for reflections of the living
real problem:
money is the sun that makes us shine.

◆◆◆

IN MEMORIAM:
MARTIN LUTHER KING, JR.

1

honey people murder mercy U.S.A.
the milkland turn to monsters teach
to kill to violate pull down destroy
the weakly freedom growing fruit
from being born

America

tomorrow yesterday rip rape
exacerbate despoil disfigure
crazy running threat the
deadly thrall
appall belief dispel
the wildlife burn the breast
the onward tongue
the outward hand
deform the normal rainy
riot sunshine shelter wreck
of darkness derogate
delimit blank
explode deprive
assassinate and batten up
like bullets fatten up
the raving greed
reactivate a springtime
terrorizing

by death by men by more
than you or I can

STOP

2

They sleep who know a regulated place
or pulse or tide or changing sky
according to some universal
stage direction obvious
like shorewashed shells

we share an afternoon of mourning
in between no next predictable
except for wild reversal hearse rehearsal
bleach the blacklong lunging
ritual of fright insanity and more
deplorable abortion
more and
more

◆◆◆

IF YOU SAW A NEGRO LADY

If you saw a Negro lady
sitting on a Tuesday
near the whirl-sludge doors of
Horn & Hardart on the main drag
of downtown Brooklyn

solitary and conspicuous as plain
and neat as walls impossible to
fresco and you watched her self-
conscious features shape about
a Horn & Hardart teaspoon
with a pucker from a cartoon

she would not understand
with spine as straight and solid
as her years of bending over floors

allowed

skin cleared of interest by a ruthless
soap   nails square and yellowclean
from metal files

sitting in a forty-year-old-flush
of solitude and prickling
from the new white cotton blouse
concealing nothing she had ever noticed
even when she bathed and never
hummed a bathtub tune nor knew one

If you saw her square
above the dirty
mopped-on antiseptic floors
before the rag-wiped table tops

little finger   broad and stiff
in heavy emulation of a cockney

mannerism
would you turn her treat
into surprise
observing

happy birthday

◆◆◆

JUICE OF A LEMON ON THE TRAIL OF LITTLE YELLOW

Little Yellow looked at the banana tree and
he looked at the moon and he heard a banana tree baboon
beneath the moon and he sat on the grass
and fell asleep there

Little Yellow nine years old underneath the moon beside
a big banana tree smiled a mango smile as he
listened to a lullaby palm and a naked woman broke
coconuts for him and fed him meat from her mango
mammaries

Little Yellow curled himself in a large banana leaf
and he deeply sailed asleep toward the mango moon
Little Yellow traveled to a place where coolies worked
to build a bathtub for the rough and tribal Caribbean

There on that lush cerulean plateau and trapped he
was kept by his boss   brother who positively took
out his teeth and left the mango mouth of Little Yellow
empty

◆◆◆

WHEN I OR ELSE

when I or else when you
and I or we
deliberate I lose I
cannot choose if you if
we then near or where
unless I stand as loser
of that losing possibility
that something that I have
or always want more than much
more at
least to have as less and
yes directed by desire

◆◆◆

TOWARD A PERSONAL SEMANTICS

if I do take somebody's word on
it means I don't know and you have to
believe if you just don't know
how do I dare to stand as
still as I am still standing

arrows create me
but I am no wish

after all the plunging
myself is no sanctuary
birds feed and fly inside me shattering
the sullen spell of any
accidental

eyeless storm to twist and sting
the tree of my remaining
like the wind

◆◆◆

FOR CHRISTOPHER

Tonight
        the machinery of shadow
                moves into the light

He is lying there
        not a true invalid
                        not dying
Now his face looks blue
        but all of that small body
                will more than do
                        as life.

The lady radiologist
                  regardless how and where
                          she turns the knob
will never know
                  the plenty of pain
                              growing
parts to arm
        a man inside the boy

practically asleep

◆◆◆

WHAT WOULD I DO WHITE?

What would I do white?
What would I do clearly full
of not exactly beans nor
pearls my nose a manicure
my eyes a picture of your wall?

I would disturb the streets by
passing by so pretty kids
on stolen petty cash would look
at me like foreign
writing in the sky

I would forget my furs on any chair.
I would ignore the doormen at the knob
the social sanskrit of my life
unwilling to disclose my cosmetology,
I would forget.

Over my wine I would acquire
I would inspire big returns to equity
the equity of capital I am

accustomed to accept

like wintertime.

I would do nothing.
That would be enough.

OKAY "NEGROES"

Okay "Negroes"
American Negroes
looking for milk
crying out loud
in the nursery of freedomland:
the rides are rough.
Tell me where you got that image
of a male white mammy.
God is vague and he don't take no sides.
You think clean fingernails crossed legs a smile
shined shoes
a crucifix around your neck
good manners
no more noise
you think who's gonna give you something?

Come a little closer.
Where you from?

UHURU IN THE O.R.

The only successful heart transplant, of the first
five attempts, meant that a black heart kept alive a

white man — a white man who upheld apartheid.

I like love anonymous
more than murder incorporated or
shall we say South Africa
I like the Valentine the heart the power
incorruptible but failing body
flowers of the world

From my death the white man
takes new breath he stands as
formerly he stood and he commands me
for his good he overlooks
my land my people
in transition transplantations
hearts   and power
beating beating beating beating
hearts in transplantation
power in transition

◆◆◆

EXERCISE IN QUITS

November 15, 1969

1

moratorium means well what
you think it means you
dense? Stop it means stop.

We move and we march sing songs
move march sing songs move march move

It/stop means stop.
                    hey mister man

how long you been fixing to kill somebody?
Waste of time
        the preparation training
you was born a bullet.

2
we be wondering what they gone do
all them others left and right
what they have in mind

about us
and who by the way is "us"

listen you got a match you got the light
you got two eyes two hands
why you taking pictures of the people

what you sposed to be you
got to photograph the people?
you afraid you will (otherwise) forget
what people look like?

man
or however you been paying dues

we look like you

        on second thought
there is a clear resemblance to the dead
among the living so
go ahead go on
and take my picture

quick

◆◆◆

IN MY OWN QUIETLY EXPLOSIVE HERE

In my own quietly explosive here
all silence isolates
to kill the artificial suffocates
a hunger

Likely dying underground
in circles hold together
wings
develop still regardless

◆◆◆

LAST POEM FOR A LITTLE WHILE

1
Thanksgiving 1969
Dear God I thank you for the problems that are mine
and evidently mine alone

By mine I mean just ours
crooked perishable blue like blood
problems yielding to no powers
we can muster we can only starve or stud
the sky the soil the stomach of the human hewn

2
(I am in this crazy room
where people all over the place
look at people all over the place
For instance Emperors in Bronze Black Face
Or Buddha Bodhisattva sandstone trickled old and dirty
    into inexpensive, public space.)

Insanity goes back a long time I suppose.

An alien religion strikes me lightly
And I wonder if it shows
then how?

3

Immediately prior to the messed-up statues that inspire
monographs and fake mistakes
the Greco-Roman paraplegic tricks
the permanently unbent knee
that indoor amphitheater that celebrates the amputee —

Immediately prior to the messed-up statues
just before the lucratively mutilated choir
of worthless lying recollection

There the aged sit and sleep;
for them museum histories spread too far too deep
for actual exploration

(aged men and women) sit and sleep
before the costly exhibition can begin

to tire what remains of life.

4

If love and sex were easier
we would choose something else
to suffer.

5

Holidays do loosen up the holocaust
the memories (sting tides) of rain and refuge
patterns hurt across the stranger city
holidays do loosen up the holocaust
They liberate the stolen totem tongue

The cripples fill the temple
palace entertainment under glass
the cripples crutching near the columns swayed
by plastic wrap
disfiguring haven halls or veils the void
impromptu void
where formerly
Egyptian sarcasucker or more recently
where European painting
turns out nothing
no one
I have ever known.

These environments these
artifacts facsimiles these
metaphors these
earrings vase that sword
none of it
none of it
is somehow what I own.

6
Symbols like the bridge.
Like bridges generally.
Today a flag a red and white and blue new flag
confused the symbols in confusion
bridge over the river
flag over the bridge
The flag hung like a loincloth flicked in drag.

7
Can't cross that bridge. You listen
things is pretty bad
you want to reach New Jersey
got to underslide the lying spangled banner.

Bad enough New Jersey.
Now Songmy.
Songmy. A sorry song. Songmy.
The massacre of sorrow songs.
Songmy. Songmy. Vietnam.
Goddamn. Vietnam.
I would go pray about the bridge.
I would go pray a sorrow Songmy song.
But last time I looked the American flag was flying
from the center of the crucifix.

8
"Well, where you want to go?"
he asks. "I don't know. It's a long
walk to the subway."
"Well," he says, "there's nothing at home."
"That's a sure thing," she answers.
"That's a sure thing: Nothing's at home."

9
Please pass the dark meat.
Turkey's one thing I can eat
and eat.
eeney eeney meeney mo
It's hard to know
whether I should head into
a movie
or take the highway to the airport.
Pass the salt.
Pass the white meat.
Pass the massacre.
o eeney eeney myney mo.
How bad was it, exactly?
What's your evidence?
Songmy o my sorrow
eeney meeney myney mo

Please pass the ham.
I want to show
Vietnam how we give thanks
around here.
Pass the ham.
And wipe your fingers on the flag.

10
Hang my haven
Jesus Christ
is temporarily off
the wall.

11
American existence twists
you finally
into a separatist.

12
I am spiders
on the ceiling of a shadow.

13
Daumier was not mistaken.
Old people sleep with their mouths open
and their hands closed flat
like an empty wallet.

So do I.

"IF IT'S WRONG IN STANDARD ENGLISH IT'S PROBABLY RIGHT IN BLACK ENGLISH, OR, AT LEAST, YOU'RE HOT"

JORDAN ON THE POLITICS OF LANGUAGE (1972-1985)

[Jordan's use of Black English in *His Own Where* (1971) received serious blowback. Some school librarians refused to put it on their shelves; some Black parents denounced it as threat: for their children to gain access to the colleges and jobs that were essential to their success, they were convinced that Black English had no place in the schools. Jordan responded to the controversy with characteristic energy. She spoke with parents' groups, librarians, school officials, gave talks, and wrote—over the course of a dozen years—several landmark essays on language and power.]

"WHITE ENGLISH / BLACK ENGLISH: THE POLITICS OF TRANSLATION"

(1972)

["White English/Black English: The Politics of Translation," is as incisive and important as George Orwell's 1946 famous essay "Politics and the English Language." Orwell wrote about the obfuscating clichés of his time; Jordan celebrates the clarity and expressiveness of Black English, contrasting it with the perilous inanities of White English government-speak, as practiced by the Nixon administration. Jordan originally published the text as two articles in 1972: "White English: The Politics of Language" in *Black World* and "Towards a Politics of Language" in *Publishers Weekly*. She included the essay in *Civil Wars* (1981).]

◆◆◆

WHITE ENGLISH

By now, most Blackfolks—even the most stubbornly duped and desperately light-headed nigger behind his walnut, "anti-poverty" desk—has heard The Man talking that talk, and the necessary translation into Black—*on white terms*—has taken place. Yeah. The Man has made his standard English speech, his second inaugural address, his budget statements, and ain' no body left who don't understand the meaning of them words falling out that mouth: In the *New York Times*, February 25, 1973, Dick Nixon has described the genocide perpetrated by America in Vietnam as "*one of the most unselfish missions ever undertaken by one nation in the defense of another.*"

Now, you just go ahead and let any little Black child lead you to the truth behind that particular, monstrous lie: let him tell you about the twelve days of Christmas "carpet bombing," My Lai, day-by-day incineration of human lives, the mining of rivers, the bombing of hospitals, and "defoliation" of the land, over there. They all—all of them whitefolks ruling the country—they all talk that talk, that "standard (white) English." It is the language of the powerful. Language is political. That's why you and me, my Brother and my Sister, that's why we sposed to choke our natural self into the weird, lying, barbarous, unreal, white speech and writing habits that the schools lay down like holy law. Because, in other words, the powerful don't play; they mean to keep that power, and those who are the powerless (you and me) better shape up—mimic/ape/suck—in the very image of the powerful, or the powerful will destroy you—you and our children.

Dick Nixon has declared that, since the U.S. of A. has completed its "unselfish mission" in Vietnam, America can turn "more fully to the works of compassion, concern and social progress at home." Sounds pretty good, right? Translation: He means the death of all human welfare programs to end hunger, hazardous housing, inequity in court, injustice, and the suffering of poor health. Check it out; I'm not lying to you. Standard English use of the word "compassion" actually means the end of milk programs for needy school kids, an 18-month halt to every form of federal assistance for low-income new housing/rehabilitation, the terminating of Community Action Programs across the nation, and the subtraction of federal aid from elementary and junior high and high school systems especially intended to enable impoverished youngsters. And, since that's what "compassion" means in White English, I most definitely do not see why any child should learn *that* English/prize it/participate in this debasement of this human means to human community: this debasement of language, per se.

See, the issue of white English is inseparable from the issues of mental health and bodily survival. If we succumb to phrases such as "winding down the war," or if we accept "pacification" to mean the murdering of unarmed villagers, and "self-reliance" to mean bail money for Lockheed Corporation and bail money for the mis-managers of the Pennsylvania Railroad, on the one hand, but also, if we allow "self-reliance" to mean starvation and sickness and misery for poor families, for the aged, and for the permanently disabled/permanently discriminated against—then our mental health is seriously in peril: we have entered the world of doublespeak-bullshit, and our lives may soon be lost behind that entry. In any event, The Man has brought the war home, where it's always really been at: sometimes explosive, sometimes smoldering, but currently, as stark, inhuman, and deliberate as the "perfect grammar" of Nixon's war cries raised, calm as a killer, against the weak, the wanting, and the ones who cannot fight back: How will we survive this new—this, to use a standard English term, "escalated"—phase of white war against Black life?

Well, first let me run down some of the ways we will *not* survive:

1/ We will not survive by joining the game according to the rules set up by our enemies; we will not survive by imitating the doublespeak/ bullshit/nonthink standard English of the powers that be: Therefore, if the F.B.I. asks you do you know so-and-so, a member of the Black Panther Party, for example, you will not respond in this Watergate "wise": "I do seem to recall having had some association with the person in question during, or should I say, sometime during, the past." You will say, instead, for example: "What's it to you? What do I look like to you? What right do you have to ask me that question?"

2/ We will *not* try to pretend that we are the Pennsylvania Railroad or some enormous, profiteering corporation such as Grumman Aerospace, and consider the government pennies to "small businesses" initiated by "minority businessmen" to be anything other than what they are: pennies copping out on the mass situation of increasing disparity between the white Have-group and the Black Have-nots.

3/ We will not help ourselves into extinction by deluding our Black selves into the belief that we should/can become white, that we can/ should sound white, think white because then we will be *like* the powerful and therefore we will *be* powerful: that is just a terrible, sad joke: you cannot obliterate yourself and do anything else, whatever, let alone be powerful: that is a logical impossibility; we must cease this self-loathing delusion and recognize that power and happiness and every good thing that we want and need and deserve must come to us as we truly are: must come to us, a Black people, on our terms, respecting our definitions of our goals, our choice of names, our styles of speech, dress, poetry, and jive. Otherwise, clearly, the "victory" is pyrrhic. You have won a job, you think, because you have "successfully" hidden away your history—your mother and your father and the man or woman that you love and *how* you love them, *how* you dance that love, and sing it. That is victory by obliteration of the self. That is not survival.

4/ We will not survive unless we realize that we remain jeopardized, as a people, by a fully conscious political system to annihilate whoever/whatever does not emulate its mainstream vocabulary, values, deceit, arrogance, and killer mentality. This is a time when those of us who believe in people, first, must become political, in every way possible: we must devise and pursue every means for survival as the people we are, as the people we want to become. Therefore, when a magazine like *Newsweek* has the insolence to ask, on its cover: WHATEVER HAPPENED TO BLACK AMERICA?, we must be together, ready, and strong to answer, on our own terms, on our own *political* terms: none of your goddamned business; you know, anyway; you did it; you stripped the programs; you ridiculed/humiliated the poor; you laughed when we wept: don't ask: we gone make you *answer* for this shit.

White power uses white English as a calculated, political display of power to control and eliminate the powerless. In America, that power belongs to white power. School, compulsory public school education, is the process whereby Black children first encounter the punishing force of this white power. "First grade" equals first contact with the politics of white language, and its incalculably destructive consequences for Black lives. This is what I mean, exactly: both Black and white youngsters are compelled to attend school. Once inside this system, the white child is rewarded for mastery of his standard, white English: the language he learned at his mother's white and standard knee. But the Black child is punished for mastery of his non-standard, Black English; for the ruling elite of America have decided that *non*-standard is *sub*-standard, and even dangerous, and must be eradicated. Moreover, the white child receives formal instruction in his standard English, and endless opportunities for the exercise and creative display of his language. But where is the elementary school course in Afro-American language, and where are the opportunities for the *accredited* exercise, and creative exploration, of Black language?

The two languages are not interchangeable. They cannot, nor do they attempt to communicate equal or identical thoughts, or feelings. And, since the experience to be conveyed is quite different, Black from white, these lingual dissimilarities should not surprise or worry anyone. However, they are both communication systems with regularities, exceptions, and values governing their word designs. Both are equally liable to poor, good, better, and creative use. In short, they are both accessible to critical criteria such as clarity, force, message, tone, and imagination. Besides this, standard English is comprehensible to Black children, even as Black language is comprehensible to white teachers—supposing that the teachers are willing to make half the effort they demand of Black students.

Then what is the difficulty? The problem is that we are saying *language*, but really dealing with power. The word "standard" is just not the same as the word "technical" or "rural" or "straight." *Standard* means the rule, the norm. Anyone deviating from the standard is therefore "wrong." As a result, literally millions of Black children are "wrong" from the moment they begin to absorb and imitate the language of their Black lives. Is that an acceptable idea?

As things stand, childhood fluency in Afro-American language leads to reading problems that worsen, course failure in diverse subjects dependent on reading skills, and a thoroughly wounded self-esteem. Afterward, an abject school career is eclipsed by an abject life career. "Failing" white English leads straight to a "failure" of adult life. This, I submit, is a fundamental, nationwide experience of Black life up against white English used to destroy us: literally accept the terms of the oppressor, or perish: that is the irreducible, horrifying truth of the politics of language.

Well, number one, we grownups: we, the Black mothers and Black fathers, and Black teachers, and Black writers, and grown Blackfolk, in general: we do not have to let this damnable situation continue; we must make it stop. We cannot accept the terms, the language of our enemy and expect to win anything; we cannot accept the coercion of our children into failure and expect to survive, as a people. The legitimacy of our language must be fully acknowledged by all of us. That will mean insisting that white/standard English be presented simply as the Second Language. That will mean presenting the second language, obviously, with perpetual reference to the first language, and the culture the first language bespeaks.

Sincere recognition of Black language as legitimate will mean formal instruction and encouragement in its use, within the regular curriculum. It will mean the respectful approaching of Black children, *in the language of Black children.* Yes: it's true that we need to acquire competence in the language of the currently powerful: Black children in America must acquire competence in white English, for the sake of self-preservation: BUT YOU WILL NEVER TEACH A CHILD A NEW LANGUAGE BY SCORNING AND RIDICULING AND FORCIBLY ERASING HIS FIRST LANGUAGE.

We can and we ought to join together to protect our Black children, our Black language, our terms of our reality, and our defining of the future we dream and desire. The public school is one, ready-made battleground. But the war is all around us and the outcome depends on how we understand or fail to perceive the serious, political intention to homogenize us, Blackfolks, out of existence. In our daily, business phone calls, in our "formal" correspondence with whites, in what we publish let us dedicate ourselves to the revelation of our true selves, on our given terms, and demand respect for us, as we are. Let us study and use our Black language, more and more: it is not A Mistake, or A Verbal Deficiency. It is a communication system subsuming dialect/regional variations that leave intact, nevertheless, a language that is invariable in profound respects. For example:

A/ Black language practices minimal inflection of verb forms. (E.g. *I go, we go, he go,* and *I be, you be,* etc.) This is *non*-standard and, also, an obviously more logical use of verbs. It is also evidence of a value system that considers the person—the actor—more important than the action.

B/ Consistency of syntax:

You going to the store.	(Depending on the tone, can be a question.)
You going to the store.	(Depending: can be a command.)
You going to the store.	(Depending: can be a simple, declarative statement.)

C/ Infrequent, irregular use of the possessive case.

D/ Clear, logical use of multiple negatives within a single sentence, to express an unmistakably negative idea. E.g., You ain gone bother me no way no more, you hear?

E/ Other logical consistencies, such as: *ours, his, theirs,* and, therefore, *mines.*

Our Black language is a political fact suffering from political persecution and political malice. Let us understand this and meet the man, politically; let us meet the man *talking the way we talk*; let us not fail to seize this means to our survival, despite white English and its power. Let us condemn white English for what it is: a threat to mental health, integrity of person, and persistence as a people of our own choosing.

And, as for our children: let us make sure that the whole world will welcome and applaud and promote the words they bring into our reality; in the struggle to reach each other, there can be no right or wrong words for our longing and our needs; there can only be the names that we trust and we try.

◆◆◆

BLACK ENGLISH

As a poet and writer, I deeply love and I deeply hate words. I love the infinite evidence and change and requirements and possibilities of language; every human use of words that is joyful, or honest, or new because experience is new, or old because each personal history testifies to inherited pleasures and/or inherited, collective memories of peril, pain, and even genocide.

As a human being, I delight in this miraculous, universal means of communion: I rejoice in this communing means that leading linguists, such as Noam Chomsky, have now shown to be innate, rather than learned; thanks to the revolutionary work of such linguists, we now understand that word patterns connecting person to reality, and reflecting and/or responding to reality, are no more learned than the brain is learned or the intestine is learned: language is a communal means intrinsic to human life. And I celebrate this fact of language that man and womankind have been privileged to explore and extend always as a means of discovery and/or revelation and of coming together and/or reaching closer to social conditions that will justify and summon forth the lyrical, hallelujah telegrams of love and peace and victory for merciful, just, and life-supporting human conduct.

But, as a Black poet and writer, I hate words that cancel my name and my history and the freedom of my future: I hate the words that condemn and refuse the language of my people in America; I am talking about a language deriving from the Niger-Congo congeries of language. I am talking about a language that joins with the Russian, Hungarian, and Arabic languages, among others, in its elimination of what technicians call a "present copula"—a verb interjected between subject and language where I will tell you simply that, "*They mine*." (And, incidentally, if I tell you "*they mine*," you don't have no kind of trouble understanding exactly what I mean, do you?)

As a Black poet and writer, I am proud of our Black, verbally bonding system born of our struggle to avoid annihilation—as Afro-American self, Afro-American marriage, community, and Afro-American culture. I am proud of this language that our continuing battle just to be has brought into currency. And so I hate the arrogant, prevailing rejection of this, our Afro-American language. And so I work, as a poet and writer, against the eradication of this system, this language, this carrier of Black-survivor consciousness.

But we are talking about power, and poetry, and books—history books, novels, what have you—none of these can win against the schools, the teachers, the media, the fearful parents, and the ruling elite of this country, unless we understand the politics of language. In America, the politics of language, the willful debasement of this human means to human communion has jeopardized the willingness of young people to believe anything they hear or read—even if it's just about the time of day.

And what is anybody going to do about it? I suggest that, for one, we join forces to cherish and protect our various, multi-foliate lives against pacification, homogenization, the silence of terror, and surrender to standards that despise and disregard the sanctity of each and every human life. We can begin by looking at language. Because it brings us together, as folks, because it makes known the unknown strangers we otherwise remain to each other, language is a process of translation; and a political process, taking place on the basis of who has the power to use, abuse, accept or reject the words—the lingual messages we must attempt to transmit—to each other and/or against each other.

In short, the subject of "Black English" cannot be intelligently separate from the subject of language as a translation and translation as a political process distinguishing between the powerless and the powerful, in no uncertain terms. Here are a few facts to illustrate my meaning:

1/ Apparently, "Black English" needs defense even though it is demonstrably a language; a perfectly adequate, verbal means of communication that can be understood by anyone but the most outrightly, retarded, standard racist.

2/ On the other hand, where is the defense, who among the standard, grammatical white English mainstreamers feels the need, even, to defend his imposition of his language on me and my children?

3/ Thou know'st the mask of night is on my face,
Else would a maiden blush bepaint my check
For that which thou has heard me speak tonight.
Fain would I dwell on form, fain, fain deny
what I have spoke: but farewell compliment:
Dost thou love me? I know thou wilt say "Ay"
And I will take thy word: yet, if thou swear'st
Thou mayst prove false: at lovers' perjuries,
They say, Jove laughs.

—*Romeo and Juliet* (Act 2, Scene 2)

Now that ain hardly standard English. But just about every kid forced into school has to grapple with that particular rap. Why? Because the powers that control the language that controls the process of translation have deiced that *Romeo and Juliet* is *necessary*, nay, *indispensable*, to passage through compulsory, public school education.

4/ "You be different from all the dead. All them tombstones tearing up the ground, look like a little city, like a small Manhattan, not exactly. Here is not the same. Here, you be bigger than the buildings, bigger than the little city. You be really different from the rest, the resting other ones.

"Moved in his arms, she make him feel like smiling. Him, his head an Afro-bush spread free beside the stones, headstones thinning in the heavy air. Him, a ready father, public lover, privately alone with her, with Angela, a half an hour walk from the hallway where they start out to hold themselves together in the noisy darkness, kissing, kissed him, kissed her, kissing.

"Cemetery let them lie there belly close, their shoulders now undressed down to the color of the heat they feel, in lying close, their legs a strong disturbing of the dust. His own where, own place for loving made for making love, the cemetery where nobody guard the dead."

—*His Own Where*

Now that ain no kind of standard English, neither. Both excerpts come from love stories about white and Black teenagers, respectively. But the Elizabethan, nonstandard English of *Romeo and Juliet* has been adjudged, by the powerful, as something students should tackle and absorb. By contrast, the Black, nonstandard language of my novel, *His Own Where*, has been adjudged, by the powerful, as substandard and even injurious to young readers.

I am one among a growing number of Black poets and writers dedicated to the preservation of Black language within our lives, and dedicated to the health of our children as they prepare themselves for a life within this standard, white America which has despised even our speech and our prayers and our love. As long as we shall survive, Black, in white America, we, and our children, require and deserve the power of Black language, Black history, Black literature, as well as the power of standard English, standard history, and standard literature. To the extent that Black survival fails on these terms, it will be a political failure: it will be the result of our not recognizing and not revolting against the political use of language, to extinguish the people we want to be and the people we have been. Politics is power. Language is political. And language, its reward, currency, punishment, and/or eradication—is political in its meaning and in its consequence.

A few days ago, a white woman telephoned to ask me to appear on her television program: she felt free to tell me that if I sounded "Black" then she would not "hire" me. This is what I am trying to say to you: language is power. And that woman is simply one of the ruling powerful people in white America who feel free to reject and strangle whoever will not mimic them—in language, values, goals. In fact, I answered her in this way: You are a typical racist. And that is the political truth of the matter, as I see it, as I hope you will begin to see it: for no one has the right to control and sentence to poverty anyone—because he or she is different and proud and honest in his or her difference and his or her pride.

Let me end by focusing on Black language, per se: A young friend of mine went through some scarifying times, leaving her homeless. During this period of intense, relentless dread and abuse, she wrote poems, trying to cope. Here are two lines from her poetry: "what have life meanted to me" and, "you are forgotten you use to exist- ed." There is no adequate, standard English translation possible for either expression of her spirit. They are intrinsically Black language cries of extreme pain so telling that even the possibilities of meaning and existence have been formulated in a past tense that is emphatic, severe. I deeply hope that more of us will want to learn and pro- tect Black language. If we lose our fluency in our language, we may irreversibly forsake elements of the spirit that have provided for our survival.

"PROBLEMS OF LANGUAGE IN A DEMOCRATIC STATE"

(1982)

[Black English and Standard English were *both* in trouble by the 1980s. The media reported that most college students could no longer think analytically, read with understanding, or express themselves with clarity. Jordan responded to the "crisis" with alacrity and acumen. She delivered "Problems of Language in a Democratic State" as the keynote address for the 1982 Annual Meeting of the National Council of Teachers of English in Washington D.C. She included it in *On Call* (1985).]

In America, you can segregate the people, but the problems will trav- el. From slavery to equal rights, from state suppression of dissent to crime, drugs and unemployment, I can't think of a single supposedly Black issue that hasn't wasted the original Black target group and then spread like the measles to outlying white experience.

If slavery was all right, for example, is state violence and law could protect property rights against people, then the Bossman could call out the state against striking white workers. And he did. And nobody bothered to track this diseased idea of the state back to the first victims: Black people. Concepts of the state as the equal servant of all people, as the resource for jobs or subsistence income; concepts of the state as a regulator of the economy to preserve the people from hunger and sickness and doom, these are ideas about a democratic state that have been raised, repeatedly, by minority Americans without majority support.

Most Americans have imagined that problem affecting Black life follow from pathogenic attributes of Black people and not from malfunctions of the state. Most Americans have sought to identify themselves with the powerful interests that oppress poor and minority peoples, perhaps hoping to keep themselves on the shooting side of the target range.

Nevertheless and notwithstanding differences of power, money, race, gender, age and class, there remains one currency common to all of us. There remains one thing that makes possible exchange, shared memory, self-affirmation and collective identity. And isn't that currency known and available to everybody regardless of this and that? And isn't that common currency therefore the basis for a democratic state that will not discriminate, or non-discriminating, currency our language? Isn't that so?

I remember very clearly how, when I first became a teacher, back in the 60s, popular wisdom had it that the only American boys and girls who could neither read nor write were Black. This was a function of the poverty of culture or vice versa: I forget which. But anyway, Black children had something wrong with them. They couldn't talk right. They couldn't see straight. They never heard a word you said to them. They seemed to think that they should throw their books around the rooms or out the windows. And another thing, their parents were no good or they were alcoholics or illiterate or, anyhow, uninterested, inept, and rotten models.

Obviously, school was cool. It was just the students who kept messing up. In those days teachers were frequently brave, depressed, dedicated, idealistic, tireless, and overworked, but they were never accountable for their failures to teach Black children how to read and write. That was not their responsibility. That was a minority problem of language, in a democratic state.

At the least, most Americans have tried to avoid what they call trouble: opposition to the powerful is a pretty sure way to get yourself in trouble.

But lately these same Americans have begun to understand that trouble does not start somewhere on the other side of town. It seems to originate inside the absolute middle of the homemade cherry pie. In our history, the state has failed to respond to the weak. State power serves the powerful. You could be white, male, Presbyterian and heterosexual besides, but if you get fired or if you get sick tomorrow, you might as well be Black, for all the state will want to hear from you. More and more of the majority is entering that old minority experience of no power: unless you stay strong, state power does not want to sweetly wait upon you.

And when minority problems become the problem of the majority, or when the weak stay weak and the strong become weak, then something does seem to be mighty wrong with the whole situation.

I suggest that as long as state power serves the powerful, more and more of the people of this democracy will become the powerless. As long as we have an economic system protected by the state rather than state protection against economic vagaries and depredations, then your and my welfare become expandable considerations.

Less than two decades after the 60s and I find national reports of a dismal discovery occurring at Harvard, at the nearby community college and on the state campus where I teach. Apparently the minority próblem of language has become a majority problem of low-level reading and writing skills. Every university in the nation now recognizes that most of its students seriously lack those analytical abilities that devolve from disciplined and critical and confident and regular exercise of the mind. Students cannot express themselves, clearly. They cannot judge if an essay is gibberish or coherent. They cannot defend a point of view. They cannot examine a written document and then accurately relate its meaning or uncover its purpose.

And either they have nothing to say, or else they talk funny. How did this happen?

I know what went down for Black kids, the ones people dismissed as unruly, unteachable. What those children brought into the classroom: their language, their style, their sense of humor, their ideas of smart, their music, their need for a valid history and a valid literature—history and literature that included their faces and their voices—and serious teachers who would tell them, "C'mon, I see you. Let me give you a hand,"—all of this was pretty well ridiculed and rejected, or denied to them.

Mostly Black kids ran into a censorship of their living particular truth, past and present. Nobody wanted to know what they felt or to teach them to think for themselves. Nobody wanted to learn anything from them. Education was a one-way number leading from the powerful teacher to the trapped parolee. Nobody wanted to hear any more political arguments raised by the fact of certain children whom the compulsory school system consistently failed. Not too many people wanted to grant that maybe schools really are political institutions teaching power to the powerful and something unpalatable and self-destructive to the weak. Not too many people wanted to reexamine their fantasies about the democratizing function of American education.

And when Black dropout rates across the country soared and stabilized at irreversible tragic heights because the kids figured, "If you don't know and don't care about who I am then why should I give a damn about what you say you do know about." The popular wisdom smiled, satisfied: Good riddance to a minority uproar.

But meanwhile, white youngsters fared only somewhat better. These are American kids required to master something described as the English language. These are American kids required to study what's accurately described as English literature. When will a legitimately American language, a language including Nebraska, Harlem, New Mexico, Oregon, Puerto Rico, Alabama and working-class life and freeways and Pac-Man become the language studied and written and glorified in the classroom?

When will a legitimate American literature rightfully supplant nostalgia for Queen Mary? Who teaches white kids to think for themselves? Who has ever wanted white children to see their own faces, clearly, to hear their own voices, clearly?

I believe Americans have wanted their sons and daughters to write just well enough to fill out a job application. Americans have wanted their children to think just well enough to hold that job. Not too many people have wanted to start trouble, or get into it.

So I would say that our schools have served most of us extremely well. We have silenced or eliminated minority children. We have pacified white children into barely competent imitations of their fear-ridden parents.

But now there are no jobs and, consequently, somebody needs to write aggressive new editorials. Somebody needs to write aggressive new statements of social design and demand. More and more Americans finally want to hear new sentences, new ideas, to articulate this unprecedented, and painful, *majority* situation. But is there anybody new around the house? Someone who can think and organize a solution to this loss of privilege, this loss of power?

I am talking about majority problems of language in a democratic state, problems of a currency that someone has stolen and hidden away and then homogenized into an official "English" language that can only express non-events involving nobody responsible, or lies. If we lived in a democratic state our language would have to hurtle, fly, curse, and sing, in all the common American names, all the undeniable and representative and participating voices of everybody here. We would not tolerate the language of the powerful and, thereby, lose all respects for words, *per se*. We would make our language conform to the truth of our many selves and we would make our language lead us into the equality of power that a democratic state must represent.

This is not a democratic state. And we put up with that. We do not have a democratic language. And we put up with that. We have the language of the powerful that perpetuates that power through the censorship of dissenting views.

This morning I watched TV. Four white men sat around talking about some ostensibly important public issue. Everyone of them was wealthy, powerful, unaccountable to you and me and also accustomed to the nationwide delivery of his opinions on a lot of subjects. Except for Tom Wicker, who can't shake his trembling southern drawl for the life of him, they might be quadruplets from an identical Ma and Pa. After about half an hour of this incestuous display, the moderator announced that, after the commercial, he'd send these "experts" out of the studio and replace them with quote a fee for all unquote.

I could hardly wait.

After the break, the moderator returned with his new guests: four white men, everyone of them wealthy, powerful, unaccountable to you and me and also accustomed to the nationwide delivery of his opinions! So much for a quote free for all unquote.

When I say that those particular white men all sounded alike, I am not exaggerating. All of them used the language of the state seeking to transcend accountability to the people, as in: "The Federal reserve has been forced to raise interest rates" or "It is widely believed ..." or "While I can't comment on that I would like to emphasize that it has been said, many times ..." or "When you take all of those factors into consideration it is obvious ..." or "Unemployment has emerged as a number one concern." Is somebody really saying those words? Is any real life affected by those words? Should we really just relax into the literally non-descript, the irresponsible language of the passive voice? Will the passive voice lead us safely out of the action? Will the action and the actors behind it leave us alone so long as we do not call them by their real names?

We have begun to live in the land of Polyphemus. Poor Polyphemus! He was this ugly and gigantic, one-eyed Cyclops who liked to smash human beings on rocks and the eat them. But one day he happened to capture the wily and restless Ulysses who, one night, gave Polyphemus so much wine that the poor lunk fell into a drunken sleep. Taking advantage of his adversary's discomposure, Ulysses and a couple of his buddies seized a great stick and heated its tip in the nearby, handily burning, fire. When the tip was glowing hot, Ulysses and his buddies stuck that thing into the one eye of Polyphemus, twisting it deeply into that socket, and blinding him.

Polyphemus howled a terrible loud howl. He was in much pain. "What is the name of the man who has done this to me?" he cried.

And the wily Ulysses answered him, "My name is No One."

Later, several other Cyclops raced up to Polyphemus, because they had heard him howling.

"Who did this to you?" they asked.

Polyphemus screamed his accusation for the world to hear: "No One has done this to me!"

Well, when the fellow Cyclops heard that they decided that if No One had done this to Polyphemus, it must be the will of the gods. Hence nothing could or should be done about the blinding of Polyphemus. And so nothing was done.

And after a while, Ulysses and his men escaped, unnoticed by the blinded Cyclops.

I share this story with you because it remains one of my favorites and because it was the only reason I stayed awake during my second year of Latin.

And I tell you about Polyphemus because we seem determined to warp ourselves into iddy-biddy imitations of his foolishness. To repeat: the other Cyclops decided that if no one had done anything then nothing was to be done. What happened to him represented the will of the gods.

I worry about that notion of a democratic state. Do we really believe 11.5% unemployment represents God's will? Is that why the powerful say, "Unemployment has emerged?" If that construction strikes your ear as somehow ridiculous because, quite rightly, it conjures up the phenomenon of unemployment as if it emerges from nowhere into nothing, then what sense do you make of this very familiar construction used, very often, by the powerless: "I lost my job." Who in his or her right mind loses a job? What should I understand if you say something like that to me? Should I suppose that one morning you got up and drank your coffee and left the house, but, then, you just couldn't find your job? If that's not what anybody means then why don't we say, "GM laid off half the night shift. They fired me."

Who did what to whom? Who's responsible?

We have a rather foggy mess and not much hope for a democratic state when the powerless agree to use a language that blames the victim for the deeds of the powerful.

As in: "I was raped." What should we conclude from that most sadly passive use of language? By definition, nobody in her right mind can say that, and mean it. For rape to occur, somebody real has to rape somebody else, equally real. Rape presupposes a rapist and a victim. The victim must learn to make language tell her own truth: He raped me.

But the victim accommodates to power. The victim doesn't want any more trouble; someone has already fired him or someone has already raped her, and so the victim uses words to evade a further confrontation with the powerful.

By itself, our language cannot refuse to reflect the agonizing process of alienation from ourselves. If we collaborate with the powerful then our language will lose its currency as a means to tell the truth in order to change the truth.

In our own passive ways, we frequently validate the passive voice of a powerful state that seeks to conceal the truth from us, the people. And this seems to me an ok situation only for a carnivorous idiot like Polyphemus.

I would not care if, for example, instead of bashing men's heads against the rocks, Polyphemus decided to watch TV, every evening. I wouldn't even care if he, consequently, became addicted to that ultimate passive experience, although maybe that's why he thought that when you murder somebody it's not such a big deal: the agony will last only a couple of minutes until the much more exciting drama of Ajax the Foaming Cleanser takes over the screen. Some people *should* be pacified. Polyphemus was one of those.

But I really think that a democratic state presupposes a small number of psychopathic giants and a rather huge number of ordinary men and women who cannot afford to resemble Polyphemus.

In September of this year, a huge number of ordinary men and women came out of their houses to make an outcry against the language of the state. Four hundred thousand Israeli plunged into the streets of Tel Aviv to demand an investigation of the massacre in Lebanon. They insisted. They must know: who did what to whom?

Against official pronouncement such as: "Security measures have been taken," or "It seems that an incident has taken place inside the camps," nearly half a million Israelis, after the massacre at Sabra and Shatilah, demanded another kind of language: an inquiry into the truth, an attribution of responsibility, a forcing of the powerful intro an accountability to the people. As Jacobo Timmerman writes in his Israeli *Journal of the Longest War*, it did seem to him that the democratic nature of the state lay at risk.

All the summer leading to Sabra and Shatilah I lived with the Israeli invasion of Lebanon. It did not kill me. As Timmerman has described our remarkable endurance of the unendurable, "... nobody has yet died of anguish." But the invasion killed other people: tens of thousands died and I watched it happen. I sat down and I read the newspaper accounts or I listened to the nightly news. The uniformi ty of official state language appalled me. How could this be 1984 in 1982?

I saw American reporters respectfully quote Philip Habib as having proclaimed, "This is a ceasefire" even as the whistling bombs drowned out the broadcast. When Menachem Begin declared, "This is not an invasion," his statement appeared in print and on the screen, everywhere as the world news of the day, even as the Israeli tanks entered Beirut.

During that same September, 1982, and shortly before Sabra and Shatilah, Israeli planes bombed the houses and the hospitals and the schools of West Beirut for twenty-two hours, unceasingly. But this was something, evidently, other than a massacre. Our American newspapers and newsmen told us that this was a "tightening of the noose" in order to "speed negotiations at the peace table."

But when one word finally burst through that foggy mess of American mass media, and when that word was *massacre*, who took it to the streets? Who called for an investigation of the government and moved to put the leadership on trial? Who said *stop*?

It happened in another country where the citizens believe it matters when the state controls the language. It didn't happen here. It happened when the citizens decided that the passive voice in a democracy means something evil way beyond a horribly mixed metaphor. It didn't happen here.

It happened in Israel. And we Americans should be ashamed.

But we were looking for a language of the people; we were wondering why our children do not read or write.

Last week a delegation of Black women graduate students invited me to address a large meeting that loud yellow flyers described as "A Black Sisters Speak-Out" followed by two exclamation points. I went to the gathering with great excitement. Obviously, we would deal with one or another crisis; whether national or international, I simply wondered which enormous and current quandary would be the one most of the women wanted to discuss.

During the warm-up period one of the women announced that we should realize our debt to the great Black women who have preceded us in history. "We are here," she said, "because of the struggle of women like," and here her sentence broke down. She tried again. "We have come this far because of all the Black women who fought for us like, like ..." and here only one name came to her mouth: "Sojourner Truth!" she exclaimed, clearly relieved to think of it, but, also embarrassed because she couldn't keep going. "And," she tried to continue, nevertheless, "the other Black women like ...: but here somebody in the audience spoke to her rescue, by calling aloud the name of Harriet Tubman. At this point I interrupted to observe that now we had two names for *482* years of our Afro-American history.

"What about Mary McLeod Bethune?" somebody else ventured at last. "That's three!" I remarked, in the manner of a referee: "Do we have a fourth?"

There was silence. Thoroughly embarrassed, the first woman looked at me and said, "Listen. I could come up with a whole list of Black women if my life depended on it."

"Well," I had to tell her, "It does."

But even this official erasure of their faces and their voices was not what those students wanted to discuss. Something more hurtful than that was bothering them. As one by one these Black women rose to express themselves, the problem was this:

A lotta times and I'm walking on campus and I see another Black woman and soI'll say 'Hi' but then she won't answer me and I don't

understand it because I don't mean we have to get into a conversa-
tion or do all of that like talking to me but you could say, 'Hi.' If you
see me you could say, 'Hi.'

I was stunned. From looking around the room I knew there were
Black women right there who face critical exposure to bodily assault,
alcoholic mothers, and racist insults and graffiti in the dorms. I knew
that the academic curriculum omitted the truth of their difficult
lives. I knew that they certainly would not be found welcome in the
marketplace after they got their degrees.

But the insistent concern was more intimate and more pitiful and
more desperate than any of those threatening conditions might sug-
gest. The abject plea of those Black women students was ruthlessly
minimal: "If you see me, you could say, 'Hi.' Let me know that you see
me; let me know I exist. Never mind a conversation between us, but,
please, if you see me, you could say, 'Hi.'"

Who can tell these Americans that they should trust the lan-
guage available to them? Who will presume to criticize their fal-
tering, their monosyllables, their alienation from a literature that
condemns them to oblivion?

If you chose, you can consider this desperation a minority prob-
lem in America, today, and then try to forget about it. But I believe
this invisibility and this silence of the real and various people of our
country is a political situation of language that every one of us must
move against, because our lives depend on it.

I believe we will have to eliminate the passive voice from our de-
mocracy. We will have to drown out the official language of the pow-
erful with our own mighty and conflicting voices or we will perish as
a people. Until we can tell our children that the powerful people are
the children, themselves, then I do not see why we should expect our
children to read or write anything.

Until we can tell our children that truth is the purpose of our
American language, and that the truth is what they know and feel
and need, then I believe our children will continue to act as though
the truth is just something that will get you into trouble.

I believe that somebody real has blinded America in at least one eye. And, in the same way that so many Americans feel that "we have lost our jobs," we suspect that we have lost our country.

We know that we do not speak the language.

And I ask you: well, what are we going to do about it?

"NOBODY MEAN MORE TO ME THAN YOU AND THE FUTURE LIFE OF WILLIE JORDAN"

(1985)

[Soon after her promotion to Professor at Stony Brook University, Jordan began designing a course on Black English. She did not know of anyone else who had attempted a project like this. "Nobody Mean More to Me Than You And the Future Life of Willie Jordan" tells the story of developing and teaching that class, "The Art of Black English," and entwines it with the story of her student Willie Jordan. His twenty-five-year-old brother, Reggie, was killed midsemester by a policeman. Jordan published the essay in *On Call* (1985). She dedicated the book to "The Future Life of Willie Jordan."]

Black English[1] is not exactly a linguistic buffalo; as children, most of the thirty-five million Afro-Americans living here depend on this language for our discovery of the world. But then we approach our maturity inside a larger social body that will not support our efforts to become anything other than the clones of those who are neither our mothers nor our fathers. We begin to grow up in a house where every true mirror shows us the face of somebody who does not belong there, whose walk and whose talk will never look or sound "right,"

---

1   Black English aphorism crafted by Monica Morris, a Junior at S.U.N.Y. at Stony Brook, October, 1984. [The footnotes in this essay are Jordan's.]

because that house was meant to shelter a family that is alien and hostile to us. As we learn our way around this environment, either we hide our original word habits, or we completely surrender our own voice, hoping to please those who will never respect anyone different from themselves: Black English is not exactly a linguistic buffalo, but we should understand its status as an endangered species, as a perishing, irreplaceable system of community intelligence, or we should expect its extinction, and, along with that, the extinguishing of much that constitutes our own proud, and singular identity.

What we casually call "English," less and less defers to England and its "gentlemen." "English" is no longer a specific matter of geography or an element of class privilege; more than thirty-three countries use this tool as a means of "intranational communication."[2] Countries as disparate as Zimbabwe and Malaysia, or Israel and Uganda, use it as their non-native currency of convenience. Obviously, this tool, this "English," cannot function inside thirty-three discrete societies on the basis of rules and values absolutely determined somewhere else, in a thirty-fourth other country, for example.

In addition to that staggering congeries of non-native users of English, there are five countries, or 333,746,000 people, for whom this thing called "English" serves as a native tongue.[3] Approximately 10% of these native speakers of "English" are Afro-American citizens of the U.S.A. I cite these numbers and varieties of human beings dependent on "English" in order, quickly, to suggest how strange and how tenuous is any concept of "Standard English." Obviously, numerous forms of English now operate inside a natural, an uncontrollable, continuum of development. I would suppose "the standard" for English in Malaysia is not the same as "the standard" in Zimbabwe. I know that standard forms of English for Black people in this country do not copy that of whites. And, in fact, the structural differences between these two kinds of English have intensified, becoming more Black, or less white, despite the expected homogenizing effects of

---

2   *English is Spreading, But What Is English.* A presentation by Professor S.N. Sridahr, Dept. of Linguistics, S.U.N.Y. at Stony Brook, April 9, 1985: Deans Conversation Among the Disciplines.

3   Ibid.

television[4] and other mass media.

Nonetheless, white standards of English persist, supreme and unquestioned, in these United States. Despite our multi-lingual population, and despite the deepening Black and white cleavage within that conglomerate, white standards control our official and popular judgments of verbal proficiency and correct, or incorrect, language skills, including speech. In contrast to India, where at least fourteen languages co-exist as legitimate Indian languages, in contrast to Nicaragua, where all citizens are legally entitled to formal school instruction in their regional or tribal languages, compulsory education in America compels accommodation to exclusively white forms of "English." White English, in America, is "Standard English."

This story began two years ago. I was teaching a new course, "In Search of the Invisible Black Woman," and my rather large class seemed evenly divided between young Black women and men. Five or six white students also sat in attendance. With unexpected speed and enthusiasm we had moved through historical narratives of the 19th century to literature by and about Black women, in the 20th. I had assigned the first forty pages of Alice Walker's *The Color Purple*, and I came, eagerly, to class that morning:

"So!" I exclaimed, aloud. "What did you think? How did you like it?"

The students studied their hands, or the floor. There was no response. The tense, resistant feeling in the room fairly astounded me.

At last, one student, a young woman still not meeting my eyes, muttered something in my direction:

"What did you say?" I prompted her.

"Why she have them talk so funny. It don't sound right."

"You mean the language?"

Another student lifted his head: "It don't look right, neither. I couldn't hardly read it."

At this, several students dumped on the book. Just about unan-

---

4   *New York Times*, March 15, 1985, Section One, p. 14: Report on study by Linguistics at the University of Pennsylvania.

imously, their criticisms, targeted the language. I listened to what they wanted to say and silently marvelled at the similarities between their casual speech patterns and Alice Walker's written version of Black English.

But I decided against pointing to these identical traits of syntax; I wanted not to make them self-conscious about their own spoken language—not while they clearly felt it was "wrong." Instead I decided to swallow my astonishment. Here was a negative Black reaction to a prize winning accomplishment of Black literature that white readers across the country had selected as a best seller. Black rejection was aimed at the one irreducibly Black element of Walker's work: the language—Celie's Black English. I wrote the opening lines of *The Color Purple* on the blackboard and asked the students to help me translate these sentences into Standard English:

> *You better not never tell nobody but God. It'd kill your mammy.*
> Dear God,
>
> I am fourteen years old. I have always been a good girl. Maybe you can give me a sign letting me know what is happening to me.
>
> Last spring after Little Lucious come I heard them fussing. He was pulling on her arm. She say it too soon, Fonso. I ain't well. Finally he leave her alone. A week go by, he pulling on her arm again. She say, Naw, I ain't gonna. Can't you see I'm already half dead, an all of the children.[5]

Our process of translation exploded with hilarity and even hysterical, shocked laughter: The Black writer, Alice Walker, knew what she was doing! If rudimentary criteria for good fiction includes the manipulation of language so that the syntax and diction of sentences will tell you the identity of speakers, the probable age and sex and class of speakers, and even the locale—urban/rural/southern/western—then Walker had written, perfectly. This is the translation into Standard English that our class produced:

---

5   Alice Walker, *The Color Purple*, p. 11, Harcourt Brace, N.Y.

Absolutely, one should never confide in anybody besides God. Your
secrets could prove devastating to your mother.
Dear God,

I am fourteen years old. I have always been good. But now, could
you help me understand what is happening to me?

Last spring, after my little brother, Lucious, was born, I heard
my parents fighting. My father kept pulling at my mother's arm. But
she told him, "It's too soon for sex, Alfonso. I am still not feeling
well." Finally, my father left her alone. A week went by, and then he
began bothering my mother, again: Pulling her arm. She told him,
"No, I won't! Can't you see I'm already exhausted from all these chil-
dren?

(Our favorite line was "It's too soon for sex, Alfonso.")

Once we could stop laughing, once we could stop our exponen-
tially wild improvisations on the theme of Translated Black English,
the students pushed me to explain their own negative first reac-
tions to their spoken language on the printed page. I thought it was
probably akin to the shock of seeing yourself in a photograph for
the first time. Most of the students had never before seen a written
facsimile of the way they talk. None of the students had ever learned
how to read and write their own verbal system of communication:
Black English. Alternatively, this fact began to baffle or else bemuse
and then infuriate my students. Why not? Was it too late? Could they
learn how to do it, now? And, ultimately, the final test question, the
one testing my sincerity: Could I teach them? Because I had never
taught anyone Black English and, as far as I knew, no one, anywhere
in the United States, had ever offered such a course, the best I could
say was "I'll try."

He looked like a wrestler.

He sat dead center in the packed room and, every time our eyes
met, he quickly nodded his head as though anxious to reassure, and
encourage, me.

Short, with strikingly broad shoulders and long arms, he spoke
with a surprisingly high, soft voice that matched the soft bright

movement of his eyes. His name was Willie Jordan. He would have seemed even more unlikely in the context of Contemporary Women's Poetry, except that ten or twelve other Black men were taking the course, as well. Still, Willie was conspicuous. His extreme fitness, the muscular density of his presence underscored the riveted, gentle attention that he gave to anything anyone said. Generally, he did not join the loud and rowdy dialogue flying back and forth, but there could be no doubt about his interest in our discussions. And, when he stood to present an argument he'd prepared, overnight, that nervous smile of his vanished and an irregular stammering replaced it, as he spoke with visceral sincerity, word by word.

That was how I met Willie Jordan. It was in between "In Search of the Invisible Black Women" and "The Art of Black English." I was waiting for Departmental approval and I supposed that Willie might be, so to speak, killing time until he, too, could study Black English. But Willie really did want to explore Contemporary Women's poetry and, to that end, volunteered for extra research and never missed a class.

Towards the end of that semester, Willie approached me for an independent study on South Africa. It would commence the next semester. I thought Willie's writing needed the kind of improvement only intense practice will yield. I knew his intelligence was outstanding. But he'd wholeheartedly opted for "Standard English" at a rather late age, and the results were stilted and frequently polysyllabic, simply for the sake of having more syllables. Willie's unnatural formality of language seemed to me consistent with the formality of his research into South African apartheid. As he projected his studies, he would have little time, indeed, for newspapers. Instead, more than 90% of his research would mean saturation in strictly historical, if not archival, material. I was certainly interested. It would be tricky to guide him into a more confident and spontaneous relationship both with language and apartheid. It was going to be wonderful to see what happened when he could catch up with himself, entirely, and talk back to the world.

September, 1984: Breezy fall weather and much excitement! My class, "The Art of Black English," was full to the limit of the fire laws. And, in Independent Study, Willie Jordan showed up, weekly, fifteen minutes early for each of our sessions. I was pretty happy to be teaching, altogether!

I remember an early class when a young brother, replete with his ever present pork-pie hat, raised his hand and then told us that most of what he'd heard was "all right" except it was "too clean." "The brothers on the street," he continued, "they mix it up more. Like 'fuck' and 'motherfuck.' Or like 'shit.'" He waited. I waited. Then all of us laughed a good while, and we got into a brawl about "correct" and "realistic" Black English that led to Rule 1.

RULE 1: *Black English is about a whole lot more than motha-fuckin.*

As a criterion, we decided, "realistic" could take you anywhere you want to go. Artful places. Angry places. Eloquent and sweetalkin places. Polemical places. Church. And the local Bar & Grill. We were checking out a language, not a mood or a scene or one guy's forgettable mouthing off.

It was hard. For most of the students, learning Black English required a fallback to patterns and rhythms of speech that many of their parents had beaten out of them. I mean *beaten*. And, in a majority of cases, correct Black English could be achieved only by striving for *incorrect* Standard English, something they were still pushing at, quite uncertainly. This state of affairs led to Rule 2.

RULE 2: *If it's wrong in Standard English it's probably right in Black English, or, at least, you're hot.*

It was hard. Roommates and family members ridiculed their studies, or remained incredulous, "You studying that shit? At school?" But we were beginning to feel the companionship of pioneers. And we decided that we needed another rule that would establish each one of us as equally important to our success. This was Rule 3.

RULE 3: *If it don't sound like something that come out somebody mouth then it don't sound right. If it don't sound right then it ain't hardly right. Period.*

This rule produced two weeks of compositions in which the students agonizingly tried to spell the sound of the Black English sentence they wanted to convey. But Black English is, preeminently, an oral/spoken means of communication. *And spelling don't talk.* So we needed Rule 4.

RULE 4: *Forget about the spelling. Let the syntax carry you.*

Once we arrived at Rule 4 we started to fly because syntax, the structure of an idea, leads you to the world view of the speaker and reveals her values. The syntax of a sentence equals the structure of your consciousness. If we insisted that the language of Black English adheres to a distinctive Black syntax, then we were postulating a profound difference between white and Black people, *per se.* Was it a difference to prize or obliterate?

There are three qualities of Black English—the presence of life, voice, and clarity—that testify to a distinctive Black value system that we became excited about and self-consciously tried to maintain.

1. Black English has been produced by a pre-technocratic, if not anti-technological, culture. More, our culture has been constantly threatened by annihilation or, at least, the swallowed blurring of assimilation. Therefore, our language is a system constructed by people constantly needed to insist that we exist, that we are present. Our language devolves from a culture that abhors all abstraction, or anything tending to obscure or delete the fact of the human being who is here and now/the truth of the person who is speaking or listening. Consequently, *there is no passive voice construction possible in Black English.* For example, you cannot say, "Black English is being eliminated." You must say, instead, "White people eliminating Black English." The assumption of the presence of life governs all of Black English. Therefore, overwhelmingly, *all action takes place in the language of the present indicative.* And every sentence assumes the living and active participation of at least two human beings, the speaker and the listener.

2. A primary consequence of the person-centered values of Black English is the delivery of voice. If you speak or write Black English, your ideas will necessarily possess that otherwise elusive attribute, *voice.*

3. One main benefit following from the person-centered values of Black English is that of *clarity*. If your idea, your sentence, assumes the presence of at least two living and active people, you will make it understandable because the motivation behind every sentence is the wish to say something real to somebody real.

As the weeks piled up, translation from Standard English into Black English or vice versa occupied a hefty part of our course work.

Standard English (hereafter S.E.): "In considering the idea of studying Black English those questioned suggested—" (What's the subject? Where's the person? Is anybody alive in there, in that idea?) Black English (hereafter B.E.): "I been asking people what you think about somebody studying Black English and they answer me like this:"

But there were interesting limits. You cannot "translate" instances of Standard English preoccupied with abstraction or with nothing/nobody evidently alive, into Black English. That would warp the language into uses antithetical to the guiding perspective of its community of users. Rather you must first change those Standard English sentences, themselves, into ideas consistent with the person-centered assumptions of Black English.

Guidelines for Black English

1. Minimal number of words for every idea: This is the source for the aphoristic and/or poetic force of the language; eliminate every possible word.
2. Clarity: If the sentence is not clear it's not Black English.
3. Eliminate use of the verb *to be* whenever possible. This leads to the deployment of more descriptive and therefore, more precise verbs.
4. Use *be* or *been* only when you want to describe a chronic, ongoing state of things.
    He *be* at the office, by 9. (He is always at the office by 9.)
    He *been* with her since forever.
5. Zero copula: Always eliminate the verb *to be* whenever it would combine with another verb, in Standard English.

   S.E.: She is going out with him.

   B.E.: She going out with him.

6. Eliminate *do* as in:

   S.E.: What do you think? What do you want?

   B.E.: What you think? What you want?

 Rules number 3, 4, 5, and 6 provide for the use of the minimal number of verbs per idea and, therefore, greater accuracy in the choice of verb.

7. In general, if you wish to say something really positive, try to formulate the idea using emphatic negative structure.

   S.E.: He's fabulous.

   B.E.: He's bad.

8. Use double or triple negatives for dramatic emphasis.

   S.E.: Tina Turner sings out of this world.

   B.E.: Ain nobody sing like Tina.

9. Never use the *–ed* suffix to indicate the past tense of a verb.

   S.E.: She closed the door.

   B.E.: She close the door. Or, she have close the door.

10. Regardless of intentional verb time, only use the third person singular, present indicative, for use of the verb *to have*, as an auxiliary.

   S.E.: He had his wallet then he lost it.

   B.E.: He have him wallet then he lose it.

   S.E.: He had seen that movie.

   B.E.: We seen that movie. Or, we have see that movie.

11. Observe a minimal inflection of verbs. Particularly, never change from the first person singular forms to the third person singular.

   S.E.: Present Tense Forms: He goes to the store.

   B.E.: He go to the store.

   S.E.: Past Tense Forms: He went to the store.

   B.E.: He go to the store. Or, he gone to the store. Or, he been to the store.

12. The possessive case scarcely ever appears in Black English. Never use an apostrophe ('s) construction. If you wander into a possessive case component of an idea, then keep logically consistent: *ours, his, theirs, mines*. But, most likely, if you bump into

such a component, you have wandered outside the underlying world-view of Black English.

> S.E.: He will take their car tomorrow.
>
> B.E.: He taking they car tomorrow.

13. Plurality: Logical consistency, continued: If the modifier indicates plurality then the noun remains in the singular case.

> S.E.: He ate twelve donuts.
>
> B.E.: He eat twelve donut.
>
> S.E.: She has many books.
>
> B.E.: She have many book.

14. Listen for, or invent, special Black English forms of the past tense, such as: "He losted it. That what she felted." If they are clear and readily understood, then use them.

15. Do not hesitate to play with words, sometimes inventing them: e.g. "astropotomous" means huge like a hippo plus astronomical and, therefore, signifies real big.

16. In Black English, unless you keenly want to underscore the past tense nature of an action, stay in the present tense and rely on the overall context of your ideas for the conveyance of time and sequence.

17. Never use the suffix–*ly* form of an adverb in Black English.

> S.E.: The rain came down rather quickly.
>
> B.E.: The rain come down pretty quick.

18. Never use the indefinite article *an* in Black English.

> S.E.: He wanted to ride an elephant.
>
> B.E.: He want to ride him a elephant.

19. Invarient syntax: in correct Black English it is possible to formulate an imperative, an interrogative, and a simple declarative idea with the same syntax:

> B.E.: You going to the store?
>
> You going to the store.
>
> You going to the store!

Where was Willie Jordan? We'd reached the mid-term of the semester. Students had formulated Black English guidelines, by consensus, and they were now writing with remarkable beauty, purpose, and enjoyment:

> *I ain hardly speakin for everybody but myself so understan that.*
> *—Kim Parks*

Samples from student writings:

"Janie have a great big ole hole inside her. Tea Cake the only thing that fit that hole...

"That pear tree beautiful to Janie, especial when bees fiddlin with the blossomin pear there growin large and lovely. But personal speakin, the love she get from starin at that tree ain the love what starin back at her in them relationship." (Monica Morris)

"Love is a big theme in, *They Eye Was Watching God.* Love show people new corners inside theyself. It pull out good stuff and stuff back bad stuff...Joe worship the doing uh his own hand and need other people to worship him too. But he ain't think about Janie that she a person and ought to live like anybody common do. Queen life not for Janie." (Monica Morris)

"In both life and writin, Black womens have varietous experience of love that be cold like a iceberg or fiery like a inferno. Passion got for the other partner involve, man or woman, seem as shallow, ankle-deep water or the most profoundest abyss." (Constance Evans)

"Family love another bond that ain't never break under no pressure." (Constance Evans)

"You know it really cold / When the friend you/ Always get out the fire / Act like they don't know you / When you in the heat." (Constance Evans)

"Big classroom discussion bout love at this time. I never take no class where us have any long arguin for and against for two or three day. New to me and great. I find the class time talkin a million time more interestin than detail bout the book." (Kathy Esseks)

As these examples suggest, Black English no longer limited the students, in any way. In fact, one of them, Philip Garfield, would shortly "translate" a pivotal scene from Ibsen's *Doll House*, as his final term paper.

Nora: I didn't gived no shit. I thinked you a asshole back then, too,
you make it so hard for me save mines husband life.
Krogstad: Girl, it clear you ain't any idea what you done. You done
exact what once done, and I losed my reputation over it.
Nora: You asks me believe you once act brave save you wife life?
Krogstad: Law care less why you done it.
Nora: Law must suck.
Krogstad: Suck or no, if I wants, judge screw you wid dis paper.
Nora: No way, man. (Philip Garfield)

But where was Willie? Compulsively punctual, and always thoroughly prepared with neatly typed compositions, he had disappeared. He failed to show up for our regularly scheduled conference, and I received neither a note nor a phone call of explanation. A whole week went by. I wondered if Willie had finally been captured by the extremely current happenings in South Africa: passage of a new constitution that did not enfranchise the Black majority, and militant Black South African reaction to that affront. I wondered if he'd been hurt, somewhere. I wondered if the serious workload of weekly readings and writings had overwhelmed him and changed his mind about independent study. Where was Willie Jordan?

One week after the first conference that Willie missed, he called: "Hello, Professor Jordan? This is Willie. I'm sorry I wasn't there last week. But something has come up and I'm pretty upset. I'm sorry but I really can't deal right now."

I asked Willie to drop by my office and just let me see that he was okay. He agreed to do that. When I saw him I knew something hideous had happened. Something had hurt him and scared him to the marrow. He was all agitated and stammering and terse and incoherent. At last, his sadly jumbled account let me surmise, as follows: Brooklyn police had murdered his unarmed-twenty-five year old brother, Reggie Jordan. Neither Willie nor his elderly parents knew what to do about it. Nobody from the press was interested. His folks had no money. Police ran his family around and around, to no point. And Reggie was really dead. And Willie wanted to fight, but he felt helpless.

With Willie's permission I began to try to secure legal counsel for the Jordan family. Unfortunately Black victims of police violence are truly numerous while the resources available to prosecute their killers are truly scarce. A friend of mine at the Center for Constitutional Rights estimated that just the preparatory costs for bringing the cops into court normally approaches $180,000. Unless the execution of Reggie Jordan became a major community cause for organizing, and protest, his murder would simply become a statistical item.

Again, with Willie's permission, I contacted every newspaper and media person I could think of. But the William Bastone feature article in *The Village Voice* was the only result from that canvassing.

Again, with Willie's permission, I presented the case to my class in Black English. We had talked about the politics of language. We had talked about love and sex and child abuse and men and women. But the murder of Reggie Jordan broke like a hurricane across the room.

There are few "issues" as endemic to Black life as police violence. Most of the students knew and respected and liked Jordan. Many of them came from the very neighborhood where the murder had occurred. All of the students had known somebody close to them who had been killed by police, or had known somebody close to them who had been killed by police, or had known frightening moments of gratuitous confrontation with the cops. They wanted to do everything at once to avenge death. Number One: They decided to compose personal statements of condolence to Willie Jordan and his family written in Black English. Number Two: They decided to compose individual messages to the police, in Black English. These should be prefaced by an explanatory paragraph composed by the entire group. Number Three: These individual messages, with their lead paragraph, should be sent to *Newsday*.

The morning after we agreed on these objectives, one of the young women students appeared with an unidentified visitor, who sat through the class, smiling in a peculiar, comfortable way.

Now we had to make tactical decisions. Because we wanted the messages published, and because we thought it was imperative that our outrage be known by the police, the tactical question was this: Should the opening, group paragraph be written in Black English or Standard English?

I have seldom been privy to a discussion with so much heart at the dead heat of it. I will never forget the eloquence, the sudden haltings of speech, the fierce struggle against tears, the furious throwaway, and useless explosions that this question elicited.

That one question contained several others, each of them extraordinarily painful to even contemplate. How best to serve the memory of Reggie Jordan? Should we use the language of the killers—Standard English—in order to make our ideas more acceptable to those controlling the killers? But wouldn't what we had to say be rejected, summarily, if we said it in our own language, the language of the victim, Reggie Jordan? But if we sought to express ourselves by abandoning our language wouldn't that mean our suicide on top of Reggie's murder? But if we expressed ourselves in our own language wouldn't that be suicidal to the wish to communicate with those who, evidently, did not give a damn about us/Reggie/police violence in the Black community?

At the end of one of the longest, most difficult hours of my own life, the students voted, unanimously, to preface their individual messages with a paragraph composed in the language of Reggie Jordan. "*At least we don't give up nothing else. At least we stick to the truth: Be who we been. And stay all the way with Reggie.*"

It was heartbreaking to proceed, from that point. Everyone in the room realized that our decision in favor of Black English had doomed our writings, even as the distinctive reality of our Black lives always has doomed our efforts to "be who we been" in this country.

I went to the blackboard and took down this paragraph, dictated by the class:

"...YOU COPS!

WE THE BROTHER AND SISTER OF WILLIE JORDAN, A FELLOW STONY BROOK STUDENT WHO THE BROTHER OF THE DEAD REGGIE JORDAN. REGGIE, LIKE MANY BROTHER AND SISTER, HE A VICTIM OF BRUTAL RACIST POLICE, OCTOBER 25, 1984. US

APPALL, FED UP, BECAUSE THAT ANOTHER SENSELESS DEATH
WHAT OCCUR IN OUR COMMUNITY. THIS WHAT WE FEEL, THIS,
FROM OUR HEART, FOR WE AIN'T STAYIN' SILENT NO MORE:"

With the completion of this introduction, nobody said anything.
I asked for comments. At this invitation, the unidentified visitor, a
young Black man, ceaselessly smiling, raised his hand. He was, it
so happens, a rookie cop. He had just joined the force in September
and, he said, he thought he should clarify a few things. So he came
forward and sprawled easily into a posture of barroom, or fireside,
nostalgia:

"See," Officer Charles enlightened us, "Most times when you out
on the street and something come down you do one of two things.
Over-react or under-react. Now, if you under-react then you can get
yourself kilt. And if you over-react then maybe you kill somebody.
Fortunately it's about nine times out of ten and you will over-react.
So the brother got kilt. And I'm sorry about that, believe me. But
what you have to understand is what kilt him: Over-reaction. That's
all. Now you talk about Black people and white police but see, now,
I'm a cop myself. And (big smile) I'm Black. And just a couple months
ago I was on the other side. But see it's the same for me. You a cop,
you the ultimate authority: the Ultimate Authority. And you on the
street, most of the time you can only do one of two things: over-react
or under-react. That's all it is with the brother: Over-reaction. Didn't
have nothing to do with race."

That morning Officer Charles had the good fortune to escape
without being boiled alive. But barely. And I remember the pride of
his smile when I read about the fate of Black policemen and other
collaborators, in South Africa. I remember him, and I remember the
shock and palpable feeling of shame that filled the room. It was as
though that foolish, and deadly, young man had just relieved himself
of his foolish, and deadly, explanation, face to face with the grief
of Reggie Jordan's father and Reggie Jordan's mother. Class ended
quietly. I copied the paragraph from the blackboard, collected the
individual messages and left to type them up.

Newsday rejected the piece.

The Village Voice could not find room in their "Letters" section to print the individual messages from the students to the police.

None of the TV news reporters picked up the story.

Nobody raised $180,000 to prosecute the murder of Reggie Jordan.

Reggie Jordan is really dead.

I asked Willie Jordan to write an essay pulling together everything important to him from that semester. He was still deeply beside himself with frustration and amazement and loss. This is what he wrote, un-edited, and in its entirety:

"Throughout the course of this semester I have been researching the effects of oppression and exploitation along racial lines in South Africa and its neighboring countries. I have become aware of South African police brutalization of native Africans beyond the extent of the law, even though the laws themselves are catalyst affliction upon Black men, women, and children. Many Africans die each year as a result of the deliberate use of police force to protect the white power structure.

"Social control agents in South Africa, such as policemen, are also used to force compliance among citizens through both overt and covert tactics. It is not uncommon to find bold-faced coercion and cold-blooded killings of Blacks by South African police for undetermined and/or inadequate reasons. Perhaps the truth is that the only reasons for this heinous treatment of Blacks rests in racial differences. We should also understand that what is conveyed through the media is not always accurate and may sometimes be construed as the tip of the iceberg at best.

"I recently received a painful reminder that racism, poverty, and the abuse of power are global problems which are by no means unique to South Africa. On October 25, 1984, at approximately 3:00 p.m. my brother, Mr. Reginald Jordan, was shot and killed by two New York City policemen from the 75th precinct in the East New York section of Brooklyn. His life ended at the age of twenty-five. Even up to this current point in time the Police Department has failed to provide my family, which consists of five brothers, eight sisters, and two parents, with a plausible reason for Reggie's death. Out of the many stories that were given to my family by the Police Department, not one of them seems to hold water. In fact, I honestly believe that the Police Department's assessment of my brother's murder is nothing short of ABSOLUTE BULLSHIT, and thus far no evidence has been produced to alter perception of the situation.

"Furthermore, I believe that one of three cases may have occurred in this incident. First, Reggie's death may have been the desired outcome of the police officer's action, in which case the killing was premeditated. Or, it was a case of mistaken identity, which clarifies the fact that the two officers who killed my brother and their commanding parties are all grossly incompetent. Or, both of the above cases are correct, i.e., Reggie's murderers intended to kill him and the Police Department behaved insubordinately.

"Part of the argument of the officers who shot Reggie was that he had attacked one of them and took his gun. This was their major claim. They also said that only one of them had actually shot Reggie. The facts, however, speak for themselves. According to the Death Certificate and autopsy report, Reggie was shot eight times from point-blank range. The Doctor who performed the autopsy told me himself that two bullets entered the side of my brother's head, four bullets were sprayed into his back, and two bullets struck him in the back of his legs. It is obvious that unnecessary force was used by the police and that it is extremely difficult to shoot someone in his back when he is attacking or approaching you.

"After experiencing a situation like this and researching South Africa I believe that to a large degree, justice may only exist as rhetoric. I find it difficult to talk of true justice when the oppression of my people both at home and abroad attests to the fact that inequality and injustice are serious problems whereby Blacks and Third World people are perpetually short-changed by society. Something has to be done about the way in which this world is set up. Although it is a difficult task, we do have the power to make a change."

—Willie J. Jordan Jr.
EGL 487, Section 58,
November 14, 1984

"THEY MINING THE RIVERS / WE MAKING LOVE REAL"

FROM *NEW DAYS: POEMS OF EXILE AND RETURN* (1974)

[In the first half of 1970, Nixon nominated G. Harrold Carswell for the Supreme Court, a man who in an earlier bid for the Georgia legislature had affirmed his "firm and vigorous belief in the principles of white supremacy"; in January 1970, journalist Christopher Pyle published reports of the U.S. Army and CIA monitoring millions of Americans for lawful political activity; four protesting students where shot and killed by the National Guard on the campus of Kent State; and presidential advisor Daniel Patrick Moynihan was continuing to analyze what he called the "pathology" of Black family life as the source of urban unrest. That same year Buckminster Fuller encouraged Jordan to accept a yearlong fellowship in Environmental Design at the American Academy in Rome, which she did. From the section of *New Days* entitled "Conditions for Leaving" we have included her scathing poetic response to Moynihan's "The Negro Family: the Case for National

Action" (issued by the U.S. Department of Labor) that shamelessly blamed single Black mothers for the conditions that led to teenage delinquency, crime, and drug use.

In September, Jordan arrived at the American Academy and began her series called the Roman Poems, included in the section "Poems of Exile." In the earliest poem of the sequence, Jordan contemplates the dark-bronze figure of a small boy in the fountain outside her window; the figure of a brown child becomes a stand-in for Jordan herself as she negotiates life in a foreign country: "there alone/and listening to a sound that is/not his." The Roman Poems are a complex fugue of love and psychic conflict, of cultural estrangement and personal reckoning, and document her coming to terms with who she will be as an American and as an artist.

Cutting short her stay, in January 1971 Jordan returned home to work on a variety of projects, among them *Okay Now*, a nonfiction-work-become-novel based on her research on Mississippi land use. She also resumed and deepened her friendships with other poets and writers who were rethinking what American literature could and should be. In "Thinking about My Poetry" (1977) she writes that it seemed to her "that we were all of us working on the same poem of a life of perpetual, difficult birth" and that if she attended to her own situation, and could "trace the provocations for [her] own voice" she could "hope to count upon myself to be serving a positive and collective function, without pretending to be more than the one Black woman poet I am." Thus, the "Poems of Return" can be candid, ironic, coy, endearing, or vociferous—and some are all at the same time—and show the full, rich range of the poet she is and the poet she is becoming.]

FROM SECTION ONE: CONDITIONS FOR LEAVING
♦♦♦
MEMO TO DANIEL PRETTY MOYNIHAN

You done what you done
I do what I can

Don't you liberate me
from my female black pathology

I been working off my knees
I been drinking what I please

And when I vine
I know I'm fine
I mean
All right for each and every Friday night

But you been screwing me so long
I got a idea something's wrong
with you

I got a simple proposition
You takeover my position

Clean your own house, babyface.

FROM SECTION TWO: POEMS OF EXILE
♦♦♦
ROMAN POEM NUMBER ONE

1
Only my own room is gray

from morning on
those high those closing windows
may divide

to make an open wall

(that's maybe nine or ten feet tall)

and when you pulley up the wooden blinds
the outdoor cypress trees
confront
consume
caress the (relatively) small and starving eyes
that mark your face

for love

2
How old is Jesus?

for example well

the dark bronze fountain boy

(behold him)

wet
perpetual

the running water slides his belly loose
the snake around his arm
supplies the slick delectable

the difference

the dry parts where his hard

fat fingers never reach

the area where early light
or late

the boy is there alone

and listening to a sound that is

not his

◆◆◆

ROMAN POEM NUMBER THREE

"I am so sorry to say this but
our poor are not as poor
as yours.
In Italy you will never see the
terrible
sad face the hopelessness
and very dry eyes of America."
And now
my teacher turns to bargain
for three small handkerchiefs
to send to Wisconsin for Christmas.

◆◆◆

ROMAN POEM NUMBER FOUR

The tiny electrical coffee pot
takes a long time to make
toy bubbles of hot water while
we wait we laugh a lot in a stiff
and a stuffy chair jokes about the world

the war the regular material for
belly laughing through
and "By the way
do you know anyone in Greece? I have/
I had some friends who went there after
the coup. But they have not
written suddenly
for several months and the telephone
operator says that no
such persons as
The Cacoullos
exist."

       — "If you give me the stamps
I will write to somebody who can find out
if your friends are still alive or what."
I hand over the stamps.
It is a good thing sometimes
to buy a few extra.

◆◆◆

ROMAN POEM NUMBER SIX

You walk downstairs
to see this man who moves so
quietly in a dark room
where there are balancing
scales on every table.
Signore D'Ettore can tell
you anything about
communications if you mean
the weight the price
of letters
packages
and special post cards.

Hunch-back
short
his gray hair always groomed
meticulous
with a comb and just a touch
of grease
           for three months
he has worn the same well
tailored suit
a gray suit quite unlike
his hair.
           I find it restful
just to watch him making
judgments all of us accept.
"But are you sad?" he asks
me looking up.

"The world is beautiful
but men are bad," he says in
slow Italian.
I smile with him but still the problem
is not solved.
The photographs of Rome
must reach my father but the big
official looking book seems blank
the finger-nail of Signore D'Ettore
seems blind and wandering
from line to line among the countries
of a long
small-printed list.
"Jamaica? Where is Jamaica?"
I am silent. My Italian
is not good enough to say, "Jamaica
is an island where you can find
calypso roses sunlight and an old man
my father

on his knees."

◆◆◆

ROMAN POEM NUMBER THIRTEEN

For Eddie

Only our hearts will argue hard
against the small lights letting in the news
and who can choose between the worst possibility
and the last
between the winners of the wars against the breathing
and the last
war everyone will lose
and who can choose between the dry gas
domination of the future
and the past
between the consequences of the killers
and the past
of all the killing? There
is no choice in these.
Your voice
breaks very close to me my love.

◆◆◆

ROMAN POEM NUMBER FOURTEEN

believe it love
believe

        my lover
lying down he
lifts me up and high
and I am

high on him

believe it love
believe

the carnage scores around
the corner

o believe it love
believe

the bleeding fills the carnage cup
my lover lifts me
I am up
      and love is lying down

believe
believe it

crazies wear a clean shirt to the fire
o my lover
lift me higher higher

crazies take a scream and
make a speech they talk and
wash their mouths in dirt
no love will hurt
me lover lift me lying down

believe
believe it
carnage crazies
snap smash more more
(what you waiting for?)

you own the rope knife rifles the whole list

the searing bomb starch brighteners
the nuclear family whiteners

look the bridge be fallen down
look the ashes from the bones turn brown
look the mushroom hides the town
look the general wears his drip dry red
drip gown

o my lover nakedly
believe my love

believe
believe it

◆◆◆

ROMAN POEM NUMBER SEVENTEEN

In their tomb paintings the Greeks reveal
what was important to them
pitchers of wine
supine repose
flute music
leisure
sex
and love

the homosexuals with lyre
one reaching his arm around the other's
head and into his hair his hand
the other boy reaching to caress the
breast of his man
the languid grace
thick lips
sloe eyes

the really comic book depiction
of a man stiffly
diving from a cliff
into water

Hippocrates wrote of birth as a breaking
down of the roadway
so that things could move more easily

we may have to die
again
before we can understand
the grace of the dead
but
it may not be worth
the destruction
of a second birth.

FROM SECTION THREE: POEMS OF RETURN

◆◆◆

ON THE SPIRIT OF MILDRED JORDAN

After sickness and a begging
from her bed
my mother dressed herself
gray lace-up oxfords
stockings baggy on her shrunken legs
an orange topper
rhinestone buttons
and a powder blue straw
hat with plastic
flowers

Then
she took the street
in short steps toward the corner

chewing gum
no less

she let the family laugh
again

she wasn't foxy
she was strong

◆◆◆

ON THE BLACK FAMILY

we making love real
they mining the rivers

we been going without trees and going
without please and growing on —
on make-dos and breakthroughs to baby
makes three's a family
ole Charlie knows nothing
about out there
where
he burning the leaves and firing the earth
and killing and killing

we been raising the children
to hold us some love for tomorrows
that show how we won our own wars
just to come in the night
Black and Loving
Man and Woman

definitely in despite
of
all the hurdles that the murdering
masterminds threw up to stop
the comings of
Black Love

we came
we came and we come in a glory of darkness
around the true reasons for sharing
our dark and our beautiful
name
that we give to our dark and our beautiful
daughters and sons
who must make the same struggle
to love

and must win

against the tyrannical soldierly sins
of the ones who beatify plastic and steel
and who fly themselves high on the failure to feel

    —they mining the rivers
    we making love real

◆◆◆

OF NIGHTSONG AND FLIGHT

There are things lovely and dangerous still

the rain
when the heat of an evening
sweetens the darkness with mist

and the eyes cannot see what the memory will
of new pain

when the headlights deceive
like the windows wild birds believe to be air
and bash bodies and wings
on the glass

when the headlights show space
but the house and the room and the bed and your face
are still there

while I am mistaken
and try to drive by

the actual kiss
of the world everywhere

◆◆◆

AFTER ALL IS SAID AND DONE

Maybe you thought I would forget
about the sunrise
how the moon stayed in the morning
time a lower lip
your partly open partly spoken
mouth

Maybe you thought I would exaggerate
the fire of the stars
the fire of the wet wood burning by
the waterside
the fire of the fuck the sudden move
you made me make
to meet you

(fire)

BABY
I do not exaggerate and
if
I could
I would.

◆◆◆

ABOUT LONG DISTANCES ON SATURDAY

he calls me from his house and
the timing seems bad
and I offer to call him back
later
but he says "no"
I'm about to split for the weekend
so
call me yeah
early next week or
sometime
and the answer is
that the question
is

(isn't it)

where are you going
baby

without me?

◆◆◆

CALLING ON ALL SILENT MINORITIES

HEY

C'MON
COME OUT

WHEREVER YOU ARE
WE NEED TO HAVE THIS MEETING
AT THIS TREE

AIN' EVEN BEEN
PLANTED
YET

FROM SECTION FOUR: UNTITLED

◆◆◆

GETTING DOWN TO GET OVER

Dedicated to my mother

1
MOMMA MOMMA MOMMA
momma momma
mammy
nanny
granny
woman
mistress
sista

luv

blackgirl

slavegirl

gal

honeychile
sweetstuff
sugar
sweetheart
baby
Baby Baby

MOMMA MOMMA
Black Momma
Black bitch
Black pussy
piecea tail
nice piecea ass

hey daddy! hey
bro!
we walk together (an')
talk together (an')
dance and *do*
(together)
dance and do/hey!
daddy!
bro!
hey!
nina nikki nonni nommo nommo
momma Black
Momma

Black Woman
Black
Female Head of Household
Black Matriarchal Matriarchy

Black Statistical
Lowlife Lowlevel Lowdown
Lowdown and *up*
to be Low-down
Black Statistical
Low Factor
Factotum
Factitious Fictitious
Figment Figuring in Lowdown Lyin
Annual Reports

Black Woman/Black
Hallelujah Saintly
patient
smilin
humble
givin thanks
for
Annual Reports and
Monthly Dole
and
Friday night
and
(*good* God!)
Monday mornin: Black and Female
martyr masochist
(A BIG WHITE LIE)
Momma Momma

What does Mothafuckin mean?
WHO'S THE MOTHAFUCKA
FUCKED MY MOMMA
messed yours over
and right now
be trippin on my starveblack
female soul

a macktruck
mothafuck
the first primordial
the paradig/digmatic
dogmatistic mothafucka who
is he?
hey!
momma momma

dry eyes on the
shy/dark/hidden/cryin Black
face
of the loneliness
the rape
the brokeup mailbox
an' no western union roses
come inside the kitchen
and no poem
take you through the whole night
and no big
Black
burly
hand
be holdin yours
to have to hold onto
no
big Black burly hand
no nommo
no Black prince
come riding from the darkness
on a beautiful black horse
no bro
no daddy

"I was sixteen when I met my father.
In a bar.

In Baltimore.
He told me who he was
and what he does.
Paid for the drinks.
I looked.
I listened.
And I left him.
It was civil
perfectly
and absolute bull
shit.
The drinks was leakin waterweak
and never got down to my knees."

hey daddy
what they been and done to you
and what you been and done
to me
to momma
momma momma
hey
sugar daddy
big daddy
sweet daddy
Black Daddy
The Original Father Divine
the everlovin
deep
tall
bad
buck
jive
cold
strut
bop
split

tight
loose
close
hot
hot
hot
sweet SWEET DADDY
WHERE YOU BEEN AND
WHEN YOU COMIN BACK TO ME
HEY
WHEN YOU COMIN BACK
TO MOMMA
momma momma

And Suppose He Finally Say
"Look, Baby.
I Loves Me Some
Everything about You.
Let Me Be Your Man."
That reach around the hurtin
like a dream.
And I ain' never wakin up
from that one.
momma momma
momma momma

2
Consider the Queen

hand on her hip
sweat restin from
the corn/bean/greens' field
steamy under the pale/sly
suffocatin sky

Consider the Queen

she fix the cufflinks
on his Sunday shirt
and fry some chicken
bake some cake
and tell the family
"Never mine about the bossman
don' know how a human
bein spozed to act. Jus'
never mind about him.
Wash your face.
Sit down. And let
the good Lord bless this table."

Consider the Queen

her babies pullin at the nipples
pullin at the momma milk

the infant fingers gingerly
approach caress the
soft/Black/swollen/momma breast

and there
inside the mommasoft
life-spillin treasure chest
the heart
breaks

rage by grief by sorrow
weary weary
breaks
breaks quiet
silently
the weary sorrow
quiet now the furious

the adamant the broken
busted beaten down and beaten up
the beaten beaten beaten
weary heart beats
tender-steady
and the babies suck/
the seed of blood
and love glows at the
soft/Black/swollen momma breast

Consider the Queen

she works when she works
in the laundry *in jail*
in the school house *in jail*
in the office *in jail*
on the soap box *in jail*
on the desk
on the floor
on the street
on the line
at the door
lookin fine
at the head of the line
steppin sharp from behind
in the light
with a song
wearing boots
or a belt
and a gun
drinkin wine when it's time
when the long week is done
but she works when she works
in the laundry in jail
she works when she works

Consider the Queen

she sleeps when she sleeps
with the king in the kingdom
she
sleeps when she sleeps
with the wall
with whatever it is who happens
to call
with me and with you
(to survive you make
do/you explore more and more)
so she sleeps when she sleeps
a really deep sleep

Consider the Queen

a full/Black/glorious/a purple rose
aroused by the tiger breathin
beside her
a shell with the moanin
of ages inside her
a hungry one feedin the folk
what they need

Consider the Queen.

3
Blackman
let that white girl go
She know what you ought to know.
(By now.)

4
MOMMA MOMMA
momma momma

family face
face of the family alive
momma
mammy
momma
woman
sista
baby
luv

the house on fire/
poison waters/
earthquake/
and the air a nightmare/
turn
turn
turn around the
national gross product
growin
really gross/turn
turn
turn the pestilence away
the miserable killers
and Canarsie
Alabama
people beggin to be people
warfare on the welfare
of the folk/
hey
turn
turn away
the trickbag university/the
trickbag propaganda
trickbag
tricklins of prosperity/of
pseudo-"status"

lynchtree necklace
on the strong
round
neck of you
my momma
momma momma
turn away
the f.b.i./the state police/the cops/
the/everyone of the
infest/incestuous investigators
into you
and Daddy/into us
hey
turn
my mother
turn
the face of history
to your own
and please be smilin
if you can
be smilin
at the family

momma momma

let the funky forecast
be the last
one we will ever
want to listen to

And Daddy see
the stars fall down
and burn a light
into the singin
darkness of your eyes
my Daddy

my Blackman
you take my body in
your arms/you use
the oil of coconuts/of trees and
flowers/fish and new fruits
from the new world
to enflame me in this otherwise
cold place
please
meanwhile
momma
momma momma
teach me how to kiss
the king within the kingdom
teach me how to t.c.b./to make do
and be
like you
teach me to survive my
momma
teach me how to hold a new life
momma
help me
turn the face of history
to your face.

FROM SECTION FIVE: POEM AGAINST A CONCLUSION

◆◆◆

THESE POEMS

These poems
they are things that I do
in the dark
reaching for you
whoever you are

and
are you ready?

These words
they are stones in the water
running away

These skeletal lines
they are desperate arms for my longing and love.

I am a stranger
learning to worship the strangers
around me

whoever you are

whoever I may become.

"JEWELS OF OUR SOUL"

JORDAN ON COUNTEE CULLEN'S ANTHOLOGY *CAROLING DUSK*, RICHARD WRIGHT, ZORA NEALE HURSTON, LANGSTON HUGHES & PHILLIS WHEATLEY
(1974-1985)

[Writing out of community spirit, following the urge to give voice to others, it's no surprise that Jordan was an ardent booster of the work of other writers, from the students in her workshops, to up-and-coming new poets, and poets whom she did not believe had gotten the attention they deserved.]

FROM "ESSAY AND REVIEW OF COUNTEE CULLEN'S ANTHOLOGY, *CAROLING DUSK*"

[1974]

[Between 1974 and 1977 Jordan's column in *American Poetry Review*, "The Black Poet Speaks of Poetry," brought to greater attention a wide range of poets, many of them little known to *APR*'s mainstream (read: mostly white) readers. She reviewed work by Ntozake Shange, Etheridge Knight, E. Ethelbert Miller, Jessica Hagedorn. But her inclusiveness and belief in excellence crossing all kinds of borders drew her to write about Karen Swenson, Barry Wallenstein, and Millen Brand as well. She kicked off her stint as columnist by reviewing a newly re-issued edition of Countee Cullen's *Caroling Dusk: An Anthology of Verse by Negro Poets*, first published in 1927. Jordan's review points out the challenges Cullen faced in putting together an anthology of "Negro" excellence that also appeased white readers' assumptions about whiteness as a constituent of the greatest verse in English. She also takes the time to recognizes the anthology "as a marvel of historical information," a rich introduction to the diverse aims, histories, and convictions of the writers of the "Harlem Renaissance," and praises some of Cullen's choices for inclusion, such as the "ten Negro Women" poets in the anthology, including two that "startle my eyes and ears with unadulterated, proud, and grateful surprise." The review appeared in *American Poetry Review*'s May/June issue of '74. (She ended her stint in protest, in January 1977, of *APR*'s continued exclusionary policies when it came to work by minorities and women.)]

[Jordan begins the essay by reprinting Countee Cullen's "Yet Do I Marvel" in its entirety]

1. *The Black Poem: It has to be somewhere ... you can get to it ...* I've been asked to address some Black and White questions about Black poetry: "... how Black and White communities may communicate with each other beyond color lines, i.e. what aspects of the Black man's life are like that of the white man's, and vice versa ..." (*not*) "physical resemblances or obvious human things." ... (*but*) "what each of us has to contribute to one another ... without violating the differences. ..."

Well, I have studied the letter presenting these questions, a number of times; each reading provokes a mixture of puzzled, angry feelings: It seems misplaced: the burden of these inquiries: For one thing, I would not presume to tell white readers what they should look for, in Black art. Nobody has held my hand, with respect to the white poetry I read and live with, and count upon, as ordinarily as I read the news.

For another thing, the questions point to a black-and-white reality I consider quite infuriating: white people/white editors of major/ nationwide magazines and publishing houses simply do not read and do not value and do not publish what I will call The Black Poem. After the compensatory, commercial flares of Black appearance under white auspices, during the middle to late sixties, traditional, white attitudes towards distinctively Black work resumed a ruling prevalence: Black poetry was cancelled out—again. And if you think I overstate the case, I challenge you to tell me how often, within even the past 15 years, for example, you have seen a Black Poem published by *The New Republic, The N.Y. Times, The New Yorker, The New York Review of Books, New American Review, Harper's, The Atlantic,* Harper & Row, Farrar, Straus & Giroux, Doubleday, etc.

Let's be specific: although *The New Republic* regards itself as a political journal, when have you seen a political Black poem published there? Or, although The *N.Y. Times* regularly presents a full page review of one book of poems by one, white poet, how often have you seen a Black poet accorded comparable space and care? For that matter, when have you seen Black poetry, per se, reviewed in *The N.Y. Times Book Review/N.Y. Review of Books*, etcetera.

You may plead ignorance, or allude to an allegedly declining exclusion of Black poetry from general anthologies: That will not get over. The facts are these: Distinctively Black poetry continues to be written and perfected and (obscurely) available to a stunning, efflo-rescent degree, across the country; there is certainly no decrease in the dazzling abundance of terrific, wonderful, necessary Black poets writing this minute up and down. (Much of the most exciting, new Black poetry that I know, comes to me, by mail, from *un*-published manuscripts.) *Nevertheless*, my white contemporary, the poet Mark Strand, for instance, has seen fit to issue an anthology of "Ameri-can" poetry that includes *not* a single Black poet and, moreover, the overwhelming majority of major anthologies that title themselves Anthologies of American/English Language/Living/Great (and so forth) Poetry do *not* include Black poets, at all, let alone inclusion of a representative/proportional nature. At the least, this particular outrage cheats the reading public: misleads and deprives the willing, waiting reader of Black poems.

This reminds me of a few writing faculty meetings at Sarah Law-rence College where I teach these days: Last October, every Black poet I proposed as someone to invite for a campus reading turned out to be a Black poet that none of my white colleagues had ever heard of! Now, you can't have it both ways: you can't keep us out and then ease off that hook by suddenly discovering that we are not as conve-niently nearby as your nearest bookstore, or college library, or usual, literary publications.

To find us, you should check out *Black World*, *Essence*, Broadside Press, Emerson Hall Publishing Company, Third Press, Third World Press, Jihad Publications, Barlenmir House Press, and like that. Or, perhaps, an occasional, defiantly dogged, university press will bring you, perhaps, Michael Harper, maybe, or a wayward, white publish-ing house will lapse into letting out a new book of Black poetry—or, probably not that so much as a book of poetry by a Black poet, if you can dig the difference.

To catch up with The Black Poem, as things stand today, as good a means as any is the creation of or location of Black poetry readings to which you just carry pencil and paper and, afterward take down the vital information: name/address of publisher/price of book.

Obviously, this will not do: indeed, the plight of Black poetry is disgusting and destined to defy our utmost ingenuity/obduracy, if we will survive The Big, White, No.

A last word on this point, a word that expands the compass of my complaint, as it should expand: Yesterday, my son came home, talking as usual about his current, English course, entitled *The Contemporary American Novel*: do you believe there was not a solitary Black novel on the list? Believe it.

To summarize so far: *Black poetry can bring nothing to anyone white or Black, unless it becomes available*: in readings, journals, and books across the board, on a first class basis. At the moment, the availability of Black poetry heavily depends upon whitepower which is, evidently, indifferent at best.

2. *The Black Poem ... Distinctively Speaking.* What is it? Quite apart from individual volumes of Black poetry, I have learned that I hold decidedly different expectations of a Black Anthology, as compared to any other kind. If the single poem, or if the anthology qualifies as distinctively Black, then, as compared to a "white anthology" or a "white poem," I expect the following:

*A striving for collective voice, or else its actual, happy accomplishment. Even if the poem proceeds in the 1st person singular, I expect a distinctively Black poem to speak *for me*-as-part-of-an-*us*, a bounded group that the poem self-consciously assumes as an integral, guiding factor in her/his/their individual art.

*From a reaching for collective voice, as a self-conscious value, it follows that a distinctively Black poem will be accessible to random readers, rather than "hard," or arrantly inaccessible. (This does not mean that prolonged/repeated study will not yield new comprehension. But it does mean that the first time around, which may be an only time, the poem has to "hit" and "stick," clearly, and openly, in a welcoming way.)

*Collective voice necessarily refers to spoken language: Distinctively Black poems characteristically deal memories and possibilities of spoken language, as against literary, or written, language. This partially accounts for the comparative directness and force of Black poetry; it is an intentionally collective, or inclusive, people's art meant to be shared, heard and, therefore, spoken—meant to be as real as bread.

*Sound patterns, rhythmic movement and change-ups often figure as importantly as specific words, or images, in distinctively Black poetry. (Even if the poet says nothing especially new, I can expect to take pleasure in the musical, textural aspects of the poem; they will be as intrinsic to the work, as the words.)

To conclude this second point: Distinctively Black poetry adheres to certain, identifiable values—political and aesthetic—that are open to adoption, enjoyment by anyone. Overriding everything else is the striving and respect for collective voice. These distinctive values also constitute the main sum of what I look for, and prize, in The Black Poem.

3. *Caroling Dusk, An Anthology of Negro Poets,* edited by Countee Cullen when he was 24 years old, published by Harper & Bros., in 1927, and re-issued, 1974, by Harper & Row ... delivers something I am extremely delighted to recommend; it is also germane to the task of this whole column, since it presents as many as 38 "Negro" poets writing, primarily, in their early to mid-twenties, during the misnamed Harlem Renaissance.

Thirteen of the poets are "Negro" women. Ten of these arrive as brand-new news to me. And two of them startle my eyes and ears with unadulterated, proud, and grateful surprise: Gladys May Casely Hayford and Helene Johnson—*no allowances* for historic difference/ "Negro" mentality versus whatever: These two, surprising, deft poets

carry definite messages they mean to transmit: Born and raised
in Sierra Leone, Sister Hayford avows the propagation of African
beauty, in its living particulars, as her special goals. Addressing her
work to "Negroes" in America, she hopes to displace "Negro" shame,
"Negro" ignorance about Africa and to instill a loving awareness of
the humane, dear, attributes actual Africans body forth. Here's her
poem, "The Serving Girl":

[Jordan reprints the poem in its entirety]

... a very graceful lyric about grace, if I ever saw one.
Countee Cullen describes Helene Johnson as "more colloquial"
(I would say "more spoken") in the language of her poems, than most:

[Jordan reprints Helene Johnson's "Sonnet to A Negro In Harlem"]

The companion piece to Helene Johnson's sonnet is Waring Cu-
ney's poem, "No Images":

[Jordan reprints the poem.]

... feelings of Blacklove between Black men and Black women, ex-
pressed in a way that lets me trust their authenticity and motivation
and invitation to a new, loving idea about *us*: but I grip with stirrings
of rage within me because I didn't have these poems when I was
growing up; I surely, sorely needed them—to balance out the gold-
en-haired, alabaster limb, allegedly "fair" characters tripping rife
through the poetry imposed on me.

And I surely, sorely needed them to balance out the troubled
reality of relations between Black men and Black women that I lived
with, and to balance out the censorship of loved, desirable Black
male, and loved, desirable Black female images, models, concepts
that dominated American mass media—a censorship which has been
mitigated, but not blown away, by any means, in recent years.

Here, in this anthology, there is much to cherish; of course, it
was put together by Countee Cullen, a dynamite, giant poet of all

times who was, however, at embarrassing pains to present his poems and his self, and the "Negro" poems of his choosing as "A variety within a uniformity that is trying to maintain the higher traditions of English verse." (I.E.: *Not* importantly deviating from white, literary traditions.) Cullen indeed managed to assemble a book in which poems to dandelions, or "From the German of Uhland," or "Touché," "Russian Cathedral," "To An Icicle" and "An April Day" just about equal the number of poems I may claim as antecedents to the distinctively Black poem. It is interesting that only those poets who do commit themselves to a collective deviation from white traditions also achieve agreeable results when versifying on hills and summertime and robins and death and John Keats. The others produce greeting-card-drek of a quality intimated by the absurdly fey, let's-write-a-little-poem titles they have aptly selected.

On the unmistakably positive side, *Caroling Dusk* stands as a marvel of historical information: from Countee Cullen's elegant, plainly assimilationist foreword, through every biographical introduction that precedes the poems of each poet, you possess an entry into the "Harlem Renaissance"—the extremely various aims, diversified backgrounds, and personal attitudes—such as I have seen documented nowhere else, particularly in such indisputable, but succinct terms.

And when you turn the page and wander into the works of the more familiar people: Sterling Brown, Langston Hughes, Jean Toomer, Claude McKay—something definitely thrills you into the excitement of discovering them/trying to measure them, as they appear here, twenty-two or twenty-three years old, and thoroughly surrounded by competing contemporaries.

I am intensely pleased to own this anthology, to depend on its being within reach, whenever I feel stranded, or "motherless," as it were: Many of the poets and many of the poems feed a truly warm pride inside me, a pride as warm as still living breath ...

Between 1927 and 1974, the original and most recent publication dates for Caroling Dusk, I was born, along with millions and millions of my Brothers and Sisters; much of what this anthology presents was what we deeply needed ... and were absolutely denied ...

Let me end with one of my favorite poems by Countee Cullen:

[Jordan reprints *"The Dark Tower"*.]

Addendum: In forthcoming issues, I will review the poetry of white poets as well: Poets such as Karen Swenson, Nathan Whiting, and Marge Piercy: those reviews should complete my answer to the questions responsible for the columns you have just finished reading—questions about criteria and values "beyond color lines"; even as I am able to use and to enjoy these white poems, white readers should be able to explore and to enjoy the distinctively Black Poem. If not, why not? In fact, I do not believe a problem exists, except by dint of proclamation … and the consequences thereof.

"NOTES TOWARD A BLACK BALANCING OF LOVE AND HATRED"

(1974)

[When Alice Walker was visiting Jordan, she praised Zora Neale Hurston's long out-of-print novel, *Their Eyes Were Watching God*. Walker gave a copy to her friend as she left, and Jordan spent that night, "including thunderstorms, mesmerized by this fantastic writer." In this essay, Jordan contrasts the celebrity of Richard Wright with the invisibility of Zora Neale Hurston. It was first published in *Black World* in 1974; Jordan included it in *Civil Wars* (1981).]

We should take care so that we will lose none of the jewels of our soul. We must begin, now, to reject the white, either/or system of dividing the world into unnecessary conflict. For example, it is tragic and ridiculous to choose between Malcolm X and Dr. King: each of

them hurled himself against a quite different aspect of our predic-
ament, and both of them, literally, gave their lives to our ongoing
struggle.

We need everybody and all that we are. We need to know and
make known the complete, constantly unfolding, complicated her-
itage that is our Black experience. We should absolutely resist the
superstar, one-at-a-time mentality that threatens the varied and
resilient, flexible wealth of our Black future, even as it shrinks and
obliterates incalculable segments of our history.

In Black literature, we have lost many jewels to the glare of
white, massmedia manipulation. According to whitepower, Ralph
Ellison was the only Black novelist writing, in this country, while
whitepower "allowed" his star to shine. Then, the media "gave" us
James Baldwin—evidently all by himself. And then there was *only*
Eldridge Cleaver. (Remember him?)

But towering before and above these media-isolated giants, there
was always Richard Wright. He has been presented as a solitary fig-
ure on the literary landscape of his period. But, right along with him,
and six years his senior, there was Zora Neale Hurston. And the fact
is that we almost lost Zora to the choose-between games played with
Black Art; until recently, no one had ever heard of her; certainly, no
one read her books. And yet, anyone who was dipped into her work,
even once, will tell you: the long-term obscurity of her joy and wis-
dom is an appalling matter of record. So we would do well to careful-
ly reconsider these two, Hurston and Wright. Perhaps that will let us
understand the cleavage in their public reception, and prevent such
inequity and virtual erasure from taking place, again.

Each of them achieved unprecedented, powerful, and extremely
important depths of Black vision and commitment, in their lifework;
according to the usual criteria, they were both Great Writers. Yet,
while Richard Wright spawned many, many followers, and enjoyed
the rewards of well-earned fame, Zora Neale Hurston suffered
through devastating critical and popular neglect, inspired no imi-
tators, and finally died, penniless, and was buried in an unmarked
grave. Why did this happen?

I believe we were misled into the notion that *only one kind* of writing—protest writing—and that *only one kind* of protest writing—deserves our support and study.

A few years back, Hoyt Fuller posed the primary functions of Protest and Affirmation as basic to an appreciation of Black Art. Wright's *Native Son* is widely recognized as the prototypical, Black, protest novel. By comparison, Hurston's novel, *Their Eyes Were Watching God*, seems to suit, perfectly, the obvious connotations of Black affirmation.

But I would add that the functions of protest and affirmation are not, ultimately, distinct; that, for instance, affirmation of Black values and lifestyle within the American context is, indeed, an act of protest. Therefore, Hurston's affirmative work is profoundly defiant, just as Wright's protest unmistakably asserts our need for an alternative, benign environment. We have been misled to discount the one in order to revere the other. But we have been misled in a number of ways: several factors help to explain the undue contrast between the careers of Wright and Hurston.

Richard Wright was a Black man born on a white, Mississippi plantation, and carried, by fits and starts, from one white, southern town to the next. In short, he was born into the antagonistic context of hostile whites wielding power against him. In this, his background mirrors our majority Black experience. And so, we readily accept the validity of *Native Son*'s Bigger Thomas, who pits himself against overwhelming white force.

Moreover, *Native Son*, undoubtedly Wright's most influential book, conforms to white standards we have swallowed, regarding literary weight. It is apparently symbolic (rather than realistic), "serious" (unrelievedly grim), socio-political (rather than "personal") in its scale, and not so much "emotional" as impassioned in its deliberate execution.

Given the antagonistic premise of *Native Son*, the personal beginnings of Richard Wright, a Black man on enemy turf, it follows that his novel should pull you forward with its furious imagination, saturate the reader with varieties of hatred, and horror; climax in violence, and ram hard—ram hard—against a destiny of doom.

But suppose the premise is a different one?

Zora Neale Hurston was born and raised in an all-Black Florida town. In other words, she was born into a supportive, nourishing environment. And without exception, her work—as novelist, as anthropologist/diligent collector and preserver of Black folktale and myth—reflects this early and late, all-Black universe which was her actual and her creative world.

You see her immovable, all-Black orientation in *Their Eyes Were Watching God*. Whites do not figure in this story of Black love; white anything or anybody is not important; what matters is the Black woman and the Black man who come together in a believable, contagious, full Black love that makes you want to go and seek and find, likewise, soon as you finish the book.

Since white America lies outside the Hurston universe, in fact as well as in her fiction, you do not run up on the man/the enemy; protest, narrowly conceived, is therefore beside the point; rhythm or tones of outrage or desperate flight would be wholly inappropriate in her text. Instead you slip into a total, Black reality where Black people do not represent issues; they represent their own, particular selves in a Family/Community setting that permits relaxation from hunted/warrior postures, and that fosters the natural, person postures of courting, jealousy, ambition, dream, sex, work, partying, sorrow, bitterness, celebration, and fellowship.

Unquestionably, *Their Eyes Were Watching God* is the prototypical Black novel of affirmation; it is the most successful, and convincing, and exemplary novel of Black love that we have, period. But the book gives us more: the story unrolls a fabulously written film of Black life freed from the constraints of oppression; here we may learn Black possibilities of ourselves if we could ever escape the hateful and alien context that has so deeply disturbed and mutilated our rightful efflorescence—*as people*. Consequently, this novel centers itself on Black love—even as *Native Son* rivets itself upon white hatred.

But, because Zora Neale Hurston was a woman, and because we have been misled into devaluating the functions of Black affirmation, her work has been derogated as romantic, the natural purview of a woman (i.e., unimportant), "personal" (not serious) in its scope, and assessed as *sui generis,* or idiosyncratic accomplishment of no lasting reverberation, or usefulness. All such derogation derives from ignorance and/or callow thinking we cannot afford to continue. Although few of us have known the happiness of an all-Black town/ universe, every single one of us is the torn-away descendant of a completely Black/African world and, today, increasing numbers of us deem an all-Black circumstance/nation as our necessary, overriding goal. Accordingly, this Sister has given us the substance of an exceptional, but imperative vision, since her focus is both an historical truth and a contemporary aim. As for the derision of love as less important than war and violence, that is plain craziness, plain *white* craziness we do not need even to discuss.

And, is it true that *Native Son* represents you and me more than Hurston's heroine, Janie Starks? Both of them bespeak our hurt, our wished-for fulfillment, and, at various times, the nature and the level of our adjustment to complete fulfillment or, on the other hand, complete frustration. What's more, I do not accept that Wright and Hurston should be perceived, properly, as antipathetic in the wellsprings of their work. Bigger Thomas, the whole living and dying creation of him, teaches as much about the necessity of love, of being able to love without being destroyed, as Hurston's Janie Starks. Their address to this subject, this agonizingly central need, differs, perhaps, as men and women have been taught to cope with human existence differently. And, elsewhere, I submit that *Their Eyes* treats with a want and a hope and a tragic adjustment that is at least as reverberating, as universal—namely, positive (loving) self-fulfillment—as the material of *Native Son*, which emphasizes the negative trajectories of that same want, hope, and confrontation.

But, rightly, we should not choose between Bigger Thomas and Janie Starks; our lives are as big and as manifold and as pained and as happy as the two of them put together. We should equally value and equally emulate Black Protest and Black Affirmation, for we require both; one without the other is dangerous, and will leave us vulnerable to extinction of the body or the spirit. We owe thanks to both the struggle and the love: to the native sons among us, and to those whose eyes are watching their own gods.

"POEM FOR LANGSTON HUGHES ON HIS 75TH BIRTHDAY: IN MEMORIAM DEAR BIG DADDY BROTHER / MISTER LANGSTON HUGHES":

(1977)

[In March 1977, Jordan and other Black writers, poets, and teachers celebrated Langston Hughes' 75th birthday at City College, not far from where Hughes had lived in Harlem. Jordan, who considered herself a daughter of Hughes for having "inherited" *Who Look at Me* (1969), read this poem. This is the first time it appears in print. That same year, Leonard Bernstein set Jordan's poem "Okay 'Negroes'" to music in "duet" with Langston Hughes' "I, Too, Sing America."]

You would probably be surprise
They got a skyscrape shoebox on 125th Street reach
so high you havta stand back ten blocks easy just
to hold that building up
inside your eyes
And Miz Jackson back to fried fish/fried hair afta
Tryin out the natural rawstuff for a coupla superpolitical
serious years
and Willie Brown fell down the hallway stairwell in
his flyboot platform sneakers yesterday
(no I ain lyin)
And Africa
And Africa/or mostofit
be independent now/or sorta
and the news is good except we got these relatives who
imitate the Europeans and the violence sometimes

look like Hiroshima smallscale
And lemmesee
The President's a whiteboy outta Georgia
And besides they put a blackboy in the U.N. talkin to
the whole world about something or other
and
last week Brother Cory Moore, Black veteran from when,
he downright took a cop into his colored custody and
kept him there at gunpoint sayin
"YOU APOLOGIZE TO ME
GODDAMMIT
YOU/THE PRESIDENT OF THESE UNITED STATES
APOLOGIZE TO ME/TO BLACK AMERICANS
FOR ALL THE SHIT AND ALL THE LIES AND ALL THE RAPE AND
ALL THE BLASPHEMY YOU CRACKAS HAVE COMMITTED STONE
AGAINST ME/MY WOMAN/AND MY CHILDREN/YOU
APOLOGIZE, GODDAMMIT."

Well, I guess you maybe wouldn't be surprise:
They call the Brother crazy
put him under observation
and the President
that newboy
well
he did call Cory Moore, you know, he did/but
I dint hear him say "I'm sorry"
And I guess you never heard no big stick say he's sorry
neither
so we're there
about where you were
Brother/Mister/Langston Hughes
except for one thing's new

we tryin hard to live a tribute to the
lovin Blackman likes of you!

"THE DIFFICULT MIRACLE OF BLACK POETRY IN AMERICA OR SOMETHING LIKE A SONNET FOR PHILLIS WHEATLEY"

(1985)

[First delivered as the keynote address for the Bicentennial Celebration of Phillis Wheatley at the University of Massachusetts, Amherst, on February 4, 1985; published in *On Call* that same year.]

It was not natural. And she was the first. Come from a country of many tongues tortured by rupture, by theft, by travel like mismatched clothing packed down into the cargo hold of evil ships sailing, irreversible, into slavery. Come to a country to be docile and dumb, to be big and breeding, easily, to be turkey/horse/cow, to be cook/carpenter/plow, to be 5'6" 140 lbs., in good condition and answering to the name of Tom or Mary: to be bed bait: to be legally spread legs for rape by the master/the master's son/the master's overseer/the master's visiting nephew: to be nothing human nothing family nothing from nowhere nothing that screams nothing that weeps nothing that dreams nothing that keeps anything/anyone deep in your heart: to live forcibly illiterate, forcibly itinerant: to live eyes lowered head bowed: to be worked without rest, to be worked without pay, to be worked without thanks, to be worked day up to nightfall: to be three-fifths of a human being at best: to be this valuable/this hated thing among strangers who purchased your life and then cursed it unceasingly: to be a slave: to be a slave. Come to this country a slave and how should you sing? After the flogging the lynch rope the general terror and weariness what should you know of a lyrical life? How could you, belonging to no one, but property to those despising the smiles of your soul, how could you dare to create yourself: a poet?

A poet can read. A poet can write.

A poet is African in Africa, or Irish in Ireland, or French on the left bank of Paris, or white in Wisconsin. A poet writes in her own language. A poet writes of her own people, her own history, her own vision, her own room, her own house where she sits at her own table quietly placing one word after another word until she builds a line and a movement and an image and a meaning that somersaults all of these into the singing, the absolutely individual voice of the poet: at liberty. A poet is somebody free. A poet is someone at home.

How should there be Black poets in America?

It was not natural. And she was the first. It was 1761—so far back before the revolution that produced these United States, so far back before the concept of freedom disturbed the insolent crimes of this continent—in 1761, when seven year old Phillis stood, as she must, when she stood nearly naked, as small as a seven year old, by herself, standing on land at last, at last after the long, annihilating horrors of the Middle Passage. Phillis, standing on the auctioneer's rude plat-form: Phillis For Sale.

Was it a nice day?

Does it matter? Should she muse on the sky or remember the sea? Until then Phillis had been somebody's child. Now she was about to become somebody's slave.

Suzannah and John Wheatley finished their breakfast and or-dered the carriage brought 'round. They would ride to the auction. This would be an important outing. They planned to buy yet another human being to help with the happiness of the comfortable life in Boston. You don't buy a human being, you don't purchase a slave, without thinking ahead. So they had planned this excursion. They were dressed for the occasion, and excited, probably. And experi-enced, certainly. The Wheatleys already owned several slaves. They had done this before; the transaction would not startle or confound or embarrass or appall either one of them.

Was it a nice day?

When the Wheatleys arrived at the auction they greeted their neighbors, they enjoyed this business of mingling with other townsfolk politely shifting about the platform, politely adjusting positions for gain of a better view of the bodies for sale. The Wheatleys were good people. They were kind people. They were open-minded and thoughtful. They looked at the bodies for sale. They looked and they looked. This one could be useful for that. That one might be useful for this. But then they looked at that child, that Black child standing nearly naked, by herself. Seven or eight years old, at the most, and frail. Now that was a different proposal! Not a strong body, not a grown set of shoulders, not a promising wide set of hips, but a little body, a delicate body, a young, surely terrified face! John Wheatley agreed to the whim of his wife, Suzannah. He put in his bid. He put down his cash. He called out the numbers. He competed successfully. He had a good time. He got what he wanted. He purchased yet another slave. He bought that Black girl standing on the platform, nearly naked. He gave this new slave to his wife and Suzannah Wheatley was delighted. She and her husband went home. They rode there by carriage. They took that new slave with them. An old slave commanded the horses that pulled the carriage that carried the Wheatleys home, along with the new slave, that little girl they named Phillis.

Why did they give her that name?

Was it a nice day?

Does it matter?

It was not natural. And she was the first: Phillis Miracle: Phillis Miracle Wheatley: the first Black human being to be published in America. She was the second female to be published in America.

And the miracle begins in Africa. It was there that a bitterly anonymous man and a woman conjoined to create this genius, this lost child of such prodigious aptitude and such beguiling attributes that she very soon interposed the reality of her particular, dear life between the Wheatleys' notions about slaves and the predictable outcome of such usual blasphemies against Black human beings.

Seven year old Phillis changed the slaveholding Wheatleys. She altered their minds. She entered their hearts. She made them see her and when they truly saw her, Phillis, darkly amazing them with the sweetness of her spirit and the alacrity of her forbidden, strange intelligence, they, in their own way, loved her as a prodigy, as a girl mysterious but godly.

Sixteen months after her entry into the Wheatley household Phillis was talking the language of her owners. Phillis was fluently reading the Scriptures. At eight and a half years of age, this Black child, or "Africa's Muse," as she would later describe herself, was fully literate in the language of this slaveholding land. She was competent and eagerly asking for more: more books, more and more information. And Suzannah Wheatley loved this child of her whimsical good luck. It pleased her to teach and to train and to tutor this Black girl, this Black darling of God. And so Phillis delved into kitchen studies commensurate, finally, to a classical education available to young white men at Harvard.

She was nine years old.

What did she read? What did she memorize? What did the Wheatleys give to this African child? Of course, it was white, all of it: white. It was English, most of it, from England. It was written, all of it, by white men taking their pleasure, their walks, their pipes, their pens and their paper, rather seriously, while somebody else cleaned the house, washed the clothes, cooked the food, watched the children: probably not slaves, but possibly a servant, or, commonly, a wife. It was written, this white man's literature of England, while somebody else did the other things that have to be done. And that was the literature absorbed by the slave, Phillis Wheatley. That was the writing, the thoughts, the nostalgia, the lust, the conceits, the ambitions, the mannerisms, the games, the illusions, the discoveries, the filth and the flowers that filled up the mind of the African child.

At fourteen, Phillis published her first poem, "To the University of Cambridge": not a brief limerick or desultory teenager's verse, but thirty-two lines of blank verse telling those fellows what for and whereas, according to their own strict Christian codes of behavior. It is in that poem that Phillis describes the miracle of her own Black poetry in America:

> While an intrinsic ardor bids me write
> the muse doth promise to assist my pen

She says that her poetry results from "an intrinsic ardor," not to dismiss the extraordinary kindness of the Wheatleys, and not to diminish the wealth of white men's literature with which she found herself quite saturated, but it was none of these extrinsic factors that compelled the labors of her poetry. It was she who created herself a poet, notwithstanding and in despite of everything around her.

Two years later, Phillis Wheatley, at the age of sixteen, had composed three additional, noteworthy poems. This is one of them, "On Being Brought from Africa to America":

Twas mercy brought me from my Pagan land,
Taught my benighted soul to understand
That there's a God, that there's a Savior too:
Once I redemption neither sought nor knew
Some view our sable race with scornful eye,
"Their color is a diabolic die."
Remember, *Christians*, Negroes, black as Cain,
May be refin'd, and join the angelic train.

Where did Phillis get these ideas?

It's simple enough to track the nonsense about herself "benighted": *benighted* means surrounded and preyed upon by darkness. That clearly reverses what had happened to that African child, surrounded by and captured by the greed of white men. Nor should we find puzzling her depiction of Africa as "Pagan" versus somewhere "refined." Even her bizarre interpretation of slavery's theft of Black life as a merciful rescue should not bewilder anyone. These are regular kinds of iniquitous nonsense found in white literature, the literature that Phillis Wheatley assimilated, with no choice in the matter.

But here, in this surprising poem, this first Black poet presents us with something wholly her own, something entirely new. It is her matter of fact assertion that, "Once I redemption neither sought nor knew," as in: once I existed beyond and without these terms under consideration. *Once I existed on other than your terms.* And, she says, *but* since we are talking your talk about good and evil/redemption and damnation, let me tell you something you had better understand. I am Black as Cain *and* I may very well be an angel of the Lord. Take care not to offend the Lord!

Where did that thought come to Phillis Wheatley?

Was it a nice day?

Does it matter?

Following her "intrinsic ardor," and attuned to the core of her own person, this girl, the first Black poet in America, had dared to redefine herself from house slave to, possibly, an angel of the Almighty.

She was making herself at home.

And, depending whether you estimated that nearly naked Black girl on the auction block to be seven or eight years old, in 1761, by the time she was eighteen or nineteen, she had published her first book of poetry, *Poems on Various Subjects Religious and Moral.* It was published in London, in 1773, and the American edition appeared, years later, in 1786. Here are some examples from the poems of Phillis Wheatley:

From "On the Death of Rev. Dr. Sewell":
Come let us all behold with wishful eyes
The saint ascending to his native skies.

From "On the Death of the Rev. Mr. George Whitefield":
Take him, ye Africans, he longs for you,
Impartial Savior is his title due,
Washed in the fountain of redeeming blood,
You shall be sons and kings, and priest to God.

Here is an especially graceful and musical couplet, penned by the first Black poet in America:
But, see the softly stealing tears apace,
Pursue each other down the mourner's face;

This is an especially awful, virtually absurd set of lines by Ms. Wheatley:
"Go Thebons! Great nations will obey

And pious tribute to her altars pay:
With rights divine, the goddess be implor'd,
Nor be her sacred offspring nor ador'd."
Thus Manto spoke. The Thebon maids obey,
And pious tribute to the goddess pay.

Awful, yes. Virtually absurd; well, yes, except, consider what it took for that young African to undertake such personal abstraction and mythologies a million million miles remote from her own ancestry, and her own darkly formulating face! Consider what might meet her laborings, as poet, should she, instead, invent a vernacular precise to Senegal, precise to slavery, and, therefore, accurate to the secret wishings of her lost and secret heart?

If she, this genius teenager, should, instead of writing verse to comfort a white man upon the death of his wife, or a white woman upon the death of her husband, or verse commemorating weirdly fabled white characters bereft of children diabolically dispersed; if she, instead composed a poetry to speak her pain, to say her grief, to find her parents, or to stir her people into insurrection, what would we now know about God's darling girl, that Phillis?

Who would publish that poetry, then?

But Phillis Miracle, she managed, nonetheless, to write, sometimes, towards the personal truth of her experience.

For example, we find in a monumental poem entitled "Thoughts on the Works of Providence," these five provocative lines, confirming every suspicion that most of the published Phillis Wheatley represents a meager portion of her concerns and inclinations:

As reason's pow'rs by day our God disclose,
So we may trace him in the night's repose.
Say what is sleep? And dreams how passing strange!
When action ceases, and ideas range
Licentious and unbounded o'er the plains.

And, concluding this long work, there are these lines:

Infinite *love*, whene'er we turn our eyes
Appears: this ev'ry creature's wants supplies
This most is heard in Nature's constant voice,
This makes the morn, and this the eve rejoice,
This bids the fost'ring rains and dews descend,
To nourish all, to serve one gen'ral end,
The good of man: Yet man ungrateful pays
But little homage, and but little praise.

Now and again and again these surviving works of the genius
Phillis Wheatley veer incisive and unmistakable, completely away
from the verse of good girl Phillis ever compassionate upon the death
of someone else's beloved, pious Phillis modestly enraptured by the
glorious trials of virtue on the road to Christ, arcane Phillis intent
upon an "Ode to Neptune," or patriotic Phillis penning an encomium
to General George Washington ("Thee, first in peace and honor").
Then do we find that "Ethiop," as she once called herself, that "Af-
rica's muse," knowledgeable, but succinct, on "dreams how passing
strange!/When action ceases, and ideas range/Licentious and un-
bounded o'er the plains."

Phillis Licentious Wheatley?

Phillis Miracle Wheatley in contemplation of love and want of
love?

Was it a nice day?

It was not natural. And she was the first.

Repeatedly singing for liberty, singing against the tyrannical,
repeatedly avid in her trusting support of the American Revolution
(how could men want freedom enough to die for it but then want
slavery enough to die for that?) repeatedly lifting witness to the
righteous and the kindly factors of her days, this was no ordinary
teenaged poet, male or female, Black or white. Indeed, the insistent-
ly concrete content of her tribute to the revolutionaries who would
forge America, an independent nation state, indeed the specific daily
substance of her poetry establishes Phillis Wheatley as the first
decidedly American poet on this continent, Black or white, male or
female.

Nor did she only love the ones who purchased her, a slave, those ones who loved her, yes, but with astonishment. Her lifelong friend was a young Black woman, Obour Tanner, who lived in Newport, Rhode Island, and one of her few poems dedicated to a living person, neither morbid nor ethereal, was written to the young Black visual artist Scipio Moorhead, himself a slave. It is he who crafted the portrait of Phillis that serves as her frontispiece profile in her book of poems. Here are the opening lines from her poem, "To S.M., A Young African Painter, On Seeing His Works."

> To show the lab'ring bosom's deep intent,
> And thought in living characters to paint.
> When first thy pencil did those beauties give,
> And breathing figures learnt from thee to live,
> How did those prospects give my soul delight,
> A new creation rushing on my sight?
> Still, wondrous youth! each noble path pursue,
> On deathless glories fix thine ardent view:
> Still may the painter's and the poet's fire
> To aid thy pencil, and thy verse conspire!
> And many the charms of each seraphic theme
> Conduct thy footsteps to immortal fame!

Remember that the poet so generously addressing the "wondrous youth" is certainly no older than eighteen, herself. And this, years before the American Revolution, and how many many years before the 1960s! This is the first Black poet of America addressing her Brother Artist not as so-and-so's Boy, but as "Scipio Moorhead, A Young African Painter."

Where did Phillis Miracle acquire this consciousness?

Was it a nice day?

It was not natural. And she was the first.

But did she—we may persevere, critical from the ease of the 1980s—did she love, did she need, freedom?

In the poem (typically titled at such length and in such deferential rectitude as to discourage most readers from scanning what follows), in the poem titled "To the Right Honorable William, Earl of Dartmouth, His Majesty's Principal Secretary of State for North America, etc.," Phillis Miracle has written these irresistible, authentic, felt lines:

No more America in mournful strain
Of wrongs, and grievance unredress'd complain,
No longer shalt Thou dread the iron chain,
Which wanton tyranny with lawless head
Had made, and with it meant t' enslave the land.
Should you, my Lord, while you peruse my song,
Wonder from whence my love of Freedom sprung,
Whence flow these wishes for the common good,
By feeling hearts alone best understood,
I, young in life, by seeming cruel of fate
Was snatch'd from Afric's fancy'd happy seat.
What pangs excruciating must molest
What sorrows labour in my parent's breast?
Steel'd was that soul and by no misery mov'd
That from a father seized his babe belov'd
Such, such my case. And can I then but pray
Others may never feel tyrannic sway?

So did the darling girl of God compose her thoughts, prior to 1776.

And then.

And then her poetry, these poems, were published in London.

And then, during her twenty-first year, Suzannah Wheatley, the white woman slaveholder who had been changed into the white mother, the white mentor, the white protector of Phillis, died.

Without that white indulgence, that white love, without that white sponsorship, what happened to the young African daughter, the young African poet?

No one knows for sure.

With the death of Mrs. Wheatley, Phillis came of age, a Black slave in America.

Where did she live?

How did she eat?

No one knows for sure.

But four years later she met and married a Black man, John Peters. Mr. Peters apparently thought well of himself, and of his people. He comported himself with dignity, studied law, argued for the liberation of Black people, and earned the everyday dislike of white folks. His wife bore him three children; all of them died.

His wife continued to be Phillis Miracle.

His wife continued to obey the "intrinsic ardor" of her calling and she never ceased the practice of her poetry. She hoped, in fact, to publish a second volume of her verse.

This would be the poetry of Phillis the lover of John, Phillis the woman, Phillis the wife of a Black man pragmatically premature in his defiant self-respect, Phillis giving birth to three children, Phillis, the mother, who must bury the three children she delivered into American life.

None of these poems was ever published.

This would have been the poetry of someone who had chosen herself, free, and brave to be free in a land of slavery.

When she was thirty-one years old, in 1784, Phillis Wheatley, the first Black poet in America, she died.

Her husband, John Peters, advertised and begged that the manuscript of her poems she had given to someone, please be returned. But no one returned them.

And I believe we would not have seen them, anyway. I believe no one would have published the poetry of Black Phillis Wheatley, that grown woman who stayed with her chosen Black man. I believe that the death of Suzannah Wheatley, coincident with the African poet's twenty-first birthday, signalled, decisively, the end of her status as a child, as a dependent. From there we would hear from an independent Black woman poet in America.

Can you imagine that, in 1775?

Can you imagine that, today?

America has long been tolerant of Black children, compared to its reception of independent Black men and Black women.

She died in 1784.

Was it a nice day?

It was not natural. And she was the first.

Last week, as the final judge for this year's Loft McKnight Awards in creative writing, awards distributed in Minneapolis, Minnesota, I read through sixteen manuscripts of rather fine poetry.

These are the terms, the lexical items, that I encountered there:

Rock, moon, star, roses, chimney, Prague, elms, lilac, railroad tracks, lake, lilies, snow geese, crow, mountain, arrow feathers, ear of corn, marsh, sandstone, rabbit-bush, gulley, pumpkins, eagle, tundra, dwarf willow, dipper-bird, brown creek, lizards, sycamores, glacier, canteen, skate eggs, birch, spruce, pumphandle

Is anything about that listing odd? I didn't suppose so. These are the terms, the lexical items accurate to the specific white Minnesota daily life of those white poets.

And so I did not reject these poems, I did not despise them saying, "How is this possible? Sixteen different manuscripts of poetry written in 1985 and not one of them uses the terms of my own Black life! Not one of them writes about the police murder of Eleanor Bumpurs or the Bernhard Goetz shooting of four Black boys or apartheid in South Africa, or unemployment, or famine in Ethiopia, or rape, or fire escapes, or cruise missiles in the New York harbor, or medicare, or alleyways, or napalm, or $4.00 an hour, and no time off for lunch."

I did not and I would not presume to impose my urgencies upon white poets writing in America. But the miracle of Black poetry in America, the *difficult* miracle of Black poetry in America, is that we have been rejected and we are frequently dismissed as "political" or "topical" or "sloganeering" and "crude" and 'insignificant" because, like Phillis Wheatley, we have persisted for freedom. We will write against South Africa and we will seldom pen a poem about wild geese flying over Prague, or grizzlies at the rain barrel under the dwarf willow trees. We will write, published or not, however we may, like Phillis Wheatley, of the terror and the hungering and the quandaries of our African lives on this North American soil. And as long as we study white literature, as long as we assimilate the English language and its implicit English values, as long as we allude and defer to gods we "neither sought nor knew," as long as we, Black poets in America, remain the children of slavery, as long as we do not come of age and attempt, then to speak the truth of our difficult maturity in an alien place, then we will be beloved, and sheltered, and published.

But not otherwise. And yet we persist.

And it was not natural. And she was the first.

This is the difficult miracle of Black poetry in America: that we persist, published or not, and loved or unloved: we persist.

And this is: "Something Like a Sonnet for Phillis Miracle Wheatley":

Girl from the realm of birds florid and fleet
flying full feather in far or near weather
Who fell to a dollar lust coffled like meat
Captured by avarice and hate spit together
Trembling asthmatic alone on the slave block
built by a savagery travelling by carriage
viewed like a species of flaw in the livestock
A child without safety of mother or marriage

Chosen by whimsy but born to surprise
They taught you to read but you learned how to write
Begging the universe into your eyes:
They dressed you in light but you dreamed with the night.
From Africa singing of justice and grace,
Your early verse sweetens the fame of our Race.

And because we Black people in North America persist in an irony profound, Black poetry persists in this way:

Like the trees of winter and
like the snow which has no power
makes very little sound
but comes and collects itself
edible light on the black trees

The tall black trees of winter
lifting up a poetry of snow
so that we may be astounded
by the poems of Black
trees inside a cold environment

"I MUST BECOME A MENACE TO MY ENEMIES"

FROM *THINGS THAT I DO IN THE DARK: NEW AND SELECTED POEMS* (1977)

[For her first *New and Selected Poems*, Jordan made an interesting decision. Rather than presenting her poems chronologically, she arranged them in thematic sections, mixing poems old and new, published and unpublished. For a poet who responded so immediately to what was happening in the world—who was vulnerable to being called "topical" and relegated to the category of agitprop—this was a stroke of her ingenious contrariness: to mix it all up—to show that her subjects were as various as her forms.

Her new poems included her satire on the notion of the Black superwoman in the form of a dramatic monologue by the outspoken Miss Valentine Jones, two contemporary Shakespearean sonnets ("I guess the sonnet represents, to most people, traditional canonized poetry. And traditional canonized poetry has been traditionally closed to black people, so that's my attraction to it."), and one of her most powerful and most frequently reprinted poems, "I Must Become a Menace to My Enemies."]

◆◆◆

FROM *THE TALKING BACK OF MISS VALENTINE JONES*: POEM # ONE

well I wanted to braid my hair
bathe and bedeck my
self so fine
so fully aforethought for
your pleasure
see:
I wanted to travel and read
and runaround fantastic
into war and peace:
I wanted to
surf
dive
fly
climb
conquer
and be conquered
THEN
I wanted to pickup the phone
and find you asking me
if I might possibly be alone
some night
(so I could answer cool
as the jewels I would wear
on bareskin for your
digmedaddy delectation:)
"WHEN
you comin ova?"

But
I had to remember to write down
margarine on the list
and shoepolish and a can of
sliced pineapples in casea company
and a quarta skim milk cause Teresa's
gainin weight and don' nobody groove on
that much
girl
and next I hadta sort for darks and lights before
the laundry hit the water which I had
to kinda keep a eye on be-
cause if the big hose jumps the sink again that
Mrs. Thompson gointa come upstairs
and brain me with a mop don' smell too
nice even though she hang
it headfirst out the winda
and I had to check
on William like to
burn hisself to death with fever
boy so thin be
callin all day "Momma! Sing to me?"
"Ma! Am I gone die?" and me not
wake enough to sit beside him longer than
to wipeaway the sweat or change the sheets/
his shirt and feed him orange
juice before I fall out sleep and
Sweet My Jesus ain' but one can
left
and we not thru the afternoon
and now
you (temporarily) shownup with a thing
you say's a poem and you
call it
"Will The Real Miss Black America Standup?"

guilty po' mouth
about duty beauties of my
headrag
boozedup doozies about
never mind
cause love is blind

well
I can't use it

and the very next bodacious Blackman
call me queen
because my life ain' shit
because (in any case) he ain' been here to share it
with me
(dish for dish and do for do and
dream for dream)
I'm gone scream him out my house
be-
cause what I wanted was
to braid my hair/bathe and bedeck my
self so fully be-
cause what I wanted was
your love
not pity
be-
cause what I wanted was
your love
your love

◆◆◆

ONE MINUS ONE MINUS ONE

This is a first map of territory
I will have to explore as poems,

again and again

My mother murdering me
to have a life of her own

What would I say
(if I could speak about it?)

My father raising me
to be a life that he
owns

What can I say
(in this loneliness)

◆◆◆

SUNFLOWER SONNET NUMBER TWO

Supposing we could just go on and on as two
voracious in the days apart as well as when
we side by side (the many ways we do
that) well! I would consider then
perfection possible, or else worthwhile
to think about. Which is to say
I guess the costs of long term tend to pile
up, block and complicate, erase away
the accidental, temporary, near
thing/pulsebeat promises one makes
because the chance, the easy new, is there
in front of you. But still, perfection takes
some sacrifice of falling stars for rare.
And there are stars, but none of you, to spare.

◆◆◆

META-RHETORIC

Homophobia
racism
self-definition
revolutionary struggle

the subject tonight for
public discussion is
our love

we sit apart
apparently at opposite ends of a line
and I feel the distance
between my eyes
between my legs
a dry
dust topography of our separation

In the meantime people
dispute the probabilities
of union

They reminisce about the chasmic histories
no ideology yet dares to surmount

I disagree with you
You disagree with me
The problem seems to be a matter of scale

Can you give me the statistical dimensions
of your mouth on my mouth
your breasts resting on my own?

I believe the agenda involves
several inches (at least)

of coincidence and endless recovery

My hope is that our lives will declare
this meeting
open

◆◆◆

I MUST BECOME A MENACE TO MY ENEMIES

Dedicated to the Poet Agostinho Neto,
President of The People's Republic of Angola: 1976

1
I will no longer lightly walk behind
a one of you who fear me:
                Be afraid.
I plan to give you reasons for your jumpy fits
and facial tics
I will not walk politely on the pavements anymore
and this is dedicated in particular
to those who hear my footsteps
or the insubstantial rattling of my grocery
cart
then turn around
see me
and hurry on
away from this impressive terror I must be:
I plan to blossom bloody on an afternoon
surrounded by my comrades singing
terrible revenge in merciless
accelerating
rhythms
But
I have watched a blind man studying his face.
I have set the table in the evening and sat down

to eat the news.
Regularly
I have gone to sleep.
There is no one to forgive me.
The dead do not give a damn.
I live like a lover
who drops her dime into the phone
just as the subway shakes into the station
wasting her message
canceling the question of her call:

fulminating or forgetful but late
and always after the fact that could save or
condemn me

I must become the action of my fate.

2

How many of my brothers and my sisters
will they kill
before I teach myself
retaliation?
Shall we pick a number?
South Africa for instance:
do we agree that more than ten thousand
in less than a year but that less than
five thousand slaughtered in more than six
months will
WHAT IS THE MATTER WITH ME?

I must become a menace to my enemies.

3

And if I
if I ever let you slide
who should be extirpated from my universe

who should be cauterized from earth
completely
(lawandorder jerkoffs of the first the
terrorist degree)
then let my body fail my soul
in its bedeviled lecheries

And if I
if I ever let love go
because the hatred and the whisperings
become a phantom dictate I o-
bey in lieu of impulse and realities
(the blossoming flamingos of my
wild mimosa trees)
then let love freeze me
out.

I must become
I must become a menace to my enemies.

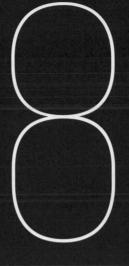

"THIS IS MY PERSPECTIVE, AND THIS IS MY FAITH"

JORDAN ON HER LIFE AND WORK (1977-2000)

"THINKING ABOUT MY POETRY"

(1977)

[Even though Jordan was a supporter and frequent contributor to feminist journals such as *Chrysalis*, *13th Moon*, *Off Our Backs*, and *Ms. Magazine*, not a single feminist publication reviewed *Things that I Do in the Dark* (1977). In reaction to this "unexpected silence," she wrote "Thinking about My Poetry," which *Chrysalis* then *did* print. Jordan included it in *Civil Wars* (1981).]

Nailed to my wooden bedroom door is a poem by Adrienne Rich, a response to my new book from the Black critic Stephen Henderson, a glossy of Monique Wittig and myself talking together, excitedly, a torn-out article on Alaska as an example of environmental crisis, a love poem from a friend, and a recent, angry limerick that I wrote "after cleaning the house on a Sunday afternoon by myself, as usual." This particular door separates my room from the kitchen; it is seldom shut. On the floor around my bed you can find the poems of John Ashbery, a novel by Mishima, two books by Alta, the first issue of *Conditions*, a recent issue of *Black Scholar*, and Jarrell's *Poetry and the Age.*

"What," I sometimes wonder, "am I trying to do, exactly?" I think that I am trying to keep myself free, that I am trying to become responsive and responsible to every aspect of my human being. I think that I am trying to learn whatever I can that will make freedom of choice an intelligent, increasing possibility. Often, these desires, these needs, translate into the sweltering sensation of a half-assed effort to explore and accomplish everything at once. But, thankfully, not always.

At first, say roughly from the age of seven through my mid-twenties, poetry was the inside dictator to whom I more or less simply submitted myself, writing down whatever the poem turned out to be, wording myself as precisely, and with whatever ambiguity, as was necessary in the interest of truthfulness. For example, the poem entitled "Pygmalion" came to me, entirely given, after reading Huxley's *Doors to Perception*, in my freshman year at Barnard. It begins:

blood mist bemuses meditation
bewilders stone cathedral sipping clemency to needs
derides impulsive incantations sacred golden full
removes ascendant pyres from raw hidden origins
despises skin simplicity which bled and bleeds in silence

young Christ   sweet Lord   avoided in austere closures

Exceptions to this quasi-automatic process were the regular

exercises that I invented for myself so that I should feel competent, as regards craft, to write in the manner of Herrick, Shelley, Eliot, or whoever, and whenever. These disciplined emulations/transmutations absorbed a great part of my working time, as a poet, although I did not consider them achievements of any kind; they served as means, strictly, and not ends. I guess my theory was that if apprenticeship was essential to painting then apprenticeship was essential to being a poet, an identity I assumed from childhood with rather unquestioning, and even religious, feelings of sobriety. It is certain that I did not regard these studies as optional. All my life, the rule was that if you were Black, you had to be twice as good/smart as anyone else just to get started. I was started, all right, but I felt it imperative to protect myself, my coming voice, from easy/categorical rejection.

Of course, preoccupation with one's self and with technique does not yield an art of interest to anyone else, necessarily, as I finally decided. In order to deserve the attention of people-out-there, I would have to concern myself with accessibility and with subjects of general consequence: indebtedness to parents, isolation, strangers, marriage, race, war, rage, love. I would have to decide, beforehand, the purpose of the poem. What did I want anyone else to see, smell, feel, understand? And, why? This last emerging concern centered me upon a conscious desire to change our environment, to scrape and ax away at the status quo. As this decision coincided approximately with the 1954 Supreme Court ruling, I found myself well supported; I was speeded forward, outside and beyond the simply personal, even as collective interests and collective action became the dominant public realities of the day. In addition, I was fortunate enough to be sponsored by the Academy of American Poets as a poet reading her works throughout the public school system of New York City—every level and every borough of the system. As you know, kids are pretty tough. And the repeated, regular, direct exposure to kids as an audience for my work irresistibly propelled me outward into new (for me) aesthetic values and new (for me) subjects just so I could hope to stand in front of them without being the biggest bore of the morning.

Although the musical potentiality of language persisted as a primary love and goal, from childhood, rhythm as vertical event, and/or rhythm as the cohesive structure of a poem only emerged as a central quest after I found myself face to face with children, and teenagers, who have a natural affinity for movement as in palpable momentum. For instance, the horizontal rhythms of Shelley, and the amazing music of "I bring fresh showers for the thirsting flowers, / From the seas and the streams; / I bear light shade for the leaves when laid / In their noonday dreams," in his poem "The Cloud," indelibly excited my ear to what I called the "Spanish" possibilities of English. And Shelley's "Queen Mab," especially sections IV to VII, utterly persuaded me that you could write political poetry that would stand as legitimate as any other poetry, as in his lines: "All things are sold: the very light of Heaven / is venal; earth's unsparing gifts of love, / The smallest and most despicable things / That lurk in the abyss of the deep, / All objects of our life, even life itself..." But I had never seen rhythm and political concept merged into a vertical event. "In Memoriam: Martin Luther King, Jr.," an excerpt of which follows, was perhaps my first attempt:

honey people murder mercy U.S.A.
the milkland turn to monsters teach
to kill to violate pull down destroy
the weakly freedom growing fruit
from being born

America

tomorrow yesterday rip rape
exacerbate despoil *disfigure...*

And as far as changes in subject are concerned, while I did not make my "self" disappear, my self-conscious criterion became that of comprehensible relationship between the person (me) and the public, by which I meant either the reader and/or the public issue under treatment.

Toward the close of the sixties, I reconsidered, and decided that I wanted to aim for the achievement of a collective voice, that I

wanted to speak as a community to a community, that to do other-
wise was not easily defensible, nor useful, and would be, in any case,
at variance with clarified political values I held as my own, by then. I
think it was in 1973 that Radcliffe convened a Black Women's Con-
ference, and invited me to be "the wrap-up" poet. With this function
in mind, I conceived a poem about the collective experience of Black
womanhood. Accordingly, some of the events within the poem would
not necessarily reflect my personal history, but all of the events, and
all of the personae, would represent my felt, collective perspective
on our collective heritage and predicament. The poem that resulted,
"Getting Down to Get Over: Dedicated to My Mother[6]," was, in fact,
a breakthrough for me, on several levels, simultaneously. I had the
rare and extraordinary chance to test this collective voice upon some
five hundred or so Black women sisters of mine. And, happily, they
accepted the representation of their and my lives, in the poem that
begins:

MOMMA MOMMA MOMMA

momma momma
mammy
nanny
granny
woman
mistress
sista

luv...

But a few years into the seventies, and I reconsidered again;
aspirations toward a collective voice seemed to me conceitful, at
least. Instead, I came to the idea of myself as ordinary. As I came to
know other poets as friends, particularly other living Black poets—
Clarence Major, Calvin Hernton, David Henderson—and other living

---

6   [see entire poem pp. 166-177]

women poets—Audre Lorde, Sonia Sanchez, Adrienne Rich, Susan Griffin—it did seem to me that we were all of us working on the same poem of a life of perpetual, difficult birth and that, therefore, I should trust myself in this way: that if I could truthfully attend to my own perpetual birth, if I could trace the provocations for my own voice and then trace its reverberations through love, Alaska, whatever, that then I could hope to count upon myself to be serving a positive and collective function, without pretending to be more than the one Black women poet I am, as a matter of fact.

This last concept of my work remains the governing criterion, as I write these thoughts, tonight: to be accurate about myself, and to force my mind into a constantly expanding apprehension of my political and moral situation. Necessarily, this changed, ruling value has altered my attitudes about movement in poetry, and about comprehensibility. There is stillness, there is sometimes paralysis in my experience, and there is much that I do not understand and that I need to confront as the incoherency, the mystery, it may mean, or be, even ultimately. And as I wish to be truthful, so my poems must reflect these other elements of being, as well.

Besides conscious changes in the purpose perceived and, consequently, changes in the techniques explored in my work, there have been changes of influence and perspective at least equal in their determining importance. (Some sources of influence have remained unalterable, such as Shelley, and such as these lines by Coleridge: "Hence viper thoughts that coil about my mind / reality's dark dream / I turn from thee and listen to the wind / which long hath rav'd unnotic'd.") "Greatness" figured as a deeply motivating notion for me, throughout my childhood. I wanted to be a "great poet"; indeed, anything less than greatness, anything less than acknowledged excellence, did not interest me. And the poets pushed upon me by my father, before my tenth birthday, were the poets of the Scriptures, Shakespeare, Edgar Allan Poe, along with the dialect poetry of Paul Laurence Dunbar. And so I thought I recognized a rather serious dilemma: how could I become a "great poet," being female, and not much taken either with Dunbar's southern dialect or with Elizabethan English, which were, both of them, altogether weird to my ears.

I even pondered the fact that these four founts were dead, so to speak. That posed a clear difficulty that left me feeling uncomfortable, but not suicidal—except that their remoteness from my world and my language, coupled with their redoubtable acclaim, crippled my trust in my own sensibilities, coerced me into eclectic compulsions I had to struggle against, later, and generally delayed my creative embracing of my own, known life as the very stuff of my art.

In my twenties, the political—racist and sexist—factors involved in "literary acknowledgement" capsized my earlier respect for the concept of "greatness," and buried it; with the shattering of my political naiveté, passed through a period of years during which I pretty much refused to read, or hear, any poetry that was not Black; I was no longer interested to become part of a tradition that dared to silence the poetry of my people. I could no longer countenance such standards as dared to reject the distinctively Black elements of our consciousness and our art. Margaret Walker, Robert Hayden, Langston Hughes were some of the Black poets whose work I most enjoyed. And there was the exquisite articulation of ambivalence that I very much admired in Le Roi Jones' "Dead Lecturer." And there was the astonishing, irrepressible beauty and force of the allegedly verbally deficient Black and Puerto Rican teenagers in Fort Greene, Brooklyn, with whom I had the privilege of working, for a few years, in our Saturday workshop that came to be known as The Voice of the Children. Consider this poem by thirteen-year-old Linda Curry which appeared in our book *The Voice of the Children*.

MY ENEMY

    My Enemy is The World
    The world hates me   it's trying
    to get rid of me   Somebody
    up there don't like me
    Why I don't know
    I've try to prove them
        Wrong but it doesn't seem
    to work

I don't know what to think
    or do I just
wonder till I find
what I am searching
for And then I will kill
the one who hates me.

More than anything else, it was the poetry of Linda Curry, it was the fighting for these kids, it was the living with them through inevitable insults in "white territory," it was the attempt to carry them through the unspeakably brutal year of 1968, that riveted my heart and mind to the preservation of Black English and to distinctively Black poetry. Indeed, my first novel, *His Own Where*, which was written entirely in Black English, was based upon two "regulars" of our workshop, and, of course, upon my own, personal life as a child growing up in Bedford-Stuyvesant.

Toward the end of my twenties, and continuing through my thirties, the poetry of women, contemporary and past, became fundamental to my spirit, and joined Black poetry as a part of the literature I was willing to respect, and wanted to incorporate into my being. Emily Dickinson, Jane Cooper, Adrienne Rich, Audre Lorde, Marge Piercy, Alice Walker, Honor Moore are some of the women who have awakened me to another dimension of love, and of struggle.

At this point in time, I refuse nothing. I am concerned to keep myself open and aware of all that I can. Hence, while women's poetry (particularly today's poetry as it issues from the embattled lives of feminist poets and writers) occupies a first place of influence, and while Third World Poetry continues to function as the fundamental testimony I wish to serve, I do read and I do indeed listen to the poetry of white male poets: Ted Hughes, Charles Simic, David Ignatow, Charles Bukowski. (Neruda and Nicanor Parra are not "white," as far as I know.)

I think this present orientation, this perhaps catholicity of interest, if not always a matter of enthusiasm, reflects my changed perspective. I have moved from an infantile reception of the universe, as given, into a progressively political self-assertion that is now reaching beyond the limitations of a victim mentality. I choose to exist unafraid of my enemies; instead, I choose to become an enemy to my enemies. And I choose to believe that my enemies can either be vanquished or else converted into allies, into Brothers. And I choose to disregard the death-obsessed, extravagantly depressed and depressing doomsayers around. As a woman, as a Black woman, as a Black woman poet and writer, I choose to believe that we, women and Third World peoples, will in fact succeed in saving ourselves, *and* our traditional assassins, from the meaning of their fear and their hatred. Even more deeply, I believe we can save ourselves from the power of our own fear and our own self-hatred.

This is my perspective, and this is my faith.

FROM "CREATION IS REVOLUTIONARY"

INTERVIEW WITH KARLA HAMMOND (1978)

[By 1978, Jordan had published four volumes of poetry, three books for children, and a young adult novel. She wrote regularly for newspapers, magazines, journals. She'd gone up against the infamous conservative talk show host William Buckley, Jr. (on the topic, "Should Books Like *Little Black Sambo* Be on Library Shelves?"), and not only held her ground, but took some of his. She gave readings at literary venues, at colleges, schools, conferences, demonstrations for social justice, libraries. Karla Hammond conducted this "mid-career" interview with Jordan in 1978, published in *Kalliope*, Volume 4, No.1, 1981. Here are excerpts.]

KH: Can you envision what it might be like to be a woman in a non-patriarchal society?

JJ: No, I can't envision it and I don't have the time. I'm living right now and I'm concerned with this situation as it is. This kind of language is jargon. I'm a poet and I don't talk about "patriarchal." What kind of word is that except a joke? "Matriarchal" doesn't improve it. They're both ugly sounding. I can't envision a non-patriarchal society because this is all I know.

What I can envision is the possibility that enough people will come to understand that because I have power equal to your power doesn't mean you have less power. Right now the people who have the power are white men and this is central to the whole resistance whether we're talking about Black people or women or children. The current idea is that if other people (not like me) have as much freedom and power as I have, then what I have is less meaningful, less valuable or just plain less. This is a hideous, fatal, long-standing error of conceptualization that has really condemned the whole western world to conceivably its own suicide.

In 1964 when Bucky Fuller and I met for the first time, he said that the problem was that the fundamental habit of Western thought was the "either/or" formulation. It's so unimaginatively malevolent and antithetical to the nature of the universe in which we all exist. You can have a fantastic house and all the rest of it and I can, too, and it's not going to hurt you (*laughs*). That's why the Women's Movement came to public attention. Many of the spokeswomen tried to explain that the liberation of women would really liberate men.

KH: How do you respond to Audre Lorde's statement that "for women…poetry is not a luxury. It is a vital necessity of our existence"?

JJ: I'm not sure that I know what Audre is saying there. Certainly she's speaking as a poet. I know that most women are not poets. If she's talking about the necessity to create yourself from your basis of self-love and self-respect in an environment hostile to your self-respect and self-love then what she's saying is to be said about all Black people. For many people poetry is a luxury. For Audre, it is not a luxury because Audre is a poet. For me it is not a luxury because that's my life. But I am not all women nor am I all Black women. Frances Piven is an activist humanitarian and she never even reads poetry. I would certainly never presume to denigrate her work. She conceived the Welfare Movement. She's been in jail more times than I have and out on more lines on the street. [...]

KH: In a recent correspondence with Ethelbert Miller, he spoke of looking at your work, Alice Walker's, Gayl Jones', Audre Lorde's, Thulani Davis' and Ntozake Shange's—looking at the concept of violence and determining whether women have been colonized by men.

JJ: I'll give you an anecdote that might be germane to that. I sent Ethelbert a copy of the "Poem about My Rights" and he said "you should take your mother out of that." And I said "Why?" And he said "Because until you get to your mother, everything that you're talking about who has done something to you—whether it's South Africa or the guys in France—is male. It's a man in some form violating you." And I said, "Listen, I don't give a damn who it is that violates me. Violation is violation. When my mother asked me to have braces on my teeth, plastic surgery on my nose and straighten my hair, she violated me and that was the first woman I ever knew. She stays in that poem." I really have a horror of generic anything. You've probably surmised that. I'm not saying that I am against the colonialization of my life by men. I'm against colonialization (*laughs*) period. It's a mistake to assume that anyone—be it women, Black people, or any one of us, generically speaking, has a corner on virtue. It's dangerous to think otherwise because you're deceiving yourself about your own capabilities to be harmful. [...]

KH: Is it important for a woman writing today to disassociate herself from all of the conflict of her own history or from the conflict of the Women's Movement to gain a perspective on her own writing?

JJ: No, that doesn't follow at all in a logical way. I'm talking about recognizing that regardless of the passion, the depth or the extent of your engagement, it is only your one person engagement. You can only speak honestly from that reality. Just because I'm absolutely committed to libertarian struggles all over the world, doesn't mean that I can speak for the Vietnamese. I can speak from my understanding of their liberation struggle and how it relates to my liberation struggle. I can speak *from* that, but I cannot speak *for* them. And I can only say *we* after I have made the intellectual humility, the limit of my one self, clear. After that has been established, then I can say we in an asking fashion and see what the response is.

KH: In speaking of the way a poem begins for you, would you say that words and phrases come to you more from a sense of their sound than from their meaning? Would this be part of the automatic process you've spoken of?

JJ: No, because the sound is in itself a statement. There are different ways of making a statement. But, for example, "Getting Down to Get Over"—the purpose of that poem was very clear in my mind before I wrote it. Very clear. But then it was a question of how to serve that purpose. And what came to me was "Momma, Momma, Momma, Momma, Momma, Momma, Momma, Momma." That's all I had. It took me two weeks to get past that. I used to walk around saying that and dancing to that. Then I had to figure out how to move from there to the rest of the poem, and to keep that fundamental rhythmical structure as the spine of the poem. Finally it came. [...]

KH: What is your impression of Hayden Carruth's classification of your "experimental impulses" falling "into two varieties: 'one is technical, arty, formalistic, *avante-gardiste*, in the manner of the New York Poets of the 1950s; two, that which 'is much less self-conscious, almost unconscious—spontaneous and natural'"?

JJ: [...] I'm sure that Carruth's intention was benign, if not very flattering. For someone, however, who has come along as self-consciously as I have in the acquirement of craft and who writes the way I do with an understanding of what every word, every letter, every consonant is doing and not doing, then it's impossible to label it "unconscious." Stephen Henderson talks about [...] what he called my "unashamed virtuosity." That's much more to the point. The virtuosity, yes, but not unconscious. What would that mean? "Unconscious virtuosity" smacks a little of the "Noble Savage." It's as if I don't really know what I'm doing, but it's terrific. When I was a sophomore at Barnard I showed a poem to one of my professors and he read it and said "you can't possibly know what this means, what you've written here—but it's very beautiful." And I thought (*laughs*) "What does he mean that I don't know what it means? I wrote it!" I've never written anything in my life that I didn't understand the meaning of when I wrote it. It wouldn't bother me if I were white and male and he had talked about unconscious virtuosity. But we (Black people and women) still have something to prove, in the sense of this hostile environment. Hayden Carruth should have asked (*laughs*), or interviewed me and in that way found out if I knew what I was talking about—determine why I wrote something this way and not in another way. [...] To be sure there are unconscious elements in everything. This is true of everyone. In the writing of poetry, however, I'm more conscious of what I am doing that I am about anything else in my life. This isn't a statement I'm making in a grand fashion. I'm talking about hours and hours and hours of days and days and days and years and years and years of reading and reading and reading and writing and writing and writing. I didn't even send out a poem for publication until I was twenty-nine. I was writing all the time from seven on. I felt that there was an apprenticeship to serve. I didn't feel that I was ready yet. When I came out in print I wanted it to be unassailable. My first book, *Who Look at Me* (1969), was published when I was thirty-three. I felt, at that point, that I was ready to be judged. But in the meantime I was working all the time. So that "*unconscious* virtuosity" is an impossible concept to me.

KH: Then you must have a large body of work that hasn't been published?

JJ: Yes, both prose and poetry. Much of the poetry that hasn't been published is what I consider work: exercises in which I'm engaged to learn how to do something. I was interested in how other people wrote and I worked at those exercises in order to serve my own sensibilities. I don't think that most of those poems would be of interest to anyone other than a poet coming along just to see the kinds of exercises, in effect, that I devised for myself to test myself.

KH: Is there a standard process for revision?

JJ: Generally speaking, the first twenty or thirty drafts are usually in pen by hand. Then I'll take it to the typewriter where it goes through a series of drafts because it looks totally different to me in that stage. If the poem isn't long, it usually comes whole within two days or so. I just work and work and work. [....] "Poem for Nana" took over three years to write. It just wasn't coming. I'd send it to Adrienne [Rich], who is a friend of mine, and she would say, "June, you still don't have it." And I would say "Yes, I know that I don't have it, but what do you think?" And she would say, "This looks really strained or forced." It took three years to get everything that I wanted in it from a "felt" level—so that it wasn't rhetoric and it wasn't "my Indian poem"—to make it a workable poem. [....] What's definite about the process of revision is that there is a process of revision (*laughs*), and there are few given poems that come entire. [...] Most of the time, if you count every single draft, I have over a hundred. [....]

KH: In saying "there is sometimes paralysis in my experience," is that equivalent to being, as [Muriel] Rukeyser puts it, "beached"?

JJ: No, it wasn't meant essentially in a writing context. I meant apart from writing. There's much paralysis, inability to move because of not knowing why I should move or what move I should make. But there's the wanting not to be like that, wanting to be moving, acting, making the decisions, but not able to do it. That's integral to much of contemporary life and it should be expressed in addition to the other aspects of our lives: otherwise, we're being dishonest. [...]

KH: An occasional theme of your relationship poems is loneliness or aloneness. Does writing necessitate an "aloneness" not shared by other fields of art?

JJ: It's so much a cultural factor that I really couldn't say. We could be having this interview and Ntozake Shange could be sitting right over there (pointing to a couch in another corner of the room). She writes that way: all the time. With me it depends. I can't finish anything with other people around, but I certainly can start poems and work on them while I'm laughing and kidding around. Very often I do that as well as when I'm by myself. But to finish a poem, I find that it is necessary to be by myself—totally concentrated in that way. To really, really hear a poem you have to be by yourself, yes. [...]

KH: You've written familial poems and spoken of growing up in New York. What attitude or conviction of your parents has stayed with you longest?

JJ: My father was a very proud man and a fighter. The men who knew him called him the "Little Bull" as a matter of fact. He was relatively short but very powerful. He had a flagrant and consistent contempt for the way in which other people labeled him, whether it was to call him a Negro, a Black or a West Indian. He would always say, "This is a man by the name of Granville Ivanhoe Jordan" because that was his name. It was not a label. That had a great impact on me. His general West Indian pride relates to having an intact ego which is not particularly vulnerable to outside manipulation where self-regard is concerned. My mother was a masochist most of her life. That had an enormous influence on me because it hurt and angered me to see her like that. At the same time, she was deeply religious and faithful and certainly imparted a religious sense of experience and purpose to me. The concept of service which figured importantly in her life figures very importantly in my life. If there was any family friction or associated problem, other people on the block or children would seek her help. Whatever the hour, she would go. My parents had the conviction that life is a battleground. So there were things that you did to win: You studied, you became very well-educated, you were quite consciously competitive. You were always trying to better yourself in ways that you could articulate. They certainly articulated ambitions to me repeatedly. Their influence on me was particularly great while I was young. It's not as though I had a tremendous choice about whether or not to accept their value system at that time.

KH: Can you speak of some of the "eclectic compulsions," [as you've described them in "Thinking about My Poetry," that] you struggled against?

JJ: It was difficult for this Black poet to master a number of craft elements because the content of the poems was so alien to my experience. So I was very excited when I was finally able to do it. But I wanted to say "Listen, I can alliterate for hours (*laughs*). I can do an iambic pentameter number that will never stop." It was a power technical display tendency that I saw in myself. It's partly showing off...partly to say "yes, I am a Black poet; and yes, Goddamn it, I can do anything you guys can do and I can do something you can't do (*laughs*) because I'm Black." But, on the other hand, what I was trying to say was "don't say she's a good poet because she's Black and she's not doing so badly." Say, "She can do anything we can do and she can do something we can't do." This was my goal and it's related to what my father and mother always used to say to me: "You're Black and so that means you can't be a good student. You've got to be twice as good a student as anyone else. You have to be the best athlete, the most popular, the best looking, etc. You know why?—in order to qualify as a B grade candidate of any other description racially." Do you know what I'm saying? You have to do all of this in order to say "I'd really like to go to City College, is it all right?" (*laughs*) So that was my attitude which I transferred to poetry.

Also understanding everything about my art—poetry is a tremendous concern for beauty. What craft knowledge makes possible is the creation of beautiful things. Shirley Clarke and I discussed this. We worked together on the film *The Cool World* (about Harlem before the 60s) and she said that what I'm talking about is really a problem. If you're talking about something which is horrifying or which is agonizing then, because of your craft, you're going to talk about what is really beautiful. She had pictures of these young Black kids walking down garbage-lined streets—garbage which should be picked up and housing that is garbage standing up. But in shooting the film she waits until it's dark and it's raining. So the street is slick and luscious looking almost like a fruit. A fruit that they're walking upon. And you think "God, is that beautiful." But that's not the purpose of the film. The purpose of that film is to say, "These children are dying and we are the ones murdering them." So there's this problem. Now that you've learned how to look at something and say "This is really beautiful regardless of what it is" you have to say "Now wait a minute" because you don't want people getting off on what a fantastic image this or that is. Or suppose it's an irreversible rhythm in [a] poem. I'm saying "The boy who should be alive is dead now." I want you to understand that. I want to say it in a way that will not be beautiful but that will have all the effectiveness that my craft can let me accomplish. So it's tricky. That's what I meant by "eclectic compulsions" (all the ways in which you learn to make your use of language beautiful regardless of the subject matter," regardless of the ideational intent of the work). If you don't resist it, sometimes, you can risk making pretty what is truly despicable. [....]

KH: How have Jane Cooper and Honor Moore's work awakened you to "another dimension of love..."?

JJ: Jane Cooper and Honor Moore are what I call distinctively white. Jane Cooper, for example, is an extremely different person from myself and from the people with whom I grew up (my family). When I was working at Sarah Lawrence, Jane Cooper (the Head of the Creative Writing Faculty) and I became friends. She would ask me to look at her manuscripts of poetry. At first I couldn't understand why anyone would write about what she writes about—it's a totally different understanding of life experience (*laughs*), which I considered then, and I think I'd say now, is white. By comparison it's much more individualistic. There's an assumption that if you wake up in the morning, go for a walk, and see a leaf fall of a tree, that's an event that justifies a poem. As a Black woman poet, it would never occur to me that that would be used for a poem. I would notice it, but that's not enough for me. Something else has to happen. But I read Jane's poetry because I was a friend of hers and I tried to understand it. Finally, I realized that her emotions are different from mine, but that they were genuine. That was serious material for her. What I meant by love is that there are different dimensions—legitimate other ways that people go through the days, nights and years in a way that's really different from my own and that they're valid. It's another way of loving, of caring about things.

KH: Is this similar to what Hayden Carruth implied in his equation "politics equals love equals language" (*The New York Times Book Review*) that he attributes to you?

JJ: No, because I'm not similar to Jane Cooper or Honor Moore (*laughs*). Not only in my poetry, but in my life. He was speaking of how I'm different from them because I wouldn't just take the walk... that in order to make a statement about anything, my understanding of what I want to say has to acquire levels of reference that lead me far away from myself and include many more people than just myself. It has to begin with this one self because that's all I am. That's the process he was trying to describe: it's not until I've started here and gone out and come back in that sense of love that I have anything appropriate to say because it won't only be about me.

KH: At the "Lesbians and Literature" discussion at the 1976

Modern Language Association Convention, Bertha Harris suggested that "if in a woman writer's work a sentence refuses to do what it is supposed to do; if there are strong images of women and if there is a refusal to be mean, the result is innately lesbian literature." In "Toward a Black Feminist Criticism," Barbara Smith, in referring to Harris' statement, replies that in applying these ideas to Black women writers she "realized that many of their works were, in Harris' sense lesbian. Not because women are 'lovers,' but because they are the central figures, are positively portrayed and have pivotal relationships with one another. The form and language of these works is also nothing like what white patriarchal culture requires or expects."

JJ: You can define anything any way. When I was at the MLA (on the same panel with Adrienne), Marilyn Hacker was in the audience and she said "how are you defining the world 'lesbian?'" And Adrienne said that the lesbian in you is whatever lets you do something that is really worthwhile. Now wait a minute. I really have a problem with this extension of the word 'lesbian'. What you want to be able to say is that you're a woman and that you want to be able to love another woman without having that mean societal disapprobation, the loss of your job, your ability to rent an apartment. You want to be able to say "I am a lesbian" without having that mean the death of a whole lot of possibilities for you. My grandmother was a very, very strong Black woman. Let me assure you that she was not a lesbian. In the sixties everyone wanted to be part of the whole Black Movement. I was saying "I'm Black and because I'm Black I can do whatever I want to do." But then everyone started saying that Beethoven was Black, Copernicus was Black, Switzerland was Black. This is ridiculous and it isn't the point. The point is that I'm Black and I'm saying "Hey! Don't mess with me because I'm Black."

KH: Have you been influenced at all by E.E. Cummings? ("When I or Else")

JJ: I used to read almost anyone whom you could mention on a crush basis. Sometimes you just read Thomas Mann forever. I used to read Eliot forever. I read E.E. Cummings. I don't know if he's been an influence. Several of his lyrics were probably the first lyrics that I ever saw which suggested to me that you could write in a way that acknowledged an urban context and bespeak a lyrical sensibility. It was significant to know that the two things were not incompatible. "Somewhere I have never traveled," for example, just a line like that is a mind expanding statement when you're very young especially and you didn't know anyone would think that it was important enough to write it down and say it in a way that people would remember.

KH: Painting, as a visual art, has influenced your writing. Is there a particular painting in *Who Look at Me* you'd care to speak about?

JJ: The frontispiece—the portrait of a gentleman, painter unknown. I thought that was amazing. That's why I placed it in front. I don't remember what year it was, that painting. It goes back a long time—obviously some time shortly after slavery was abolished in the formal sense. But I had never seen a painting of a Black man who was being described and depicted as a gentleman. And here he was—a gentleman, a lord or a squire. Not only was he painted that way, but looking at him you know he's a gentleman (*laughs*). I loved "painter anonymous" because it seemed perfectly appropriate that whoever did it (*laughs*) would not take responsibility for having found this man and then having rendered him accurately in a way that has nothing to do with socio-statistical descriptions of Black people of any time, does it? He's a lord in America, a Black man! The beauty, the elegance of his demeanor, and his grace just astounded me. That someone saw it and did not block it out, but actually went ahead and made this painting which is well done is startling. Also I like the idea of the painting enormously in that it refers back to what I was saying about my father. Whoever this Black gentleman was, he obviously created himself and named himself to himself and to others.

KH: Who are some of your musical influences?

JJ: It's not who but what music. The answer is all music by which I mean all sound that is organized by an intelligence. This is determined to some effect—whether it's the effect of having people dance, suggesting what used to be called celestial levels of perception or whether it's a Mozart sonata or a straight monotonous hard driving disco number. There's an intelligence manipulating sound in a way to produce a particular effect. In that respect, music has always been an overriding influence in my life.

KH: By saying that from age seven through your mid-twenties "poetry was the inside dictator to whom (you) more or less simply submitted," are you suggesting that poetry was largely an unconscious act as opposed to your approach to poetry today?

JJ: Now I always decide first what I'm going to write. It doesn't just come to me. Now the poem can come to me in different ways but the purpose of it is already decided. When I begin the revisions of the poem, I'm checking it against that purpose.

KH: Can formalism be a protective device early in one's writing? ("It allowed me to handle materials I couldn't pick up barehanded"— Adrienne Rich).

JJ: Yes, certainly, of course, that's true. But it's not merely protective. Formalism serves other purposes (*laughs*) of needing whatever the content needs. For instance, the content may really need to be presented in an apparently ordered fashion so that it is seemingly palpable. Therefore, a readership that otherwise might feel they couldn't handle the subject matter—be it grief or whatever—realizes that it's also a frequent means of assisting a poet in handling material. It might be that the material, the feeling or the image, might really escape your artistic control. So this is a way of gaining artistic control over what you need to communicate. I view all formalism as absolutely essential craft information. I teach that in a very rigorous way in all my workshops. What you might call formalistic, for example, "da dum da dum da dum..." [Eds. note: Jordan imitates the rhythm of an iambic tetrameter line] people might think of as doggerel because it's obvious. Well, once you know that that's an expectation: "da dum da dum da dum..." then you can do something Brechtian. You can say something that is really outrageous according to prevailing norms. People will just move along with you. I don't like the term "formalism" because what you're really talking about is intelligible components of the craft of poetry. Poetry really is based on a huge body of craft elements that are all intelligible. The more you write and read, the more you recognize the craft responsible for the effect. It doesn't in any way demystify or despoil the experience to understand why it is that you are moved in a particular way. I'm not afraid of knowing anything. An artist can't afford to pretend that her accomplishment derives from an unconscious spontaneous happenstance because that's not true. We're talking about discipline, a knowledge that is very complicated and that deserves all the serious, self-conscious commitment that any high calling requires. What I mean by high calling is that it's not immediately obvious. The usefulness of it may not always be immediately obvious. It's like faith. Love is a high calling to me. It's not about usefulness. It's just there, but you really care about it more than you care about anything else. Like your car. Or your clothes. So, to me, it's a high calling in the sense that it's not amenable to utilitarian analysis. It derives from a spiritual orientation.

KH: "If apprenticeship was essential to painting then apprenticeship was essential to being a poet" (J. Jordan). Would you say (from your work in the schools) that this is less than conscious today?

JJ: You can't validly generalize that way. People regard poetry not so much as an art or as a calling, but as something everyone does particularly when they're depressed, lonely, or in love. So in the context of commonplace opinion, I'd say poetry, in this country, has seldom commanded the kind of respect that, say, being a concert pianist would. One would assume that a concert pianist is one who works exceedingly hard daily and has done a great deal of research. But where poetry is concerned many people think that it's about how one feels (*laughs*). But, on the other hand, the students whom I'm in touch with and have been at the various schools where I've taught always present me with at least two or three in a group of, say, ten to twenty who are quite serious and gifted. That means that they read omnivorously and that they take it for granted that arduous rewriting and self-conscious stretching of yourself in a technical sense are integral to any successful fruition as a poet.

KH: Have you seen any recent attempts on the part of reviewers, essayists or critics to focus attention on Margaret Walker's, Gwendolyn Brooks' or their contemporaries' work?

JJ: The awareness is there of the value of Margaret Walker's work but her own work has been under-evaluated until now. Let me give you an example in my own life. This is the first time that I've ever been interviewed about my poetry in my entire life. Now I have been a published poet for over twenty years. Compare me to Adrienne Rich. How many times a week is Adrienne interviewed (*laughs*)? [...]. Do you know that there are only three times that a major publishing house has published a Black poet's work?—Langston Hughes,' Gwendolyn Brooks' *Selected Poems* and my *Things that I Do in the Dark*. That's in the history of this country. So at the same time that I said "feminism" I wanted to know about this sisterhood. Let's have it both ways. There's a very, very deep attitude, in this country, that is racist. It's very upsetting to me. You can't close out anything and hope for excellence or for greatness. The reason Walt Whitman was a great poet was because his arms were open. That's how you have to be and that's why I'm mentioning all these things about boxes: Black poets, feminists, etc.

KH: Has there been a particularly memorable moment professionally for you?

JJ: Many moments are memorable, but it would be difficult to isolate one from another. Perhaps writing "Poem about My Rights" (another break-through poem) to have been able to write it and be able to read it is memorable. Now it's going to be published in *Essence* which amazes me. There was a commemoration of South African Women's Day at the United Nations in Dag Hammarskjold Auditorium on August 9th [1978] and I read at that occasion. When I finished reading that poem all the men in the audience stood up. They were the first people on their feet! Ambassadors, and so on. Everyone went crazy. I had another poem I'd written for the occasion. I didn't know what to do because dramatically I should have left the stage at that moment (*laughs*) but I wanted to read this other poem. I just stood there and looked at this auditorium which was packed (aisles full of people and folks on their feet screaming, yelling, clapping) and I thought "Look at this!" This poem comes from my gut. It's taken me so long to even formulate it let alone write it. There were men and women and they were white and they were Black and everyone was on their feet. It was an astonishing moment. I've had standing ovations before but what stunned me was because it was this poem that they were staggered by in such a happy way.

Then, again recently...the end of last semester...a student came up to me after I gave a presentation and she said, "You know, I have to ask you to forgive me because I have wasted two thirds of this semester like most of the other students. I don't know if you know it or not but from the time you came into the classroom we thought you were jive." See, I never teach standing up. I always say "this is not my class / this is your class. And I want to hear what you have to say." We get into a democratic circle. And she said "we thought you were jive because you said 'look, I'm not going to talk anymore.'" They even thought that I hadn't done the reading (*laughs*) because it was so totally different from anything else. And then she heard my speech to the faculty and the students about what I'm trying to do and how it's so different from what everyone else does. It's despised, you know. I was amazed because I thought that the situation was bad, but I didn't know that it was that bad (*laughs*). I didn't know that they didn't allow courses to figure as credit toward the major. It was worse than I'd thought. And she said "I'm never going to forgive myself for having wasted so much time!" I wish I could show you the difference in the students between then and the end of the semester and the term papers that those kids put out. Unbelievable! Beautiful!

KH: Is there anything that you want to say about the new work?

JJ: They're breakthrough poems and each one of them is a big poem. "Taking Care" is shorter in word number, but the space that you really need between the sections makes it a big poem. I'm very gratified and encouraged that in the same year, within three months, that I wrote "Poem about My Rights" that I could also write "Taking Care" and mean it. "Taking Care" has been a long time coming. Often when I go around reading, people say to me "you're so angry and then you're so calm." I kid around, too, and I'm really basically a very happy person. I'm very angry, but I'm also very happy (*laughs*) and I realized that I needed to write a poem about why I'm happy, too. I'm happy because of this religious thing. I believe that we're going to make it through and I mean all of us. And I'm happy to be part of that. So the poem finally came through. The kids last year wanted me to be the commencement poet at Stony Brook (I'm the first tenured Black faculty member of the University. Speaking of how things have changed...) There was so much love among us by that time that I wanted to do something by way of a graduation present and I just didn't have it in me to write this poem. I wanted it, but I wanted a poem that was going to say "It's going to be alright. It's going to be alright." Finally, about three and a half weeks ago I wrote it in two days. This is the title poem of the new book. [Eds. note: "Taking Care" is included in *Passion*, but didn't become the "title poem."] It's going to be in *American Rag*. That's why it's Baltimore, Berkeley...I wanted to really open it up because we're all going to make it. I really believe that. I'm glad that I could write it and mean it and that I could write the other one and mean it. The other one about my "Rights" is just different because there's so much anger and hurt. But I feel good.

"MANY RIVERS TO CROSS"

(1982)

[Jordan's father, Granville, dominated her family life, and her mother, Mildred, stoically submitted to his tyranny. At a 1973 Black Women's Conference at Radcliffe, Jordan read a poem for her mother, "Getting Down to Get Over" (see pp. 166-177) that brought an audience of 500 to a standing ovation. In this keynote address to the conference on "Women and Work" at Barnard on December 11, 1981, she spoke openly and eloquently of her mother's love, life, and her suicide in 1966, and of the importance of the other women in her life who had seen her through with love. She called for a "new women's work [that means] we will not die trying to stand up: we will live that way: standing up." The speech was published in *Savvy* in July 1982, and appeared in *On Call* (1985).

When my mother killed herself I was looking for a job. That was fifteen years ago. I had no money and no food. On the pleasure side I was down to my last pack of Pall Malls plus half a bottle of J & B. I needed to find work because I needed to be able fully to support myself and my eight-year-old son, very fast. My plan was to raise enough big bucks so that I could take an okay apartment inside an acceptable public school district, by September. That deadline left me less than three months to turn my fortunes right side up.

It seemed that I had everything to do at once. Somehow I must move all of our things, mostly books and toys, out of the housing project before the rent fell due, again. I must do this without letting my neighbors know because destitution and divorce added up to personal shame, and failure. Those same neighbors had looked upon my husband and me as an ideal young couple, in many ways: insepa-rable, doting, ambitious. They had kept me busy and laughing in the hard weeks following my husband's departure for graduate school in Chicago; they had been the ones to remember him warmly through teasing remarks and questions all that long year that I remained alone, waiting for his return while I became the "temporary," sole breadwinner of our peculiar long-distance family by telephone. They had been the ones who kindly stopped the teasing and the queries when the year ended and my husband, the father of my child, did not come back. They never asked me and I never told them what that meant, altogether. I don't think I really knew.

I could see how my husband would proceed more or less naturally from graduate school to a professional occupation of his choice, just as he had shifted rather easily from me, his wife, to another man's wife—another woman. What I could not see was how I should go forward, now, in any natural, coherent way. As a mother without a husband, as a poet without a publisher, a freelance journalist without assignment, a city planner without a contract, it seemed to me that several incontestable and conflicting necessities had suddenly elimi-nated the whole realm of choice from my life.

My husband and I agreed that he would have the divorce that he wanted, and I would have the child. This ordinary settlement is, as millions of women will testify, as absurd as saying, "I'll give you a call, you handle everything else." At any rate, as my lawyer explained, the law was then the same as the law today; the courts would surely award me a reasonable amount of the father's income as child support, but the courts would also insist that they could not enforce their own decree. In other words, according to the law, what a father owes to his child is not serious compared to what a man owes to the bank for a car, or a vacation. Hence, as they say, it is extremely regrettable but nonetheless true that the courts cannot garnish a father's salary, nor freeze his account, nor seize his property on behalf of his children, in our society. Apparently this is because a child is not a car or a couch or a boat. (I would suppose this is the very best available definition of the difference between an American child and a car.)

Anyway, I wanted to get out of the projects as quickly as possible. But I was going to need help because I couldn't bend down and I couldn't carry anything heavy and I couldn't let my parents know about these problems because I didn't want to fight with them about the reasons behind the problems—which was the same reason I couldn't walk around or sit up straight to read or write without vomiting and acute abdominal pain. My parents would have evaluated that reason as a terrible secret compounded by a terrible crime; once again an unmarried woman, I had, nevertheless, become pregnant. What's more I had tried to interrupt this pregnancy even though this particular effort required not one but a total of three abortions— each of them illegal and amazingly expensive, as well as, evidently, somewhat poorly executed.

My mother, against my father's furious rejections of me and what he viewed as my failure, offered what she could; she had no money herself but there was space in the old brownstone of my childhood. I would live with them during the summer while I pursued my crash schedule for cash, and she would spend as much time with Christopher, her only and beloved grandchild, as her worsening but partially undiagnosed illness allowed.

After she suffered a stroke, her serenely imposing figure had shrunk into an unevenly balanced, starved shell of chronic disorder. In the last two years, her physical condition had forced her retirement from nursing, and she spent most of her days on a makeshift cot pushed against the wall of the dining room next to the kitchen. She could do very few things for herself, besides snack on crackers, or pour ready-made juice into a cup and then drink it.

In June, 1966, I moved from the projects into my parents' house with the help of a woman named Mrs. Hazel Griffin. Since my teens, she had been my hairdresser. Every day, all day, she stood on her feet, washing and straightening hair in her crowded shop, the Arch of Beauty. Mrs. Griffin had never been married, had never finished high school, and she ran the Arch of Beauty with an imperturbable and contagious sense of success. She had a daughter as old as I who worked alongside her mother, coddling customer fantasy into confidence. Gradually, Mrs. Griffin and I became close; as my own mother became more and more bedridden and demoralized, Mrs. Griffin extended herself—dropping by my parents' house to make dinner for them, or calling me to wish me good luck on a special freelance venture, and so forth. It was Mrs. Griffin who closed her shop for a whole day and drove all the way from Brooklyn to my housing project apartment in Queens. It was Mrs. Griffin who packed me up, so to speak, and carried me and the boxes back to Brooklyn, back to the house of my parents. It was Mrs. Griffin who ignored my father standing hateful at the top of the stone steps of the house and not saying a word of thanks and not once relieving her of a single load she wrestled up the stairs and past him. My father hated Mrs. Griffin because he was proud and because she was a stranger of mercy. My father hated Mrs. Griffin because he was like that sometimes: hateful and crazy.

My father alternated between weeping bouts of self-pity and storm explosions of wrath against the gods apparently determined to ruin him. These were his alternating reactions to my mother's increasing enfeeblement, her stoic depression. I think he was scared; who would take care of him? Would she get well again and make everything all right again?

This is how we organized the brownstone; I fixed a room for my son on the top floor of the house. I slept on the parlor floor in the front room. My father slept on the same floor, in the back. My mother stayed downstairs.

About a week after moving in, my mother asked me about the progress of my plans. I told her things were not terrific but that there were two different planning jobs I hoped to secure within the next few days. One of them involved a study of new towns in Sweden and the other one involved an analysis of the social consequences of a huge hydro-electric dam under construction in Ghana. My mother stared at me uncomprehendingly and then urged me to look for work in the local post office. We bitterly argued about what she dismissed as my "high-falutin" ideas and, I believe, that was the last substantial conversation between us.

From my first memory of him, my father had always worked at the post office. His favorite was the night shift, which brought him home usually between three and four o'clock in the morning.

It was hot. I finally fell asleep that night, a few nights after the argument between my mother and myself. She seemed to be rallying; that afternoon, she and my son had spent a long time in the backyard, oblivious to the heat and the mosquitoes. They were both tired but peaceful when they noisily re-entered the house, holding hands awkwardly.

But someone was knocking at the door to my room. Why should I wake up? It would be impossible to fall asleep again. It was so hot. The knocking continued. I switched on the light by the bed: 3:30 a.m. It must be my father. Furious, I pulled on a pair of shorts and a t-shirt. "What do you want? What's the matter?" I asked him, through the door. Had he gone berserk? What could he have to talk about at that ridiculous hour?

"OK, all right," I said, rubbing my eyes awake as I stepped to the door and opened it. "What?"

To my surprise, my father stood there looking very uncertain.

"It's your mother," he told me, in a burly, formal voice. "I think she's dead, but I'm not sure." He was avoiding my eyes.

"What do you mean," I answered.

"I want you to go downstairs and figure it out."

I could not believe what he was saying to me. "You want me to figure out if my mother is dead or alive?"

"I can't tell! I don't know!" he shouted angrily.

"Jesus Christ," I muttered, angry and beside myself.

I turned and glanced around my room, wondering if I could find anything to carry with me on this mission; what do you use to determine a life or a death? I couldn't see anything obvious that might be useful.

"I'll wait up here," my father said. "You call up and let me know."

I could not believe it; a man married to a woman more than forty years and he can't tell if she's alive or dead and he wakes up his kid and tells her, "You figure it out."

I was at the bottom of the stairs. I halted just outside the dining room where my mother slept. Suppose she really was dead? Suppose my father was not just being crazy and hateful? "Naw," I shook my head and confidently entered the room.

"Momma?!" I called, aloud. At the edge of the cot, my mother was leaning forward, one arm braced to hoist her body up. She was trying to stand up! I rushed over. "Wait. Here, I'll help you!" I said.

And I reached out my hands to give her a lift. The body of my mother was stiff. She was not yet cold, but she was stiff. Maybe I had come downstairs just in time! I tried to loosen her arms, to change her position, to ease her into lying down.

"Momma!" I kept saying. "Momma, listen to me! It's OK! I'm here and everything. Just relax. Relax! Give me a hand, now. I'm trying to help you lie down!"

Her body did not relax. She did not answer me. But she was not cold. Her eyes were not shut.

From upstairs my father was yelling, "Is she dead? Is she dead?"

"No!" I screamed at him. "No! She's not dead!"

At this, my father tore down the stairs and into the room. Then he braked.

"Milly?" he called out, tentative. Then he shouted at me and banged around the walls. "You damn fool. Don't you see now she's gone. Now she's gone!" We began to argue.

"She's alive! Call the doctor!"

"No!"

"Yes!"

At last my father left the room to call the doctor.

I straightened up. I felt completely exhausted from trying to gain a response from my mother. There she was, stiff on the edge of her bed, just about to stand up. Her lips were set, determined. She would manage it, but by herself. I could not help. Her eyes fixed on some point below the floor.

"Momma!" I shook her hard as I could to rouse her into focus. Now she fell back on the cot, but frozen and in the wrong position. It hit me that she might be dead. She might be dead.

My father reappeared at the door. He would not come any closer. "Dr. Davis says he will come. And he call the police."

The police? Would they know if my mother was dead or alive? Who would know?

I went to the phone and called my aunt. "Come quick," I said. "My father thinks Momma has died but she's here but she's stiff."

Soon the house was weird and ugly and crowded and I thought I was losing my mind.

Three white policemen stood around telling me my mother was dead. "How do you know?" I asked, and they shrugged and then they repeated themselves. And the doctor never came. But my aunt came and my uncle and they said she was dead.

After a conference with the cops, my aunt disappeared and when she came back she held a bottle in one of her hands. She and the police whispered together some more. Then one of the cops said, "Don't worry about it. We won't say anything." My aunt signaled me to follow her into the hallway where she let me understand that, in fact, my mother had committed suicide.

I could not assimilate this information: suicide.

I broke away from my aunt and ran to the telephone. I called a friend of mine, a woman who talked back loud to me so that I could realize my growing hysteria, and check it. then I called my cousin Valerie who lived in Harlem; she woke up instantly and urged me to come right away.

I hurried to the top floor and stood my sleeping son on his feet. I wanted to get him out of this house of death more than I ever wanted anything. He could not stand by himself so I carried him down the two flights to the street and laid him on the backseat and then took off.

At Valerie's, my son continued to sleep, so we put him to bed, closed the door, and talked. My cousin made me eat eggs, drink whiskey, and shower. She would take care of Christopher, she said. I should go back and deal with the situation in Brooklyn.

When I arrived, the house was absolutely full of women from the church dressed as though they were going to Sunday communion. It seemed to me they were, every one of them, wearing hats and gloves and drinking coffee and solemnly addressing invitations to a funeral and I could not find my mother anywhere and I could not find an empty spot in the house where I could sit and smoke a cigarette.

My mother was dead.

Feeling completely out of place, I headed for the front door, ready to leave. My father grabbed my shoulder from behind and forcibly spun me around.

"You see this?" he smiled, waving a large document in the air. "This am insurance paper for you!" He waved it in my face. "Your mother, she left you insurance, see?"

I watched him.

"But I gwine burn it in the furnace before I give it to you to t'row away on trash!"

"Is that money?" I demanded. "Did my mother leave me money?"

"Eh-heh!" he laughed. "And you don't get it from me. Not today, not tomorrow. Not until I dead and buried!"

My father grabbed for my arm and I swung away from him. He hit me on my head and I hit back. We were fighting.

Suddenly, the ladies from the church bustled about and pushed, horrified, between us. This was a sin, they said, for a father and a child to fight in the house of the dead and the mother not yet in the ground! Such a good woman she was, they said. She was a good woman, a good woman, they all agreed. Out of respect for the memory of this good woman, in deference to my mother who had committed suicide, the ladies shook their hats and insisted we should not fight; I should not fight with my father.

Utterly disgusted and disoriented, I went back to Harlem. By the time I reached my cousin's place I had begun to bleed, heavily. Valerie said I was hemorrhaging so she called up her boyfriend and the two of them hobbled me into Harlem Hospital.

I don't know how long I remained unconscious, but when I opened my eyes I found myself on the women's ward, with an intravenous setup feeding into my arm. After a while, Valerie showed up. Christopher was fine, she told me; my friends were taking turns with him. Whatever I did, I should not admit I'd had an abortion or I'd get her into trouble, and myself in trouble. Just play dumb and rest. I'd have to stay on the ward for several days. My mother's funeral was tomorrow afternoon. What did I want her to tell people to explain why I wouldn't be there? She meant, what lie?

I thought about it and decided I had nothing to say; if I couldn't tell the truth then the hell with it.

I lay in that bed at Harlem Hospital, thinking and sleeping. I wanted to get well.

I wanted to be strong. I never wanted to be weak again as long as I lived. I thought about my mother and her suicide and I thought about how my father could not tell whether she was dead or alive.

I wanted to get well and what I wanted to do as soon as I was strong again, actually, what I wanted to do was I wanted to live my life so that people would know unmistakably that I am alive, so that when I finally die people will know the difference for sure between my living and my death.

And I thought about the idea of my mother as a good woman and I rejected that, because I don't see why it's a good thing when you give up, or when you cooperate with those who hate you or when you polish and iron and mend and endlessly mollify for the sake of the people who love the way that you kill yourself day by day silently.

And I think all of this is really about women and work. Certainly this is all about me as a woman and my life work. I mean I am not sure my mother's suicide was something extraordinary. Perhaps most women must deal with a similar inheritance, the legacy of a woman whose death you cannot possibly pinpoint because she died so many, many times and because, even before she became your mother, the life of that woman was taken; I say it was taken away.

And really it was to honor my mother that I did fight with my father, that man who could not tell the living from the dead.

And really it is to honor Mrs. Hazel Griffin and my cousin Valerie and all the women I love, including myself, that I am working for the courage to admit the truth that Bertolt Brecht has written; he says, "It takes courage to say that the good were defeated not because they were good, but because they were weak."

I cherish the mercy and the grace of women's work. But I know there is new work that we must undertake as well: that new work will make defeat detestable to us. That new women's work will mean we will not die trying to stand up: we will live that way: standing up.

I came too late to help my mother to her feet.

By way of everlasting thanks to all of the women who have helped me to stay alive I am working never to be late again.

FROM "OTHER KINDS OF DREAMS"
INTERVIEW WITH PRATIBHA PARMAR (1989)

[Pratibha Parmar, writer and film maker, met Jordan in 1989 in London when Jordan was on a reading tour. Parmar, who was part of the Black women's movement in the U.K. felt that the movement was disintegrating, while, at the same time, was raising important questions about racism within white feminism and lack of intersectional awareness. She wrote an essay about the challenges and political fissures triggered by a focus on identity politics called "Other Kinds of Dreams." She followed the essay with this interview with Jordan, whose "commitment to internationalism and her ability to articulate the complex links and contradictions between the deeply personal and the deeply political in a clear and passionate way is rare." In 1991, Parmar directed the documentary, *A Place of Rage*, featuring Jordan, Alice Walker, and Angela Davis. *The Feminist Review* published "Other Kinds of Dreams," in March 1989, from which we've reprinted the interview.]

Pratibha Parmar: One of the most interesting and challenging things I have found in your writings is the way in which your radicalism refuses to suppress the complexity of our identities as women and as black people. In Britain there has been a tendency in the women's movement, both black and white, to organize around the assumptions of our shared identities but in the process of political organizing many of these assumption have fallen apart. Can you talk about some of the issues raised around identity politics and what you think it means to define oneself as a political person?

June Jordan: We have been organizing on the basis of identity, around immutable attributes of gender, race and class for a long time and it doesn't seem to have worked. There are obvious reasons for getting together with other people because someone else is black or she is a woman but I think we have to try to develop habits of evaluation in whatever we attempt politically. People get set into certain ways of doing things and they don't evaluate whether it's working or not. Or if they do evaluate then it's to say it's not working but it's not our fault, there couldn't possibly be anything wrong with our thinking on this subject or this issue. The problem invariably is that the enemy is simply inflexible or impregnable. This is a doomed modus operandi. We have to find out what works and some things may work to a certain extent and not beyond that.

I don't think that gender politics or that race politics per se are isolated from other ways of organizing for change, whether reformist change or revolutionary change. I don't think that they will take us where we want to go. I think that's abundantly clear if we look at our history as black people. We as black people have enormous problems everywhere in the world and we women have colossal problems everywhere in the world. I think there is something deficient in the thinking on the part of anybody who proposes either gender identity politics or race identity politics as sufficient, because every single one of us is more than whatever race we represent or embody and more than whatever gender category we fall into. We have other kinds of allegiances, other kinds of dreams that have nothing to do with whether we are white or not white.

A lot of awareness of ourselves as women as black people and

third world people really comes out of our involuntary forced rela-
tionships with people who despise us on the basis of what we are
rather than what we do. In other words our political awareness of
ourselves derives more often than not from a necessity to find out
why it is that this particular kind of persecution continues for my
people, or myself or my kind. Once you try to answer that question
you find yourself in the territory of people who despise you, people
who are responsible for the invention of the term racism or sexism.
I think it's important that each one of us is more than what cannot
be changed about us. That seems self-evident and accordingly our
politics should reflect that understanding.

This is not at all to disparage or dismiss the necessity for what
I would call issue-oriented unity among different kinds of people,
women, black people, or black women. I am not dismissing it but just
saying that it's probably not enough. It may be enough to get started
on something but I doubt very much whether it's enough to get any-
thing finished.

PP: So you are saying that in order to move forward, a crucial
part of the political process is to go beyond the personal and expe-
riential ways of organizing? You have written, 'It occurs to me that
much organizational grief could be avoided if people understood that
partnership in misery does not necessarily provide for partnership
for change: *when we get the monsters off our backs all of us may
want to run in very different directions.*'

JJ: Yes, for example, I think that for any woman who has ever
been raped, the existence of feminist or all female rape counseling
centers is absolutely necessary, the recourse to a refuge where a
woman can retire to repair herself without fear. But the problem is
more than an individual problem. She didn't rape herself. In order
to eliminate the possibility of rape or even the likelihood of rape for
women generally we have to beyond ourselves. We have to sit down
with and/or stand up to and finally in some way impact upon men. I
don't think it's ever enough on your own. And I would say the same
thing about race identity politics. I didn't, nor did my people or my
parents, invent the problems that we as black people have to solve.
We black people, the victims of racism are not the ones that have to

learn new ways of thinking about things so that we can stop racist habits of thought. Neither do we have the power to be placed in appropriate situations to abolish the social and economic arrangements that have assured the continuity of racism in our lives. That's for white people. What we really need to do is pass the taking of succor from each other, so to speak and build on our collective confidence and pride. Some people who I have met since I have been in London have been saying, it's terrible because nothing is going on politically. But that's not the point. I don't mean to knock that at all, but okay, now you know and I know that something is terrible, what are you going to do about it. Let's not sit inside our sorrows, let's not describe things to death. My orientation is activism. Other than that it's like a kind of vanity or a decadence. I will tell you how I suffer and you tell me how you suffer. . . it's bad enough to suffer but to talk about it endlessly . . . I say to them stop it. . .. . stop it. . . .

PP: Many movements such as the women's movement, the black movement and black women's groups have been organizing for a number of years around their shared oppressions. But it seems to me that many of these movements are stagnating because there is a refusal to acknowledge the need to move away from modes of being, that is accumulating all the isms of race, sex, class, disability etc., to modes of doing. What do you think are the dangers of this? How do you think we can move forward from this paralysis?

JJ: I am sure there is a danger. The first part of the political process is to recognize that there is a political problem and then to find people who agree with you. But the last part of the process which is to get rid of it is necessary and something too many of us forget. I am not interested in struggle. I am interested in victory. Let's get rid of the problems, let's not just sit around and talk about it and hold each other's hands. That's where you make evaluation: is it getting us there, if it's not then let's have other kinds of meeting with other kinds of meetings with other kinds of people. I think people can get stuck absolutely. What is the purpose of your identity? That is the question. So what? Is the way I would put it in my abrupt American way, What do you want to do on the basis of that? You just think if you fill a room by putting out flyers, with 50 women of the same color as you, somehow, you have accomplished everything you set out to accomplish. I don't think so. Not at all, why are you meeting.

Almost every year black students at Stony Brook where I teach, come around to say to me that they want to hold a meeting and I say, yes and I ask what's it about. They say unity and I say unity for what? I am already black and you are black so we unify okay but I don't need to meet with you about that.. When we get together, what's the purpose of that, what do you want to do? I don't need to sit in a room with other people who are black to know that I am black – that's not unity. Unity has to have some purpose to it otherwise we are not talking politics. I don't know what we are talking, maybe a mode of social life. That's okay, but beyond that people have to begin to understand that just because somebody is a woman or somebody is black does not mean that he or she and I should have the same politics. I don't think that's necessarily the case.

We should try to measure each other on the basis of what we do for each other rather than on the basis of who we are.

PP: There has been a strong tendency in the women's movement to create hierarchies of oppression. What is your experience of this?

JJ: I have a tremendous instinctive aversion to the idea of ranking oppression. In other words for nobody to try and corner misery. I think it's dangerous. It seems to me to be an immoral way of going about things. The difficulty here is the sloppiness of language. We call everything an oppression, going to the dentist is an oppression, then the word does not mean anything. Revisions in our language might help and it might also steer us clear from saying something as useless as, but mine is this and yours is that. If I, a black woman poet and writer, a professor of English at State University, it I am oppressed then we need another word to describe a woman in a refugee camp in Palestine or the mother of six in a rural village in Nicaragua or any counterpart inside South Africa.

PP: In the last few years there has been much talk about the need for coalitions and alliances between different groups of women not only nationally but internationally. What is your assessment of this form of political organizing?

JJ: I would say about coalitions what I said about unity, which

is what for? The issue should determine the social configuration
of politics. I am not going to sit in a room with other people just to
demonstrate black unity, we have got to have some reason for unity.
Why should I coalesce with you and why do you coalesce with me,
three has to be a reason why we need each other. It seems to me that
an awareness of the necessity for international coalition should not
be hard to come by in many spheres of feminist discourse because so
many of our problems, apparently have universal currency. I think
that never having been to London, for example, I can still be quite
sure that most women here, whatever class or color, are going to feel
shy about walking out at night just as I do. I just assume that. That's
about safety in the street. There is a universal experience for women,
which is that physical mobility is circumscribed by our gender and
by the enemies of our gender. This is one of the ways they seek to
make us know their hatred and respect it. This holds throughout the
world for women and literally we are not to about in the world freely.
If we do then we have to understand that we may have to pay for it
with our bodies. That is the threat. They don't ask you what you are
doing on the street, they rape you and mutilate you bodily to let you
remember your place. You have no rightful place in public.

Everywhere in the world we have the least amount of income,
everywhere in the world the intensity of the bond between women is
seen to be subversive and it seems to me there would be good rea-
sons to attempt international work against some of these common
conditions. We cannot eliminate the problems unless we see them in
their global dimensions. We should not fear the enlargement of our
deliberate connections in this way. We should understand that this
is a source of strength. It also makes it more difficult for anyone to
destroy our movement. Okay, they can do whatever they want to in
London, but there is Bangladesh, it's hydra headed, it's happening
everywhere, you can't destroy it. That's not to negate the necessity
or obviate the need to work where you live but this is only part of a
greater environment. I am talking against short sightedness.

I also think it's a good idea not to have any fixed notions in one's
head. I don't want any one to tell me where I should put my attention
first. If down the line we can try to respect each other according to

the principle of self determination then we can begin to move forward. There are enough of us to go around and you don't have to do what I do and vice versa. I do this and you do that, there is plenty of room.

JORDAN ON CERTAIN KINDS OF THEORY

FROM *THE WOMEN'S REVIEW OF BOOKS*
(1991)

[*The Women's Review of Books* asked several Black feminist critics and theorists to discuss the problems, politics and possibilities of their enterprise. Nellie McKay, Patricia Hill Collins, Mae Henderson, and Jordan participated in the conversation. These are two comments Jordan made during the exchange. They were published in Vol. 8. No. 5 (February 1991) of the magazine.]

All I know about "post-structuralist" and "deconstructionist" criticism is this: it's an abject worshipping of European fathers at their worst. It's elitist by intention and by implication both. It has nothing to do with the art, life or future of literature. It's losing all of us a whole lot of potential writers and poets and graduate students who cannot and will not tolerate tyrannies of language which are obviously anti-democratic and proud of it. These schools of "new theory" are and will remain irrelevant to my work.

**

Who sets the standards for admissible and inadmissible terms/ diction/discourse controls the outcome of what should be a public, populist, democratic debate in which all of the languages of all of our different histories meet with equal and respectful consideration. I am a poet and I am a writer and I am hoping to help change the world. Therefore I am taking pains to express my thoughts and findings in ways most likely to reach the maximal number and diversity of peoples on the planet.

The imposition of "post-structuralist" or "deconstructionist" values upon the human activity of writing and reading should be seen as nothing more than that: a cloud passing over a big, big sky that will outlast every one of us who loves the world and lives inside it.

FROM *SOLDIER: A POET'S CHILDHOOD*

(2000)

[Jordan called children "the only blameless people alive." As children, she said, we are under the control of adults; it is truly the first power relationship we experience. She spoke and wrote of her own childhood in poems, essays, and interviews. In 1997, she began a memoir of her childhood, originally called *Portrait of the Poet as a Little Black Girl*. It became *Soldier: A Poet's Childhood*, and she dedicated it to her father.

"I didn't want to leave her," her friend Toni Morrison said, "to let this little soldier go. So delightful, so proud, so loaded with expectations. There is so much always bubbling beneath the surface, and you see it all, just bubbling into these vivid recollections of a singular childhood: of yearning for and earning paternal love; of learning fearlessness and beauty and poetry. *Soldier* is such an intensely perceptive narrative. I am left, breathless, waiting for more."

Soldier continues a rich legacy of African-American autobiographical narrative from Harriet Jacobs' *Incidents in the Life of a Slave Girl* (1861) and Booker T. Washington's *Up from Slavery* (1901) to James Baldwin's *Go Tell It on the Mountain* (1953) to Maya Angelou's *I Know Why the Caged Bird Sings* (1969) and Audre Lorde's *Zami: A New*

Spelling of My Name (1982). Here are excerpts.]

[My parents] were both West Indian immigrants. Both of them came to America barefoot, peasant levels of poverty. But there the similarities disappeared.

My father quit after the first few months of grade school in Jamaica because, he said, the other children laughed at the rags he wore.

My mother completed the equivalent of high school and so, as my father reminded her, again and again, she knew how to read and write "long before" he got around to teaching himself those skills.

But my mother grew up in the dirt-floor cabin of a mountain village without electricity or running water. She would often whisper to me pictures of the frightening shadows of banana leaves below the changing message of the moon.

She came to this country because my grandmother, a domestic worker in New Jersey, finally sent for her.

My father came because his older brother, down in Panama, tried to take his teeth out with an ordinary pair of pliers.

Or: He came because he'd finished his stint as a British soldier who served in a cavalry regiment of Her Majesty's something or other in World War I.

It was hard to settle my father into a steady frame of reference.

He was a "race man," an admirer of Marcus Garvey, an enthusiast for theories about African origins of the human species, a zealous volunteer boxing instructor at the Harlem YMCA, devotedly literate in the available Negro poetry and political writings—and, also, he would angrily insist that he was *not* "black," *not* a "Negro."

Looking at him, you'd have to say that my father was extremely handsome, possibly white, and at least 50 percent Chinese.

Listening to him, you'd have to conclude that he was passionately confused and volatile.

Calling himself the Little Bull, my father was short, conspicuously fit, truculent, and generally (with women) flirtatious.

Believing that "idleness is the devil's plan," he stayed busy; reading through the night, his index finger tracking each syllable that he silently mouthed, or writing letters to government officials, or designing the next household or backyard project, or refining a schedule of forced enlightenment for me, his only child.

He was forever loquacious, argumentative, and visionary in his perspective.

And he was addicted to beauty, which is probably why he married my mother.

She had flawless brown skin and enormous dark brown eyes. She was very beautiful. She was also very sad. But my father mistook her sadness for dignity, and he treasured her reserve, her hesitant pacing, her mysterious poise. He also savored the teasing of her artificial quiet, the fullness of her bosom, and her quivering lower lip. She walked that proud Jamaican walk, allowing for no haste, no misstep, no embarrassment of clumsy impulse.

He was a man's man. She was a man's woman, thrilled to be chosen by an unemployed, ambitious West Indian who would make her his wife: He would be the stubborn provider who would take proper care of her in this strange, fast-talking city.

And on the afternoon when he did at last get work, as an elevator operator, my father ran the whole length of Manhattan, uptown to their two cramped rooms, to shout, "A job! A job! I got a job!"

He intended to keep every single promise he made to her—and to himself.

All he wanted in exchange was her fidelity, her respect, a little loosening up on the affectionate side of things, and a son.

[...]

This is when the fighting began.

I was not yet two years old.

Until then, I had assimilated everything from cereal and baby blankets to rhymes and stories and I had given nothing back, so to speak, besides a toothless gurgling or a watchful, fleeting look of concentration.

Now, my father decided, that was not enough. He wanted, he needed, to ascertain exactly what I was learning, and how. There would be no more mere listening to Sing a Song of Sixpence, a Pocketful of Rye / Four and Twenty Blackbirds Baked in a Pie!

It was my turn. He'd plod through a rhyme out loud, and then I'd be tested: Could I recite that myself?

I could.

Well then, how much was four and twenty?

Of course, even the question was meaningless to me.

No matter! Clearly I must learn to count. I must pay attention to the four and twenty pale green peas he now rolled across the floor.

He would teach me about numbers.

And further, to that end, he purchased a miniature abacus with green and blue and yellow wooden beads that easily flew back and forth on straight, colorless rods.

I was given an illustrated hardcover Mother Goose and, alternating with my mother, he read to me the rhymes I had already memorized.

Next he'd encourage me to open my large new Mother Goose and "find," for example, Jack and Jill Went Up the Hill.

Done?

Okay: Read it to him—backward.

As he assumed control, he advised my mother that she, in effect, had been dismissed.

He knew what had to be done.

He'd do it.

I'd do it.

She'd see, very soon, that his decision was the right decision.

They argued about who was more likely to "spoil" or "ruin" me.

My father's voice got loud.

My mother didn't say much, but she never said, "All right."

She was fighting.

They were fighting.

They were fighting with each other.

I had become the difference between them.

[...]

Maybe I should have been born a boy. I think I dumbfounded my father. Whatever his plans and his hopes for me, he must have noticed now and again that I, his only child, was in fact a little girl modeling pastel sunbonnets color-coordinated with puffy-sleeved dresses that had to accommodate just-in-case cotton handkerchiefs pinned to them.

I'm not sure.

Regardless of any particulars about me, he was convinced that a "Negro" parent had to produce a child who could become a virtual whiteman and therefore possess dignity and power.

Probably it seemed easier to change me than to change the meaning and complexion of power.

At any rate, he determined he'd transform me, his daughter, into something better, something more likely to succeed.

He taught me everything from the perspective of a recruiting warrior. There was a war on against colored people, against poor people. I had to become a soldier who would rise through the ranks and emerge a commander of men rather than an infantry pawn.

I would become that sturdy, brilliant soldier, or he would, well, beat me to death.

[...]

Sundays we rose even earlier than usual, consumed a quick breakfast, and walked the half mile to Brooklyn's St. Phillips Episcopal Church. I loved this church. I thought it was the most beautiful, hallowed space. And beforehand my mother would spend extra time on her minimal ablutions and she'd fidget a hat onto her hair and, rather solemnly, we'd take to the streets, a familial but awkward-looking trio. I'd notice the agreeable smell of coffee and toast still clouding my mind, but I'd be clear about our destination. We'd find tons of other children and their parents when we got there, and everyone would be acting very friendly and very formal, and the vaulted interior of the church would let all of us feel little and close and glad of such deliberate company.

My father's Sunday preparations were quite a bit more complicated. He shaved himself with a straight razor, releasing a steel blade six inches long. But before anything else, he'd spend ten minutes sharpening that blade on a "razor strap" of broad leather hanging from a bathroom hook. And while he slapped the blade this way and that against the strap he'd be singing a calypso song, trying to scandalize my mother, who often pretended she could not hear him.

In fact, you could not help but hear my father.

And after the sharpening of the razor blade, he'd unearth his "finest English bristle" shaving brush and slurp it around in a small crockery bowl of shaving soap and create a creamy, almost bubbling lather, which he'd then lavish all over his cheeks and frequently all over mine.

Then there'd be complete silence. He was now actually shaving himself, and there would be no more songs and no more horsing around until he was done and that blade had been folded and sheathed safely out of sight.

At last he'd emerge from the bathroom, beaming, and ask me to examine his skin: Was it smooth? Was it soft? It was.

Well, then, would my mother care to give him a little kiss?

She would not.

***

"The Lord be with you."

"And with thy spirit."

"Let us pray."

Week after week I waited to hear those three lines, again and again. Who had composed such magic?

Before us stood the priest, his arms lifted up, his garments sanctified, silken, and regal, and below him we stood or kneled as one body with one voice.

This unison amazed me. The oral structure of Episcopal litany calmed my heart and stirred my soul, and nobody had to try to teach me the meaning of that most mysterious Scripture:

In the beginning was the Word
and the Word was with God
and the Word was God

Did I not see and hear the truth of this assertion? Did I not long to live that truth with every fiber of my being? Did I not believe and desire and trust that truth, without understanding anything beyond the sound and the form and the consequences of that sound, that form?

It was so quiet!

There were no arguments, no cigars, no sarcasm, no jangling oddities or dangers.

I felt safe.

Everyone stayed on company behavior, or better than that.

And the stupendous height and depth of the church imparted a sense of infinite, imperturbable shelter.

Who would ever dare to desecrate the House of the Lord?

And, as my body was the temple
of God, who would dare to attack
or defile me?

"For He shall give his angels charge over you,
to keep you in all your ways."

And what about God's only "begotten" Son?

And what about the literal sip of literal sweet
red wine from the golden goblet
of Holy Communion?

"Yea, though I walk through the valley
of the shadow of death
I will fear no evil
For Thou art with me."

And what about God, who would "smite"
my enemies?

Who were my enemies?

***

I could never get enough of it: Church. I had mixed feelings about
prayer, especially my mother's prayers, which were so specific and so
apparently oblivious to whether anybody heard or "answered" them.
But church was different. Church was undeniable. A good part of
the time I was not sure what anybody was talking about, but no one
seemed to care about that:

What mattered was the magical language and its repetition that
left you feeling united and taken care of, and happy "in the Lord."

The entire congregation used the same words to invoke and
preserve that magic, and so I learned those words: I savored and I
repeated and I longed for and I thought about and I dreamed about:

"The Lord be with you."
"And with thy spirit."
"Let us pray."

I imitated the monotone but rhythmical incantations of the
priest. I memorized the patterns of his call and our response. I prid-
ed myself on being the first down on her knees.

I was eager to prove my deference, my willing belief. It was stun-
ning to consider that one word—for example, the very name Jesus—
could make the mighty bow down and the crippled rise up and walk.

Just thinking about "Jesus," I grew dizzy. I felt intoxicated.

This was Sunday worship for the fellowship of Christ. None of
that translated into anything I understood, except for the concept of
worship, which seemed to be something contagious and exalted and
extremely satisfying, even if specific to nothing known or visible.
Worship felt to me like a relief from anything regular or ordinary. I
suspected that was the point. I was wild about worship.

Best of all was the altar. Framed by stained-glass paintings, there it stood, shimmering and hushed, the gold cross hovering above a marble mantelpiece with elongated, lit candles held by gold candelabra surrounded by massive and fragrant floral displays.

Actually, if I'd had to name the four most mysterious and provocative ideas or facts I had run across by my sixth birthday, I'd have to say *dinosaur*, *Indians*, *diamonds*, and *God*.

[...]

One reason I didn't like girls too much was Valerie.

But now and then she'd make me a tuna fish sandwich with onions and a huge amount of mayonnaise and black pepper, and she'd use white bread (which my parents did not allow me to eat), and I'd think she was just the best cousin in the world.

Or she'd imitate my father or one of our uncles or aunts and put me in stitches.

But mostly I did not like her too much.

I did not appreciate having to say "thank you" for her hand-me-down jackets.

I did not like her infinite contempt and her infinite superiority based upon how old she was, which was, as far as I could tell, not something she had accomplished by herself.

I did not like listening to how much her feet hurt in her newest pair of powder blue heels, or whatever.

But I could get even with her.

After she took me to see *Isle of the Dead*, starring Boris Karloff, I could terrify Valerie by lunging into her path and pretending to be a killer walking corpse. Or I could get hold of a dead rat or a dead mouse, still in its trap, and drop that in front of her and she'd freak.

Or I could tell her I'd heard really weird noises upstairs and we'd better hide under the sink, and we'd hide under the sink for hours, even though she was four years older than I. And the entire time I'd be about to die laughing.

***

I used to laugh all the time. I used to laugh so much and so hard in church, in school, at the kitchen table, on the subway! I used to laugh so much my nose would run and my eyes would tear and I just couldn't stop.

One of my elementary-school teachers warned me that if I didn't stop laughing all the time I would literally die laughing.

And of course I thought that was one of the funniest ideas I'd ever heard, and I just laughed.

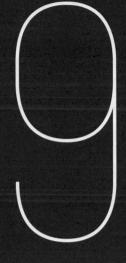

"SO HOT SO HOT SO HOT SO WHAT / SO HOT SO WHAT SO HOT SO HOT"

COLLABORATIONS: THEATER, MUSIC, TEACHING, POETRY (1981-1996)

[Poetry can be a lonely art, and Jordan loved working with people. Maybe that's why she was so drawn to collaborations. She wrote several plays over the years. "I think in one way or another," she once said, "I'm always trying to get away from being an only child, and theater is a great way to do it. It's alive and collective." She was passionate about music and wrote lyrics and libretti. ("I like music you can move to," she used to say, but that wasn't all the music she cared about. When one of the editors visited her in Berkeley in 1996, the soundtrack included everything from Bach to Babyface.) From the beginning of her teaching career, she viewed teaching as collaboration, too. She and Adrienne Rich turned writing poetry into collaboration, when they exchanged letter-poems in the early summer of 1996. Here's a sampling of Jordan's many projects working with others.]

FROM *THE ISSUE*

(1981)

[After yet another murder of a Black man by a police officer, this time in Brooklyn, Lloyd Wilson, the protagonist of Jordan's play, *The Issue*, issues an ultimatum. "Every time the cops kill a black kid, a policeman will be killed," the civil rights activist and leader of the militant Brotherhood announces in the media, furious and desperate (Jordan reframes threat as a fierce rhetorical device in "Poem about Police Violence," see pp. 328-329). The result: Wilson has to hide. Where? His white girlfriend Claudia's farmhouse provides the four walls for the continuation of all the conflicts on a private level: between the hunted Black man and the privileged white woman, between Black machismo and feminism (how can you be a *sister* in a *brotherhood*?), between Black and white feminism. The fight is on—on all fronts, behind closed doors and all over the nation. "What the fuck have we ever won? We didn't even win the Civil War," shouts Wilson. Claudia is quick to reply: "Yeah, you did. You won the war. It was the victory that got taken away." Finally, Wilson decides to come out of hiding and fight. He rejoins his movement in a Bedford-Stuyvesant church basement, preparing to lead a massive rally. Participating, he risks his life: rumors fly that the cops are ready to gun him down. The play ends with Wilson's—very Jordan-like—words: "I was born ready."

Jordan's *The Issue*, written in 1979, a year after the police murder of Arthur Miller in Brooklyn, is a searing examination of race, responsibility, rage, Black radicalism, white supremacy, fight for freedom-fighting, and moral reckoning. Jordan's alternate title for the play was *The Arrow that Flies by Day*, drawn from the 91st Psalm: "You will not fear the terror of the night, nor the arrow that flies by day, nor the pestilence that stalks in darkness, nor the destruction that wastes at noonday." The play, a link in American theater somewhere between Lorraine Hansberry, James Baldwin, Amiri Baraka, August Wilson, and Suzan-Lori Parks, has been performed only once, in a 1981 staged reading at Joseph Papp's Public Theater, under the direction of

Ntozake Shange.
   This excerpt is from Scene 2, Act 1.]

(Lights come up on the kitchen: the audience views the kitchen long enough for the character of the kitchen itself to be understood, and felt.

Then the three of them, LLOYD, CLAUDIA, and KIMAKO, more or less enter through Stage Right Front corner doorway, at once. EACH is burdened by big supermarket bags, producing French bread and an unsliced loaf of pumpernickel and a variety of cheeses and a bunch of apples and a fistful, maybe, of Nestlé's chocolate bars and wine or individual bottles of Heineken's/Perrier while CLAUDIA contributes luncheon-ware and glasses (if it's wine) that wrestle all of the stuff into an attractive, orderly setting of a light repast.

There is a lot of action but little talk: The things on the table, finally, look appetizing and the THREE of them sit around it in different postures of fatigue.

KIMAKO sits closest to the audience, Stage Right. Then there's LLOYD, as HE says, "in the fucking middle," then there's CLAUDIA. THEY poke and eat and sip.)

LLOYD: *(Meditative but then comes to an [illegible], to lighten things, begins to tease KIMAKO, by way of thanking her, at the same time)*
Sister Richardson, you really cook up a storm!
(As he stuffs the cold store-bought cheese and bread into his mouth and washes it down with a large gulp of cold beer from the bottle, or else a large, draining swallow from the wineglass which HE will immediately refill)

KIMAKO: *(Ready and glad to play, however briefly)*

I thought you'd feel like a little soul cooking stuck up here with this cold Swedish type. *(SHE winks at CLAUDIA)* So I baked this Italian-French bread last night a coupla minutes before I went to bed, don't you know. And I let the milk just mold itself into gorgonzola. And, the apples?! It was nothing, really. *(Laughing, ALL of them)* Anything for you, sweetheart. *(SHE gets up, a second, to kiss LLOYD on the forehead)* A good grease to put the Big Man at his ease!

LLOYD: I sure am glad they sent you: Can you picture Meatball in a supermarket! Shit. They would arrest the nigga for incompetence.

KIMAKO: *(Still laughing)*
Meatball looking at the truly dry cereals and thinking what the fuck does this mean? What are *the implications* of the labels?

LLOYD: How is my man?

KIMAKO: You know he wanted to come, himself. Verify for himself that you're still among the breathing. B.J. gave me so many questions for you—he's a dedicated Brother: on the case. Anyway, he knows: He's being followed, police likely to mess with a Black man by himself around this kind of territory much more than—a helpless, cute Black matriarch like me.

LLOYD: *(Frowning)*
Yeah, but still. That decision put you on the line.

KIMAKO: *(Lightly)*
There's three of us on that line. At least.

CLAUDIA: *(Her voice a little unsure of itself, a little untrue because SHE's just been listening, until now; SHE speaks to BOTH of them, almost formally/deferential)*
Do you feel you have a clear enough idea of the lay of the land around the house? Do you want to walk it again? So you're sure what we're doing if we have to move fast?

LLOYD: *(Decisively speaking for himself and KIMAKO)*
Naw, it's clear. It's cool. We might as well relax a little.

KIMAKO: *(Awkwardly)*
The thing is I'm mainly supposed to get you to leave: to come back. To Brooklyn. For a rally as big as we can make it.

CLAUDIA: *(Aghast)* When?

KIMAKO: *(Not looking at EITHER of them)* As soon as you can be ready. Tomorrow. Tomorrow night. We need a hot minute to put out the word, to organize, try to control the crowd so it's orderly and nothing happens.

(Involuntarily CLAUDIA jolts her body away in a partial turning away from LLOYD's view of her face)

CLAUDIA: *(Flushed, angry, and muttering)* Something has happened already! The point is to keep the cops "orderly!" Can you "organize" to do that?

KIMAKO: *(Looking past LLOYD, to CLAUDIA, and slightly puzzled)* What are you saying?

CLAUDIA: I can't believe the Brotherhood is setting up another one-sided nonviolent mass demonstration by thousands of people who will stand there the same as Lloyd—sitting ducks among pigs.

KIMAKO: *(Heated, but handling it)* I really can't get into an argument with you: anyway, I'm just the messenger.

CLAUDIA: *(Tauntingly)* "Messenger?"

KIMAKO: *(Self-effacing but with an angry edge to her words)* I would imagine that the idea is that enough Black people have been killed: it has to be nonviolent, otherwise they—the police—will mow us down.

CLAUDIA: *(Openly baiting KIMAKO now)*
You "would imagine?" The evidence for nonviolence as a way to embarrass violent police is not what you would call terrific!

LLOYD: *(Gesturing with his arms outstretched as though to push the TWO WOMEN apart)* Whoa! The Brotherhood has made a decision, right? *(Looking at KIMAKO)* They want me back? Fast? Why? What is it? *(Arms down and face rearranged into an impassive expression)*

KIMAKO: Things are pretty tense. Another young brother was shot, by the police. His name is Larry Rhodes. He's in Kings County, in a coma. *(Bites her lip)* A very beautiful little guy. *(Pause. Speaking with difficulty)* He used to be one of my star troublemakers. *(Slowly but picking up spirit)* Full of questions and then he'd start carrying on about something and he wouldn't be able to stop laughing and then all the other kids would get into it. You know how they are. *(She has begun to smile)*

LLOYD: *(Quietly)* So how did it happen?

KIMAKO: *(The smile dies as she understands the question)* He was running out one of the buildings on the projects as these cops were coming in. Somebody had called the police about a husband and wife kind of fight. When the police saw Larry running, one of them pulled the trigger, by accident, as always. The bullet caught Larry in the neck. *(Nobody says anything and KIMAKO continues. Clearing her throat and raising her voice slightly)* We got six or seven eyewitnesses, but no move to suspend the cop. As a matter of fact, the police refuse to talk with anyone from The Brotherhood. They say—*(She reaches into her backpack and takes out a stack of newspaper clippings, a pile of Xerox pages, a tape recorder, two cassettes, then a headline and hands it over to LLOYD)* "Tell Wilson to come out of hiding." They say, "Tell the Big Man to be a Big Man: Show his face." Just like we insist on talking only with the Commissioner, they insist on only talking with you.

CLAUDIA: *(Asking LLOYD about the headline)* What does it say?

LLOYD: *(Head and eyes down, and tightlipped)* COPS TAUNT: "BLACK LEADERSHIP IS HIDING." *(He reaches over to the stacks of paper on the table and pulls them close so HE can scan through the material)*

KIMAKO: *(Picking up a particular cassette and checking the label to see if it's the right one)* And you should probably listen to this one, Lloyd. So you know nobody's playing.

CLAUDIA: What is it?

KIMAKO: Your friend from Channel 5? He got this tape on some cops outside the 77th precinct having a discussion about exactly what to do with this particular Black leader soon as they catch him. How they plan to make an example out of Lloyd, to keep the rest of us in line. *(Looking across at LLOYD)* We had what turned out to be a giant demonstration in Tompkins Park, about the shooting. Right after that 1,000 of us started this march into the streets/linking arms and chanting A PEOPLE UNITED CAN NEVER BE DEFEATED—and the cops? They showed up, hundreds in a "counter-demonstration" and *rioted!* Drove the police cars full-speed into the crowd. All of a sudden there were sirens going and the lights flashing and the police cars plowing into us. Everybody was screaming, trying to get out of the way. I saw one woman knocked down to the sidewalk, trampled on. Then the TPF turned out, beating on people's heads with billy sticks and chasing us into hallways and stalking the streets, rifles out, looking for anything/anybody to move. We had to run for our lives—crawling across the concrete *(SHE turns up the palms of her hands so the long scratch marks daubed with iodine can be seen)* to get away. *(Emphatically)* We had to *try to not breathe:* they were that close! That wild to kill Black people. We have a few pictures of the cops in action but not a whole lot; most of the media split and went home after the speechmaking. And then the cops had the nerve to hold up signs—"ONE OF THEIRS IS SHOT—BUT ONE OF OURS IS

DEAD!" The mayor was and has been "unavailable" for comment.

LLOYD: They want to keep score! *(Furious and slow and clear)* Look at this garbage. All the way back to 1964. Then it was Lieutenant Gilligan. Shot the kid who was fooling around with a *water* gun. And then there was Newark: Did you ever see that cover of *Life* Magazine: Black boy bleeding to death on the street. Cops shot him through the back of the head. The kid was running with a six-pack. Of beer. Every mothafucking year they do this. All you got to do is let it be Christmas or Thanksgiving or spring or summer or Monday or Sunday and they act like killers on the loose. We getting good at funerals/ funeral oratory. Good at rallies. Good at speeches. It's a ritual: They murder our children. And what do we do about it? We cry real hard real loud. Then it's over: That's that. *(Leaning forward on his elbows, looking at KIMAKO)* If I was a pig, behind all of that crying for all of that dying, I would blow away a nigga a day. Why the hell not.

CLAUDIA*: (Alarm ringing through her voice)* You're going back to lead the rally!

LLOYD*: (Sarcastically, turning his head to CLAUDIA as HE pushes his chair away from the table, getting up from his place)* Naw. I'm gonna stay here and screw you.

CLAUDIA*: (Pissed and fed up)* Excuse me. For living. *(SHE rises, quickly, and exits Stage Rear, Stage Left, going upstairs) (There is silence. LLOYD, hands in his pockets, stands still: looking towards the stairs where SHE has disappeared)*

"OUGHTA BE A WOMAN"

WITH BERNICE JOHNSON REAGON
(1981)

[Since 1973, with its founding by singer, composer, and activist Bernice Johnson Reagon, Sweet Honey in the Rock has been performing and recording in the sonorous, spiritual, celebratory spirit of the African-American female a capella tradition. To hear them, wrote Horace Clarence Boyer, gospel singer and scholar, is to hear "[t]he sound ... of sisters sitting around the fireplace singing songs of social commentary, a female choir in rehearsal, a congregation of Wednesday evening Prayer Services singers, or a village that has come together to sing through happiness, trials or death."

Jordan worked with Reagon and Sweet Honey several times. In 1973, Reagon and Jordan, under the direction of Ntozake Shange, created an evening of song and poetry in honor of Sojourner Truth. Reagon put several of Jordan's poems to music for Sweet Honey, including "Alla Tha's All Right, but" (from *Passion* (1980), and the line "*we are the ones we have been waiting for*" from "Poem for South African Women."

We include here the lyrics of "Oughta Be A Woman," which the poet wrote after Reagon shared with Jordan details of her mother's life. The anthem of the suffering and strength of all Black women appears on *Good News*, released in 1981. Barbara Smith included the poem in her introduction to *Home Girls: A Black Feminist Anthology* (1983).]

OUGHTA BE A WOMAN

Washing the floors to send you to college
Staying at home so you can feel safe
What do you think is the soul of her knowledge
What do you think that makes her feel safe

Biting her lips and lowering her eyes
To make sure there's food on the table
What do you think would be her surprise
If the world was as willing as she's able

Hugging herself in an old kitchen chair
She listens to your hurt and your rage
What do you think she knows of despair
What is the aching of age

The fathers, the children, the brothers
Turn to her and everybody white turns to her
What about her turning around
Alone in the everyday light

There oughta be a woman can break
Down, sit down, break down, sit down
Like everybody else call it quits on Mondays
Blues on Tuesdays, sleep until Sunday
Down, sit down, break down, sit down

A way outa no way is flesh outa flesh
Courage that cries out at night
A way outa no way is flesh outa flesh
Bravery kept outa sight
A way outa no way is too much to ask
Too much of a task for any one woman

FROM *BANG BANG ÜBER ALLES*

WITH ADRIENNE TORF

(1986)

[Jordan collaborated with pianist/composer Adrienne Torf for almost two decades, beginning in 1983, on songs, readings and performances. The two also created a full-length Brecht/Weill-influenced musical drama, *Bang Bang Über Alles* (Jordan also called it a "docu-opera" and a "North American *Threepenny Opera*"). Together, Jordan's ingenious lyrics and Torf's multi-faceted score tell the story of anti-Ku Klux Klan activists trying to overturn racist beliefs and violence, and using the music they love to do it—new wave, gospel, classical, blues, rock. After staged readings and concerts in New York, the full work premiered on June 12, 1986 at 7 Stages Theatre in Atlanta, Georgia. Soon, life imitated art: on the third night of the show's run, real Klansmen protested, threatening to burn the theater down if the show wasn't cancelled. The police arrived to disperse the Klan, and that evening's performances took place on schedule.

Here are two songs from *Bang Bang*: "The Custodian's Song," sung by Tom, a character torn between his loyalties to his activist friends and to his Klansman father, and "Song of the Law-Abiding Citizen," which makes rap out of food stamps and nuclear waste. It is sung by Buddy, a tremendously talented Black singer/ songwriter, whose political concern is defined by a moral right-or-wrong perspective. Jordan included the lyrics of "Song of the Law-Abiding Citizen" in *Living Room* (1985). On the CD of her work with Jordan, *Collaboration: Selected Works, 1983-2000*, Torf included the song as well, and listeners can hear Jordan herself performing the piece, under the title "So Hot."]

◆◆◆

THE CUSTODIAN'S SONG

I don't believe there was much of a plan.
There never is with these kind of people.
They do what they feel like/they do what they can.
I don't believe there was much of a plan.

They figure their hearts will show them the way
They want to do right/or that's what they say
But I want to know: If you mean to do right
Shouldn't you welcome the chance for a fight?

But no! They complain and they scream for protection
You can scare them to death if you just disagree!
The men that they have can't hold an erection
And the women whine endlessly: "Let me be free!"

Dancers and singers! To take on the Klan?
They must have been dreaming! My old man's a man!
My old man's a patriot down to his shoes
He's got the real story on colored and Jews

Who asked for their commyrot inside our school?
They don't even live here: we have our own rules!
But no! They insisted: They took us for fools.
We taught them a lesson. And they lost the duel.

Or that's what I think. You'll see for yourself!
How do-gooder busybodies stepped out of bounds
Which is the habit with these kind of people
They should stay home with their books on a shelf

But they didn't. And now you can watch
how a weird idea for a musical show
turned into a pretty bad botch
of things: A show

down
that showed somebody
up!

And I don't believe there was much of a plan
There never is with these kind of people.
They do what they feel like/they do what they can.
I don't believe there was much of a plan.

◆◆◆

SONG OF THE LAW-ABIDING CITIZEN (*AKA* "SO HOT")

so hot so hot so hot so what
so hot so what so hot so hot

They made a mistake
I got more than I usually take
I got food stamps food stamps I got
so many stamps in the mail
I thought maybe I should put them on sale
How lucky I am
I got food stamps: Hot damn!
I made up my mind
to be decent and kind
to let my upright character shine
I sent 10,000 food stamps
back to the President (and his beautiful wife)
and I can't pay the rent
but I sent 10,000 food stamps
back to the President (and his beautiful wife)
how lucky I am
hot damn
They made a mistake
for Chrissake
And I gave it away to the President

I thought that was legal I thought that was kind
and I can't pay the rent
but I sent 10,000 food stamps
back back back to the President

so hot so hot so hot so what
so hot so what so hot so hot

Trucks cruisin' down the avenue
carrying nuclear garbage right next to you
and it's legal
it's radioaction ridin' like a regal
load of jewels
past the bars the cruel
school house and the church and if
the trucks wipeout or crash
or even lurch too hard around a corner
we will just be goners
and it's legal
it's radioaction ridin' regal
through the skittery city street
and don't be jittery
because it's legal
radioaction ridin' the road
Avenue A Avenue B Avenue C Avenue D
Avenue of the Americas

so hot so hot so hot so what
so hot so what so hot so hot
so hot so hot so hot so what

FROM *I WAS LOOKING AT THE CEILING AND THEN I SAW THE SKY*

WITH JOHN ADAMS AND PETER SELLARS

(1995)

[*I was Looking at the Ceiling and Then I Saw the Sky* was a close collaboration with director Peter Sellars and composer John Adams. Jordan called the two-act opera/song cycle, with musical forms ranging from gospel to jazz, from funk to rock, "a lot of good news coming out of a lot of bad news," and subtitled it "earthquake/romance." "My idea of romance is that it's like an earthquake," she said. *Ceiling/Sky* featured a cast of seven young Los Angeles residents—including a womanizing Black minister, a white rookie cop unable to come to terms with being gay, a Black gang leader and his girlfriend, and an undocumented Salvadoran immigrant. They all must come to grip with themselves, each other, their community, and their future in the devastating aftermath of the 1994 Northridge earthquake. The opera premiered in Berkeley on May 13, 1995, and played over fifty performances in New York, Montreal, Helsinki, Paris, and Hamburg. The libretto was published in book form in 1995 and, in 2005, Naxos released *Ceiling/Sky* as one of its American Opera Classics. *The Los Angeles Times*, reviewing a 2014 revival of the work at Southern California's Long Beach Opera, praised *Ceiling/Sky* as "a richly existential 'earthquake/romance,'" with "songs [that] do indeed find that elusive sweet spot between pop and opera..." and which, in its daring hybrid has both a "hook that stays with you longer than you might like and...an emotional depth that Broadway wouldn't dare attempt."]

◆◆◆

YOUR HONOR MY CLIENT HE'S A YOUNG BLACK MAN (RICK'S SOLO)

Your Honor my Client He's a Young Black man
Your Honor my Client He's Not Really Impossible to Understand
So I ask you to try
Just as I/Just as I
Have to trust what I know/where I stand
in relationship to
This remarkable Black man!
He's enjoying the day on the street
He's heading in no particular direction
He's following the drift of his feet
But his beeper goes off
His girlfriend's number comes up
And because he hopes (of course) to keep her
this girlfriend the mother of his first and only child
a seven-month-old
a baby daughter he's wild
to protect and to hold
my Client is not inclined to delay or to scoff
at this sudden alarm
So he does what he believes
a Black man oughta do
He calls this young lady to inquire/to make sure that no harm
has befallen her out of the blue
Your Honor my Client He's a Young Black man
Your Honor my Client He's Not Really Impossible to Understand
He's just this minute back from a second term in jail
for a couple of wobblers with little or no reason
except that this man's a natural-born leader
and as you probably know it's always open season
on a Young Black man set up to fail!
I apologize if I digress
To get back to the point:
My Client/He's recently released. I guess

you could say he's just back from the joint
and his girlfriend/well, clearly he needs her!
She's waited for him and She wants him Right now!
Over the phone She tells him She can't find her son!
Immigration has taken him somewhere as bait!
She's screaming and crying! She's completely undone!
Maybe she should hide! Maybe he should bring her a gun!
What if they come to the house for the baby girl too!
Your Honor my Client He's a Young Black man!
He's familiar with the terror of the armies of the State
He will do/he will do
Whatever he must whatever he can
And he doesn't know why and he doesn't know how
But he'll Rush to his girlfriend and chill out her fears
He'll rescue her boy and Stop all her tears
He's Racing to stand there in front of her face—
Now here is where
(I would say) it's a cultural thing:
Momentarily
My Client strays from the path on his way:
(*Spoken*) One for his girlfriend and another one he figures
will help him to calm
Things down but then there's a crowd and he can't wait around just
to pay
for two bottles of beer
Two cold forties from a local convenience store/Okay:
He steals them: Four Dollars and Thirty-nine Cents'
          worth of ice-cold brew
He's Thinking this has been a hella day
          for him and his girlfriend and two
          bottles of beer is not more than he's due!

Your Honor my Client He's a Young Black man
Your Honor my Client He's Not Really Impossible to Understand
They've stolen a Child! He's taken two beers!
Three strikes and he's facing forty-five years!

And one witness claims that my Client/
Allegedly he
(almost) took away her breath/But!
There was no injury!
There is no death!
Who has he hurt?
And what will we lose
if the law rules
inert
(which is what you may choose)
Your Honor my Client He's a Young Black man
Your Honor my Client He's Not Really Impossible to Understand
(I think) it's a Cultural Thing
His rage and his petty mistake!
Two bottles of beer and his life's now at stake!
I give you five dollars to cover the brew/it's a bargain!
For five bucks/for five bucks the Court
Can be through
with my Client or
if all of us lose we spend twenty-five *Thousand* a year
for the rest of his time incarcerated for
two bottles of beer!

◆◆◆

LEILA'S SONG: ALONE (AGAIN OR AT LAST)

After all is said and done
I want to be somebody's straight-up Number One
After every crisis every problem like the setting of the sun
I want/somebody hold me close and tell me stories when it rains
I need/somebody break apart
        the meaning of the chains
        that chock my heart
After all is said and done

I want to be the reason for the for the sunrise and the flowers out of
season
I want to be
I need to be somebody's
> dressed up
> dressed down
> naked
> three hundred sixty-five nights of one light
> year's piercing
> us tight
> together
> tight
> tight
> 1 x 1

After all is said and done
I need to be
I want to be somebody's straight-up Number One!

FROM *JUNE JORDAN'S POETRY FOR THE PEOPLE: A REVOLUTIONARY BLUEPRINT*

WITH EDITOR LAUREN MULLER AND THE BLUEPRINT COLLECTIVE
(1995)

[Jordan taught her first poetry classes at Berkeley in the fall of 1990. She was immediately impressed and moved by her students; their "society of competing opinions and conflicting/commingling identities" inspired her to create Poetry for the People (also known as P4P). This unique program went beyond student workshopping of their poems, though it certainly did that, too. Jordan tapped the energy and talents of her students, and had them spreading the word about the power and truth-telling of poetry. Classes were designed around themes of urgency—such as "The Politics of Childhood"—and published anthologies on these subjects. After three semesters, students became "Student Teacher Poets," conducting workshops at community and religious centers, nursing homes, area schools, and correctional facilities. They organized readings, radio programming, teach-ins. A self-sustaining enterprise, but also missionary in spirit in the best sense of the word, in 1995 they found a way to teach other colleges and universities how to do the same thing—thus *June Jordan's Poetry for the People: A Revolutionary Blueprint*, a how-to-guide, produced by Jordan's students, including guidelines for creating trust and community in the classroom, striving for excellence, advice on teaching and creating meaningful syllabi, tips on organizing public readings, teach-ins, community workshops, working with children, and a bibliography of resources. Jordan was very proud. "I teach and I write and I walk and I talk among people who want what I want: Good health, safety, a fair chance at happiness, and a growing environment of friends." It sounds like something close to Martin Luther King, Jr.'s Beloved Community, and indeed it was. It was something she found—and created—at Berkeley with her friends and her students. At the time of this writing, P4P is still alive and well at Berkeley, and P4P programs, using this revolutionary blueprint and being sensitive to their own communities, now exist in colleges and cultural institutions across the country. The following is an excerpt from Jordan's introduction to the book.]

This is an important, big book of good news. While professional theoreticians and politicians debate "student participation" and while cheap-shot opinion-makers bemoan the "balkanization" of America or the "decline" of "Western civilization," something actual and positive and tested and new and very American has been happening where I teach. While very well-paid and unqualified, non-geneticists have splashed their invidious notions of genetic destiny all over collaborating mass-media screens and printed pages, something else, something faithful and literate and individual and collective and technical and creative and systematic and unexpected and unpredictable has been taking place on the showcase campus of U.C. Berkeley.

Revered as a world-class University for scientific research and accomplishment, respected as the leading public institution of higher learning in the United States, and boasting the most heterogeneous student population on the earth, the intellectual facts about U.C. Berkeley altogether disprove and debunk those popular armchair jitters variously headlined as "The Threat of Diversity" or "Political Correctness-versus-Everything-Profound-and-Obviously-Indispensable-and-Unarguably-Critical-to-Enlightenment"—such as "Sir Gawain and the Green Knight."

But what's new inside the national example of U.C. Berkeley is not Chemistry or Nuclear Micro-Biology or Ultra-English Lit or Engineering or Women's Studies. It is not Pulitzer Prizes and MacArthur Foundation Awards regularly collected by illustrious members of the faculty. Nor is it the non-white majority freshman culled from the very top of graduating high school seniors nationwide. The news is poetry.

And this important, big book documents the meaning of impassioned embrace of language, the meaning of that highest calling: the difficult, fabulous pursuit of the power of the word/the voice/the poetry, of people who live and die together, mostly unknown to each other: mostly seen, but not heard.

You cannot write lies and write good poetry. Deceit, abstraction, euphemism: any one of these will doom a poem to the realm of "baffling" or "forgettable," or worse. Good poetry requires precision: if you do not attempt to say, accurately, truthfully, what you feel or see or need, then how will you achieve precision? What criterion will guide you to the next absolutely "right" word?

And so poetry is not a shopping list, a casual disquisition on the colors of the sky, a soporific daydream, or a bumper sticker sloganeering. Poetry is a political action undertaken for the sake of information, the faith, the exorcism, and the lyrical invention, that telling the truth makes possible. Poetry means taking control of the language of your life. Good poems can interdict a suicide, rescue a love affair, and build a revolution in which speaking and listening to somebody becomes the first and last purpose to every social encounter.

I would hope that folks throughout the U.S.A. would consider the creation of poems as a foundation for true community: a fearless democratic society.

This important, big book delivers a blueprint for poetry for the people: a testament, a manual, an anthology of new poems and new bibliographies, and an open case history. It is an academic experiment soaring past campus boundaries. It is a political movement that anybody anywhere can join, imitate, or improve. It is a literary movement that no one can stifle or erase.

But I did not wake up one morning ablaze with a coherent vision of Poetry for the People! The natural intermingling of my ideas and my observations as an educator, a poet, and the African-American daughter of poorly documented immigrants did not lead me to any limited ideological perspectives or resolve. Poetry for the People is the arduous and happy outcome of practical, day-by-day, classroom failure and success.

For anyone interested, this Blueprint will spare you most of the trial and many of the errors of my own gradual discoveries.

All of my teaching life I have tried to remember how much I always, as a student, hated school, and why. It is, in some ways, quite amazing for me to realize that, as of this date, I have been a teacher, on the University level, for almost two decades. Now it would seem very strange, and I would feel grievously deprived, if I did not need to think in new ways and read many new books and learn new names and adapt to a new and unpredictable racial and cultural heterogeneity of specific breadth in experience, every semester.

When I was going to school, too much of the time I found myself an alien body force-fed stories and facts about people entirely unrelated to me, or my family. And the regular demands upon me only required my acquiescence to a program of instruction predetermined without regard for my particular history, or future. I was made to learn about "the powerful": those who won wars or who conquered territory or whose odd ideas about poetry and love prevailed inside some distant country where neither my parents nor myself would find welcome.

When I arrived at the University of California at Berkeley, the outdoor student society of competing opinions and conflicting/comingling identities inflamed my imagination. I wondered if I could try to preserve, and even embolden, that fabulous, natural energy of assertive, polemical young hearts and minds inside the classroom.

My first semester teaching for African American Studies and Women's Studies Departments tested these ambitions, at once. When I walked into the classroom for African American Freshman Composition, to my complete surprise, I found a minority of African American students: the majority presented me with an uneasy mix of Asian American and Chicana/Chicano Americans and Euro-Americans. My task, then, was to revise and to devise a reading list and a method of handling diverse writings so as to identify, and embrace, what was distinctive to African American experience, on the one hand, and also, to identify, and to embrace, what was personally relevant (either because of commonalities or because of important differences) to every young man and woman sitting in that same space.

When I walked into my first Women's Studies classroom, I found myself facing an overwhelmingly White group of young women packed together in an expectant, rabble-rousing spirit that completely surprised me: What were they expecting? What did they want to happen?

In African American Studies Freshman Composition, I quickly developed a practical value system which invested student writing with at least as much imperative worth as anything else we might read. This meant student compositions twice weekly, at least, and this meant that, in effect, the class was producing its own literature: a literature reflecting the ideas and dreams and memories of the actual young Americans at work.

For the Women's Studies, I quickly settled upon the concept of "The Politics of Childhood" and, to my delight, the students eagerly rallied to that challenge. In addition to our assigned readings, they wrote and they shared, aloud, whatever had deeply bruised, or enabled, them as children. Before long, we had reason to declare our class "A Community of Trust." The honesty and the depth of students' sharing required no less, if we were to proceed as a collective.

Eventually, the pain of so much of the testimony became perilously keen and threatened to immobilize/demoralize all participants. At this point, I tried to invent a route to power: I asked students to conduct research into the status of children in California, and in other parts of the U.S.A. I asked them to organize their findings and then integrate their individual lives, as children, into the big picture of children's needs unmet, in our America. This they did with fantastic, evangelical energy and competence, both.

I contacted KPFA, and was able to arrange for an hour-long broadcast of student-researched/student-composed/student-performed script. So successful was this event that KPFA re-broadcast this offering and Pacifica National Radio put the show on nationwide satellite. In addition, calls and letters to the students came pouring in from people working with abused children: child advocates, moved by the power of the students' knowledge and purposes. And, at the end, a new organization advocating children's rights was formed, with University of California at Berkeley students of the class, "The Politics of Childhood," at its helm.

As a teacher I was learning how not to hate school: how to overcome the fixed, predetermined, graveyard nature of so much formal education: come and be buried here among these other (allegedly) honorable dead.

For my next semester, I undertook the presentation of Contemporary Women's Poetry and African American Poetry. Again, student writings occupied equal space and time, along with James Weldon Johnson or Adrienne Rich, for example. But, still, there seemed to be something inherently backwards and/or inert to our studies. At last, I realized it would be logical, and terrific, to publish the students' poetry in their own anthologies. We would distribute these books at public student readings organized and publicized with at least as much care and determination as we might give to a campus appearance by a visiting Hot Shot Poet.

And so, "Poetry November" was born. In this month, African American Poetry students and Contemporary Women's Poetry students would, separately, present their poems on campus. Their anthologies would be given to the audience. And their readings would receive press and radio and flyer publicity altogether commensurate to the publicity we would muster for the two visiting poets, Cornelius Eady and Sherley Anne Williams, we intended to invite.

To make all of this happen, I raised money: from the African American Studies Department to the Dean of Interdisciplinary Studies to the Department of English. And the students raised money from various student funding sources. Suddenly a huge beehive of multifaceted activity exploded into life: Poetry November was on its way!

We were listed with the *San Francisco Chronicle* Pink Pages, *Poetry Flash*, *The Daily Californian*, and the students and myself went on the air on KPFA and KQED, and, it seemed, things would come together.

Then we decided to have a reception of food and beverages and flowers after each reading. African American Poetry students would buy the food and set-up the reception and host everything for the Contemporary Women's Poetry reading. And vice-versa. As a result of this exchange plan, students met in myriad committee and errand gang activities and became allies and friends across pretty important former barriers. For example, I remember my happy shock when I saw a young White lesbian student and a young Black student, a nationalist young man, laughing and dancing around with a vacuum cleaner in the cleanup aftermath of a reception held in the English Department's lounge.

Each student reading was Standing Room Only. Ditto for the Hot Shot Poet's evening. In response to this response, and in recognition of the willingness of truly disparate students to work together, closely, when the factor of self-interest is clear (the common goal of a successful public poetry reading) I decided to try and vault beyond the demarcations of Women's Studies and African American Studies and, instead, offer something called "Poetry for the People."

This dream-reality began with my third semester at U.C. Berkeley. Students from Freshman to graduate students in their last year at Boalt Law School, men/women, African Americans, Asian Americans, Latino Americans, gay, lesbian, straight—everybody, The People—could take this course in poetry. Requirements stipulated common readings and discussion, obedience to a tyrannical set of guidelines that I composed, a hefty minimum number of acceptable poems to be written by each student, energetic help with publishing the anthology, raising monies for this objective, and participation in a public poetry reading that would include all of the tedious tasks attendant to publicity and a small reception, afterwards.

These requirements were met by the enthusiastic throng of students who came to Poetry for the People. As the Gulf War was then in progress, the students' anthology was called "Poetry for the People in A Time Of War." Various students gave interviews to the Bay Area Press and, again, appeared on KPFA and KQED, and so forth.

Towards the end of the previous semester I had conceived, organized, and directed a campus-wide "Teach-in" on the Persian Gulf War. Faculty colleagues of many disciplines, and student activists of several ideologies, and of every color and ethnicity and sexual persuasion fused their energies to create a very powerful day that was decently documented by local television, radio and press. Ours was, I might add, proudly, the first such "Teach-in" in the U.S.A.

The huge success of "Poetry November" and the Gulf War "Teach-in" transformed my expectations. Evidently, at last, I had become part of an academic community where you could love school because school did not have to be something apart from, or in denial of, your own life and the multifarious new lives of your heterogeneous students! School could become, in fact, a place where students learned about the world and then resolved, collectively and creatively, to change it!

At the conclusion of the third semester, a core of young poets wanted to make Poetry for the People a way of life. And we discussed what to do next. I decided to try and institute a course called "The Teaching and Writing of Poetry." Interested students would work closely with me and then they, in turn, would become student teachers of other students. This was something we implemented with reasonable success.

Publication of the students' work, plus presentation of the students in a public reading, of course, continued to be fundamental attributes of both the Teaching and Writing of Poetry course and (its related) Poetry for the People. Again, the diversity of my students compelled a diversity of syllabus materials that I began to find mind-boggling. And, again, students collaborated together and became friends across every possible, previous barrier of distinction. I was pretty happy!

We, Poetry for the People, brought Adrienne Rich and Thulani Davis to the University of California at Berkeley, and later, Ntozake Shange, as well. We filled Wheeler Auditorium and, again, student readings were, themselves, S.R.O.

And with the sturdy expansion of our program, it did/does seem that there really are ways to change school so that you can get out of it more alive than dead!

If you value what students can teach to each other and to you,

If you spend at least half of your energies trying to connect students with the world on important, risky, levels of exchange and collaboration,

If you delete taglines like "multi-cultural" or "gender" or "sexual preference" from your brain and, instead, look to see who are the students you hope to interest, inform, include, and enlighten—through the literature you assign as well as through the sharing of the new American writings you will invite and enable them to create,

If you dream and scheme about the self-evident, as well as the potential, reasons why public performance, publication, and media appearances are natural and necessary steps to the acquirement of power through language,

Then: You will probably find yourself launched on an unpredictable, nerve-racking, and marvelous adventure in democracy and education!

But! Why should power and language coalesce in poetry? Because poetry is the medium for telling the truth, and because a poem is antithetical to lies/evasions and superficiality, anyone who becomes a practicing poet has an excellent chance of becoming somebody real, somebody known, self-defined, and attuned to and listening and hungering for kindred real voices utterly/articulately different from his or her own voice.

This outward and inward attunement seems to me a most reasonable basis for the political beginning of a beloved community: a democratic state in which the people can trust the names they have invented for themselves and for each other. It is this trustworthy use of words that poetry requires, and inspires. It is this highest ideal of trustworthy intersection among differing peoples that poetry can realize: POETRY FOR THE PEOPLE!

DEAR JUNE, DEAR ADRIENNE

WITH ADRIENNE RICH
(1996)

[June Jordan and Adrienne Rich met in the late 1960s at City College, teaching in the SEEK program. They bonded fast, and regularly frequented their favorite Indian restaurant on the Upper West Side to talk poetry, teaching, politics, motherhood (by 1970, Rich had also become a single mother). In the early 1980s, there was a painful rift. Just as Rich was re-claiming her Jewish identity in poems like "Sources," Israel invaded Lebanon. Jordan, unaware that Rich had ever identified herself as Jewish, was shocked by the timing. "To me it would be like if Idi Amin was rampaging, as he did, and until then I had never identified myself as black." They didn't speak for three years, but reconciled; their friendship resumed and deepened. Jordan admired Rich's "startling honesty" and "brilliance of articulation" in dealing with issues of racism, the relations between men and women, and the struggles and contradictions in her own life. Rich said, "Without denying our cruel separations, Jordan went for human commonality, the opportunities for beholding and being seen by one another" and called her "one of the most musically and lyrically gifted poets of the late twentieth century." In early June 1996, they both promised to write a letter in the form of poem to one another every day. They faxed to each other, Jordan's texts written in her hand. This particular form of correspondence did not last long, but it did produce an unforgettable poetic conversation. In "Dear June, Dear Adrienne," the two writers rededicated themselves to the love that is "a summoning forever / immanent"; what Jordan called "the lens / to magnify / ignite / redeem / and willingly defy" those who "jeopardize the birdsong of our days."]

◆◆◆

6.1.96

June—

       it's the first of June
         the light is powerful
the Pacific out there
       giving back
         light for light
My heart feels sick
       not broken
         I promise you
but sick
       the Muse of Despair
         seems to have moved
next door
       sidelong I watch her
         watering snail-bitten plants
on her desolate porch
       the word is
         she's an artist
June, I don't want
       to go meet her
         look through her stacks
of self-portraits with closed eyes
       her lifework
         of repetitions

To feel equal
       To the task at hand

That is happiness
Simple—the task itself
always unfolding
and the belief
the means
unfolding too
because we could hear each other
Many others

What does not change/ is the will to change
Olson's line: I thought
he meant poetry, yes
but everything
So we tried to change
ourselves
believing we would live
to see a time we
had to get ready for

Not the most urgent letters even
will be delivered now
it's said
sensational and passionless
messages will get clicked from
screen to screen
nothing handwritten will
get through
I'm writing you
this urgent letter

anyway, by hand
to promise you
to be sick at heart is not
to have resigned
or broken faith

I'm calling in
        on your pirate station
          your talkshow of the spirits
to tell you this
        and please, dear June, write soon

But Adrienne
did we get ready
did we
prepare ourselves
beyond the family table
figuring
an honorable route   to conversations
with the stuffed
rapacious overlords
who eat
the territory   of the   breast
and then the breast?

Did we suppose
invisible might somebody mean
maquiladores
not
the golden limning
of the letters
of the poet
Reverent regardless
as she wakens the night
with words

we did what we knew how
which
leveraging the market
loading up an AK-48
will not now

or ever
fit into

And honorable remains
a neighborhood deserted
by imaginations of your Muse
and mine

(what would it mean
to talk with murder
or
to dialog with avarice
insensible
to everything beyond the needs
of greed?)

And so the conversation
of this work
persists between us
still
No widening of the circle
to include
known lunatics
or borderline
communities of mob
or merciful components   meaning critical
mass means critical
energy to pass   beyond
alternatives
beyond your dearest wish
or any of my own
and
What's wrong with that?

That we will write
and hold together

hand to hand
a full moon
lost or captured by the tides
of changing waters
seems tonight
so clear to me
dear Adrienne
a "giving back"
of "light for light"
that we live
meant
to do

    and then renew

◆◆◆

6.2.96

dear June
  did we get ready
    for a time
when public intellectuals
  movement celebrities
    of every color
and any gender
would spin the wheels of rhetoric
  in villas on Italian lakes
    while heart-
sick teachers would hang on in
  desolation's classroom
and student might-have-beens
  get stripsearched on the street
bull-rushed and hogtied
  disappeared into
sealed Lexan cells embedded in
  concrete Did we
imagine such dead-ends
  or such refined

luxury cruises of dissent
        did we
prepare an offshore art
        and are its signals strong enough?

Oh, Adrienne!

Perhaps not
on enough
or in
the water hurtling
envelopes of neutral
force
(did we believe neutrality?)
for those who welcome risk
mixed with the test
of body
surfing
obligations

Yes
we stay home

our gardens of dry land
luxuriate
and bloom domestic

but could we know about
a different history
of our heroes
running
horseback
immolated
shot
a history of Tolstoi

setting out the garbage
or Neruda
worrying about his hair
or de Beauvoir
paying the bills
or Sor Juana
worrying about what to wear?

And least
you and I
do not deny
the promise of minutiae

The daily faith of fools
who turn the lights on
without fail

we could do worse
(and many boast about the worst that they have done)

but our tormented
reaching for the task
not yet begun

well it's a torment
sacred
in its visceral
and glancing
aggravation

Don't you think?

◆◆◆

6.3.96

June, long ago

you wrote,
Where is the love?
and we have watched
the fakeries of hate
and mere compliance
coldblood
colonize
a language germinated
from wild spirit's
wildest hopes
Neruda, yes
Freire and Fanon
and, yes
Sor Juana   Mrs. Hamer
and Whitman whom we fought about
you saying
he was unrecognized
I arguing
"he's in the *canon!*"
(June, you were right...
canonization too
can be a burial)
Where is the love?
What has been taken
To the heart
and given back?
Who recognized
as in
handwriting so explicit

even a scrap of paper is
still and suddenly
dangerous and dear?
Where is the love
the lens
to magnify

—now—these minutiae?

◆◆◆

6.3.96-6.4.96

Dear Adrienne

But love was never more
than what Elijah
listened to
> **That small**
> **that still**

a summoning forever
immanent
regardless of its wavelength
pitted against tyrannies
gigantic
in a kitchen
or some other battlefield
> **computer rituals of *quit***
> **or *cancel***
> **or the friend who lies**

It is often—like the calling
of the psychopath
"a clean cut kid"—
that we mistake
the madness of the trickster
demon
for our own
or
minimize the meaning
of these words on open
opening

space

inside this cartoon
context
where it's normal
to approach a wall
for money

this then
is the lens
to magnify
ignite
redeem
and willingly defy
the maggots eager
for that moment when
our spirits die
and dying
deify the fearsome
meretricious
killer agencies
that jeopardize
the birdsong of our days

Oh, Adrienne!
This is that love

        It's here
        Between us

              growing

"WE ARE THE ONES WE HAVE BEEN WAITING FOR"

FROM *PASSION: NEW POEMS 1977-1980* (1980)
& FROM *CIVIL WARS: OBSERVATIONS FROM THE FRONT LINES OF AMERICA*
(1981)

FROM *PASSION: NEW POEMS: 1977-1980*

(1980)

[Dedicated to "everyone as scared as I used to be," Jordan's *Passion* is a landmark work. The 1970s were an exciting time for women writers who were breaking through to a new freedom and revelation in their work. Equally exciting was the recovery of lost or suppressed careers—of women writers whose work had fallen out of print, out of fashion, or had been relegated to diminished status by condescending critics. Alice Walker initiated a deep search into Zora Neale Hurston's fate and legacy with her essay "Looking for Zora" (1975) and her Hurston Reader *I Love Myself When I Am Laughing ...* (1979); Adrienne Rich's 1976 essay "Vesuvius at Home" transformed the image of Emily Dickinson as eccentric recluse into a persuasive portrait of an American genius well aware of her powers; H.D.'s extraordinary war-time *Trilogy* of the 1940s, long out of print, re-appeared in its entirety; Muriel Rukeyser was re-found and rightfully celebrated for her more than thirty years of pioneering poetry, genre-defying prose, and political activism. Jordan's 1980 contribution was just as revolutionary.

Passion begins with an essay (Jordan calls it a "preface") that celebrates "the great white father" Walt Whitman as the progenitor of the urgent, exciting new poetry being written by "New World poets"— a poetry "as personal, as public, as irresistible, as quick, as necessary, as unprecedented, as representative, as exalted, as speakably commonplace, and as musical, as an emergency phone call." Jordan heard those emergency phone calls in the voices of Black and Third World poets, women poets, self-publishing and small press poets, gay and lesbian and bisexual poets who were singing a new America and a new world.

Her Whitman essay and the poems of *Passion* are of one piece. The poems—these things that she does in the dark—take on every kind of violence practiced against human beings, both tragic and everyday. They praise ancestors like Sojourner Truth; entice a lover, whose lips are "luminous announcements" under a moonlit sky; chronicle the intricacies of friendship, love, parenting, quiet reflection, and righteous indignation. *Passion* is a tour-de-force of tenderness and provocation. With an unerring use of language, from street slang to sonnets, as the vehicle for both morality and imagination. (As Angela Davis has written, Jordan's "lifelong devotion to justice, equality, and radical democracy seemed to revolve around the pleasure she felt in hurling beautiful words at a world full of racism, poverty, homophobia, and inane politicians determined to preserve this awful state of affairs.") *Passion* includes many of Jordan's best-known, most frequently reprinted poems, including "Case in Point," "Letter to the Local Police,"

"Poem about Police Violence," "Poem about My Rights." Even Barack Obama, in his 2008 presidential campaign, used *Passion* as a source, when he declared, "we are the ones we have been waiting for"; the line comes from Jordan's "Poem for South African Women."]

♦♦♦

"FOR THE SAKE OF A PEOPLE'S POETRY: WALT WHITMAN AND THE REST OF US"

In America, the father is white; it is he who inaugurated the experiment of this republic. It is he who sailed his way into slave ownership and who availed himself of my mother—that African woman whose function was miserable—defined by his desirings, or his rage. It is he who continues to dominate the destiny of the Mississippi River, the Blue Ridge Mountains, and the life of my son. Understandably, then, I am curious about this man.

Most of the time my interest can be characterized as wary, at best. Other times, it is the interest a pedestrian feels for the fast traveling truck about to smash into him. Or her. Again. And at other times it is the curiosity of a stranger trying to figure out the system of the language that excludes her name and all of the names of all of her people. It is this last that leads me to the poet Walt Whitman. Trying to understand the system responsible for every boring, inaccessible, irrelevant, derivative and pretentious poem that is glued to the marrow of required readings in American classrooms, or trying to understand the system responsible for the exclusion of every hilarious, amazing, visionary, pertinent and unforgettable poet from National Endowment of the Arts grants and from national publications, I come back to Walt Whitman.

What in the hell happened to him? Wasn't he a white man? Wasn't he some kind of a father to American literature? Didn't he talk about this New World? Didn't he see it? Didn't he sing this New World, this America, on a New World, an American scale of his own visionary invention?

It so happens that Walt Whitman is the one white father who shares the systematic disadvantages of his heterogeneous offspring trapped inside a closet that is, in reality, as huge as the continental spread of North and South America. What Whitman envisioned, we, the people and the poets of the New World, embody. He has been punished for the moral questions that our very lives arouse.

At home as a child, I learned the poetry of the Bible and the poetry of Paul Laurence Dunbar. As a student, I diligently followed orthodox directions from *The Canterbury Tales* right through *The Wasteland* by that consummate Anglophile whose name I can never remember. And I kept waiting. It was, I thought, all right to deal with daffodils in the 17th century of an island as much like Manhattan as I resemble Queen Mary. But what about Dunbar? When was he coming up again? And where were the Black poets, altogether? And who were the women poets I might reasonably emulate? And wasn't there, ever, a great poet who was crazy about Brooklyn or furious about war? And I kept waiting. And I kept writing my own poetry. And I kept reading apparently underground poetry: poetry kept strictly off campus. I kept reading the poetry of so many gifted students when I became a teacher. I kept listening to the wonderful poetry of the multiplying numbers of my friends who were and who are New World poets until I knew, for a fact, that there was and that there is an American, a New World poetry that is as personal, as public, as irresistible, as quick, as necessary, as unprecedented, as representative, as exalted, as speakably commonplace, and as musical as an emergency phone call.

But I didn't know about Walt Whitman. Yes, I had heard about this bohemian, this homosexual, even, who wrote something about The Captain and The Lilacs in The Hallway, but nobody ever told me to read his work! Not only was Whitman not required reading, he was, on the contrary, presented as a rather hairy buffoon suffering from a childish proclivity for exercise and open air.

Nevertheless, it is through the study of the poems and the ideas of this particular white father that I have reached a tactical, if not strategic, understanding of the racist, sexist, and anti-American predicament that condemns most New World writing to peripheral/unpublished manuscript status.

Before these United States came into being, the great poets of the world earned their lustre through undeniable forms of spontaneous popularity; generations of a people chose to memorize and then to further elaborate these songs and to impart them to the next generation. I am talking about people; African families and Greek families and the families of the Hebrew tribes and all that multitude to whom the Bhagavad-Gita is as daily as the sun! If these poems were not always religious, they were certainly moral in notice, or in accomplishment, or both. None of these great poems would be mistaken for the poetry of another country, another time. You do not find a single helicopter taking off or landing in any of the sonnets of Elizabethan England, nor do you run across rice and peas in any of the psalms! Evidently, one criterion for great poetry used to be the requirements of cultural nationalism.

But by the advent of the thirty-six year old poet, Walt Whitman, the phenomenon of a people's poetry, or great poetry and its spontaneous popularity, could no longer be assumed. The physical immensity and the farflung population of this New World decisively separated poets from suitable means to produce and distribute their poetry. Now there would have to be intermediaries—critics and publishers—whose marketplace principles of scarcity would, logically, oppose them to populist traditions of art.

Old World concepts would replace the democratic and these elitist notions would prevail; in the context of such considerations, an American literary establishment antithetical to the New World meanings of America took root. And this is one reason why the pre-eminently American white father of American poetry exists primarily in the realm of caricature and rumor in his own country.

As a matter of fact, if you hope to hear about Whitman your best bet is to leave home. Ignore prevailing American criticism and, instead, ask anybody anywhere else in the world this question: As Shakespeare is to England, Dante to Italy, Tolstoy to Russia, Goethe to Germany, Aghostino Neto to Angola, Pablo Neruda to Chile, Mao-Tse-Tung to China, and Ho Chi Minh to Vietnam, who is the great American writer, the distinctively American poet, the giant American "literatus?" Undoubtedly, the answer will be *Walt Whitman*.

He is the poet who wrote:

A man's body at auction
(For before the war I often go to the slave-mart and watch the sale.)
I help the auctioneer, the sloven does not half know his business. . .
Gentlemen look on this wonder.
Whatever the bids of the bidders they cannot be high enough for it.

from "I Sing the Body Electric," by Walt Whitman

I ask you, today: Who in the United States would publish those lines? They are all wrong! In the first place there is nothing obscure, nothing contrived, nothing an ordinary strap-hanger in the subway would be puzzled by! In the second place, the voice of those lines is intimate and direct, at once; it is the voice of the poet who assumes that he speaks to an equal and that he need not fear that equality. On the contrary, the intimate distance between the poet and the reader is a distance that assumes there is everything important, between them, to be shared. And what is poetic about a line of words that runs as long as a regular, a spoken idea? You could more easily imagine an actual human being speaking such lines than you could imagine an artist composing them in a room carefully separated from the real life of his family. This can't be poetry! Besides, these lines apparently serve an expressly moral purpose! Then is this didactic/political writing? Aha! This cannot be *good* poetry. And, in fact, you will never see, for example, *The New Yorker* Magazine publishing a poem marked by such splendid deficiencies.

Consider the inevitable, the irresistible, simplicity of that enormous moral idea:

Gentlemen look on this wonder.
Whatever the bids of the bidders they cannot be high enough for it .
. .
This is not only one man, this the father of those who shall be fathers in their turns
In him the start of populous states and rich republics, Of him count-

less immortal lives with countless embodiments and enjoyments

from "I Sing the Body Electric," by Walt Whitman

Crucial and obviously important and, hence, this is not an idea generally broadcast: the poet is trying to save a human being while even the *poem* cannot be saved from the insolence of marketplace evaluation!

Indeed Whitman and the traceable descendants of Walt Whitman, those who follow his democratic faith into obviously New World forms of experience and art, they suffer from establishment rejection and contempt the same as forced this archetypal American genius to publish, distribute, and review his own work, by himself. The descendants I have in mind include those unmistakably contemporaneous young poets who base themselves upon domesticities such as disco, Las Vegas, MacDonald's, and $40 running shoes. Also within the Whitman tradition, Black and First World*[7] poets traceably transform and further the egalitarian sensibility that isolates that one white father from his more powerful compatriots. I am thinking of the feminist poets evidently intent upon speaking with a maximal number and diversity of other Americans' lives. I am thinking of all the many first rank heroes of the New World who are overwhelmingly forced to publish their own works using a hand press, or whatever, or else give it up entirely.

That is to say, the only peoples who can test or verify the meaning of the United States as a democratic state, as a pluralistic culture, these are the very peoples whose contribution to a national vision and discovery meets with steadfast ridicule and disregard.

A democratic state does not, after all, exist for the few, but for the many. A democratic state is not proven by the welfare of the strong but by the welfare of the weak. And unless that many, that manifold constitution of diverse peoples can be seen as integral to the national art/the national consciousness, you might as well mean

---

7   Given that they were first to exist on the planet and currently make up the majority, the author will refer to that part of the population usually termed Third World as the First World. [The footnotes in this essay are Jordan's.]

only Czechoslovakia when you talk about the USA, or only Ireland, or merely France, or exclusively white men.

Pablo Neruda is a New World poet whose fate differs from the other Whitman descendants because he was born into a country where the majority of the citizens did not mistake themselves for Englishmen or long to find themselves struggling, at most, with cucumber sandwiches and tea. He was never European. His anguish was not aroused by thee piece suits and rolled umbrellas. When he cries, towards the conclusion of *The Heights of Machu Picchu*, "Arise and birth with me, my brother,"[8] he plainly does not allude to Lord or Colonel Anybody At All. As he writes earlier, in that amazing poem:

> I came by another way, river by river, street after street,
> city by city, one bed and another,
> forcing the salt of my mask through a wilderness;
> and there, in the shame of the ultimate hovels, lampless
> and tireless,
> lacking bread or a stone or a stillness, alone in myself,
> I whirled at my will, dying the death that was mine

from *The Heights of Macho Picchu*,
translated by Ben Bolitt, Evergreen Press

Of course Neruda has not escaped all of the untoward consequences common to Whitman descendants. American critics and translators never weary of asserting that Neruda is a quote great unquote poet *despite* the political commitment of his art and despite the artistic consequences of the commitment. Specifically, Neruda's self-conscious decision to write in a manner readily comprehensible to the masses of his countrymen, and his self-conscious decision to specify, outright, the United Fruit Company when that was the instigating subject of his poem, become unfortunate moments in an otherwise supposedly sublime, not to mention surrealist, deeply Old

---

8   from Section XII of The Heights of Macho Picchu, translated by Nathaniel Tarn, Farrar Straus and Giroux: New York

World and European but nonetheless Chilean case history. To assure the validity of this perspective, the usual American critic and translator presents you with a smattering of the unfortunate, ostensibly political poetry and, on the other hand, buries you under volumes of Neruda's early work that antedates the Spanish Civil War or, in other words, that antedates Neruda's serious conversion to a political world view.

This kind of artistically indefensible censorship would have you perceive qualitative and even irreconcilable differences between the poet who wrote:

> You, my antagonist, in that splintering dream
> like the bristling glass of gardens, like a menace of ruinous bells,
> volleys
> of blackening ivy at the perfume's center,
> enemy of the great hipbones my skin has touched
> with a harrowing dew

> from "Woes and the Furies," by Pablo
> Neruda in *Selected Poems of Neruda*,
> (translated by Ben Bolitt, p. 101)

And the poet who wrote, some twenty years later, these lines from the poem entitled "The Dictators":

> Lament was perpetual and fell, like a plant and its pollen,
> forcing a lightless increase in the blinded, big leaves
> And bludgeon by bludgeon, on the terrible waters,
> scale over scale in the bog,
> the snout filled with silence and slime
> and vendetta was born

> from "The Dictators," by Pablo
> Neruda in *Selected Poems of Neruda*,
> (translated by Ben Bolitt, p. 161)

According to prevalent American criticism, that later poem of Neruda represents a lesser achievement precisely because it can be understood by more people, more easily, than the first. It is also derogated because this poem attacks a keystone of the Old World, namely dictatorship or, in other words, power and privilege for the few.

The peculiar North American vendetta against Walt Whitman, against the first son of this democratic union, can be further fathomed if you look at some facts: Neruda's eminence is now acknowledged on international levels; it is known to encompass profound impact upon North American poets who do not realize the North American/Walt Whitman origins for so much that is singular and worthy in the poetry of Neruda. You will even find American critics who congratulate Neruda for overcoming the "Whitmanesque" content of his art. This perfidious arrogance is as calculated as it is common. You cannot persuade anyone seriously familiar with Neruda's life and art that he could have found cause, at any point, to disagree with the tenets, the analysis and the authentic New World vision presented by Walt Whitman in his essay, *Democratic Vistas*, which remains the most signal and persuasive manifesto of New World thinking and belief in print.

Let me define my terms, in brief: New World does not mean New England. New World means non-European; it means new; it means big; it means heterogeneous; it means unknown; it means free; it means an end to feudalism, caste, privilege, and the violence of power. It means *wild* in the sense that a tree growing away from the earth enacts a wild event. It means *democratic* in the sense that, as Whitman wrote:

> I believe a leaf of grass is no less than
> the journey-work of the stars. . .
> And a mouse is miracle enough to stagger
> sextillions of infidels

> from "Song of Myself"

New World means that, as Whitman wrote, "I keep as delicate

around the bowels as around the head and heart." New World means, as Whitman said, "By God! I will accept nothing which all cannot have their counterpart of on the same terms."

In *Democratic Vistas*, Whitman declared,

> As the greatest lessons of Nature through the universe are perhaps the lessons of variety and freedom, the same present the greatest lessons also in New World politics and progress . . . Sole among nationalities, these States have assumed the task to put in forms of history, power and practicality, on areas of amplitude rivaling the operations of the physical kosmos, the moral political speculations of ages, long, long deffer'd, the democratic republican principle, and the theory of development and perfection by voluntary standards and self-reliance.

Listen to this white father; he is so weird! Here he is calling aloud for an American, a democratic spirit. An American, a democratic idea that could morally constrain and coordinate the material body of USA affluence and piratical outreach, more than a hundred years ago he wrote,

> The great poems, Shakespeare included, are poisonous to the idea of the pride and dignity of the common people, the lifeblood of democracy. The models of our literature, as we get it from other lands, ultra marine, have had their birth in courts, and bask'd and grown in castle sunshine; all smells of princes' favors ... Do you call those genteel little creatures American poets? Do you term that perpetual, pistareen, paste-pot work, American art, American drama, taste, verse? ... We see the sons and daughters of The New World, ignorant of its genius, not yet inaugurating the native, the universal, and the near, still importing the distant, the partial, the dead.

Abhorring the "thin sentiment of parlors, parasols, piano-song, tinkling rhymes," Whitman conjured up a poetry of America, a poetry of democracy which would not "mean the smooth walks, trimm'd hedges, poseys and nightingales of the English poets, but the whole orb, with its geologic history, the Kosmos, carrying fire and snow that rolls through the illimitable areas, light as a feather, though weighing billions of tons."

Well, what happened?

Whitman went ahead and wrote the poetry demanded by his vision. He became, by thousands upon thousands of words, a great American poet:

There was a child went forth every day,
And the first object he look'd upon, that object he became,
And that object became part of him for the day
Or a certain part of the day,
Or for many years or stretching cycles of years
The early lilacs became part of this child,
And grass and white and red morning-glories,
and white and red clover, and the song of the phoebe-bird. . .

from "There was a Child Went Forth"

And, elsewhere, he wrote:

It avails not, time nor place—distance avails not,
I am with you, you men and women of a generation,
or ever some many generations hence,
Just as you feel when you look on the river and sky,
so I felt,
Just as any of you is one of a living crowd, I was one of a crowd,
Just as you are refresh'd by the gladness of the river
and the bright flow, I was refresh'd,
Just as you stand and lean on the rail, yet
hurry with the swift current, I stood yet was hurried,
Just as you look on the numberless masts of ships and the
thick-stemm'd pipes of steamboats,
I look'd. . .

from "Crossing Brooklyn Ferry"

This great American poet of democracy as cosmos, this poet of a continent as consciousness, this poet of the many people as one people, this poet of diction comprehensible to all, of a vision insisting on each, of a rhythm/a rhetorical momentum to transport the reader from the Brooklyn ferry into the hills of Alabama and back again, of line after line of bodily, concrete detail that constitutes the mysterious the cellular tissue of a nation indivisible but dependent upon and astonishing in its diversity, this white father of a great poetry deprived of its spontaneous popularity/a great poetry hidden away from the ordinary people it celebrates so well, he has been, again and again, cast aside as an undisciplined poseur, a merely freak eruption of prolix perversities.

Last year, the *New York Times Book Review* saw fit to import a European self-appointed critic of American literature to address the question: Is there a great American poet? Since this visitor was ignorant of the philosophy and the achievements of Walt Whitman, the visitor, Denis Donoghue, comfortably excluded every possible descendent of Whitman from his erstwhile cerebrations. Only one woman was mentioned (she, needless to add, did not qualify). No poets under fifty, and not one Black or First World poet received even cursory assessment. Not one poet of distinctively New World values, and their formal embodiment, managed to dent the suavity of Donoghue's public display.

This *New York Times* event perpetuated American habits of beggarly, absurd deference to the Old World. And these habits bespeak more than marketplace intrusions into cultural realms. We erase ourselves through self-hatred. We lend our silence to the American anti-American process whereby anything and anyone special to this nation state becomes liable to condemnation because it is what it is, truly.

Against self-hatred there is Whitman and there are all of the New World poets who insistently devise legitimate varieties of cultural nationalism. There is Whitman and all of the poets whose lives have been baptized by witness to blood, by witness to cataclysmic, political confrontations from the Civil War through the Civil Rights Era, through the Women's Movement, and on and on through the conflicts between the hungry and the well-fed, the wasteful, the bullies.

In the poetry of the New World, you meet with a reverence for the material world that begins with a reverence for human life. There is an intellectual trust in sensuality as a means of knowledge, an easily deciphered system of reference, aspirations to a believable, collective voice and, consequently, emphatic preference for broadly accessible, spoken language. Deliberately balancing perception with vision, it seeks to match moral exhortation with sensory report.

All of the traceable descendants of Whitman have met with an establishment, academic reception disgracefully identical; except for the New World poets who live and write beyond the boundaries of the USA, the offspring of this one white father encounter everlasting marketplace disparagement as crude or optional or simplistic or, as Whitman himself wrote "hankering, gross, mystical, nude."

I too am a descendant of Walt Whitman. And I am not by myself struggling to tell the truth about this history of so much land and so much blood, of so much that should be sacred and so much that has been desecrated and annihilated boastfully.

My brothers and my sisters of this New World, we remember that, as Whitman said,

> I do not trouble my spirit to vindicate
> itself or be understood,
> I see that the elementary laws never apologize

from "Song of Myself"

We do not apologize that we are not Emily Dickinson, Ezra Pound, T.S. Eliot, Wallace Stevens, Robert Lowell, and Elizabeth Bishop. Or, as Whitman exclaimed, "I exist as I am, that is enough."

New World poetry moves into and beyond the lives of Walt Whitman, Pablo Neruda, Aghostino Neto, Gabriela Mistral, Langston Hughes, and Margaret Walker. I follow this movement with my own life. I am calm and smiling as we go. Is it not written, somewhere very near to me:

A man's body at auction . . .
Gentlemen look on this wonder.
Whatever the bids of the bidders
they cannot be high enough for it . . .

And didn't that weird white father predict this truth that is always
growing:

I swear to you the architects shall appear without fail,
I swear to you they will understand you and justify you,
The greatest among them shall be he who best knows you
and encloses all and is faithful to all,
He and rest shall not forget you, they shall
perceive that you are not an iota less than they,
You shall be fully glorified in them

from "Song of the Rolling Earth"

Walt Whitman and all of the New World poets coming after him, we,
too, go on singing this America.

◆◆◆

POEM FOR NANA

What will we do
when there is nobody left
to kill?

*

40,000 gallons of oil gushing into
the ocean
But I
sit on top this mountainside above
the Pacific
checking out the flowers
the California poppies orange

as I meet myself in heat
                                   I'm wondering
where's the Indians?

            all this filmstrip territory
            all this cowboy sagaland:
            not
            a single Indian
            in sight

40,000 gallons gushing up poison
from the deepest seabeds
every hour

40,000 gallons
while
experts international
while
new pollutants
swallow the unfathomable
still:

        no Indians

I'm staring hard around me
past the pinks the poppies and the precipice
that let me see the wide Pacific
unsuspecting
even trivial
by virtue of its vast surrender

I am a woman searching for her savagery
even if it's doomed

Where are the Indians?

                    *

Crow Nose
Little Bear
Slim Girl
Black Elk
Fox Belly

the people of the sacred trees
and rivers precious to the stars that told
old stories to the night

how do we follow after you?

falling
snow before the firelight
and buffalo as brothers
to the man

how do we follow into that?

                                *

They found her facedown
where she would be dancing
to the shadow drums that humble
birds to silent
      flight

They found her body held
its life dispelled
by ice
my life burns to destroy

Anna Mae Pictou Aquash
slain on The Trail of Broken Treaties
bullet lodged in her brain/hands
and fingertips
dismembered

who won the only peace
that cannot pass
from mouth to mouth

*

Memory should agitate
the pierced bone crack
of one in pushed-back horror
pushed-back pain
as when I call out looking for my face
among the wounded coins
to toss about
or out
entirely
the legends of Geronimo
of Pocahontas
now become a squat
pedestrian cement inside the tomb
of all my trust

as when I feel you isolate
among the hungers of the trees
a trembling
hidden tinder so long unsolicited
by flame

as when I accept my sister dead
when there should be
a fluid holiness
of spirits wrapped around the world
redeemed by women
whispering communion

*

I find my way by following your spine

Your heart indivisible from my real wish
we

compelled the moon into the evening when
you said, "No,
I will not let go
of your hand."

*

Now I am diving for a tide to take me everywhere

Below
the soft Pacific spoils
a purple girdling of the globe
impregnable

*

Last year the South African Minister of Justice
described Anti-Government Disturbances as
Part of a Worldwide Trend toward the
Breakdown of Established Political and Cultural
Orders

*

God knows I hope he's right.

◆◆◆

CASE IN POINT

A friend of mine who raised six daughters and
who never wrote what she regards as serious
until she
was fifty-three
tells me there is no silence peculiar
to the female

I have decided I have something to say
about female silence: so to speak
these are my 2¢ on the subject:
2 weeks ago I was raped for the second
time in my life the first occasion

being a whiteman and the most recent
situation being a blackman actually
head of the local NAACP

Today is 2 weeks after the fact
of that man straddling
his knees either side of my chest
his hairy arm and powerful left hand
forcing my arms and my hands over my head
flat to the pillow while he rammed
what he described as his quote big dick
unquote into my mouth
and shouted out: "D'ya want to swallow
my big dick; well, do ya?"

He was being rhetorical.
My silence was peculiar
to the female.

◆◆◆

LETTER TO THE LOCAL POLICE

Dear Sirs:

I have been enjoying the law and order of our
community throughout the past three months since
my wife and I, our two cats, and miscellaneous
photographs of the six grandchildren belonging to
our previous neighbors (with whom we were very
close) arrived in Saratoga Springs which is clearly
prospering under your custody

Indeed, until yesterday afternoon and despite my
vigilant casting about, I have been unable to discover
a single instance of reasons for public-spirited concern,

much less complaint

You may easily appreciate, then, how it is that
I write to your office, at this date, with utmost
regret for the lamentable circumstances that force
my hand

Speaking directly to the issue of the moment:

I have encountered a regular profusion of certain
unidentified roses, growing to no discernible purpose,
and according to no perceptible control, approximately
one quarter mile west of the Northway, on the southern
side

To be specific, there are practically thousands of
the aforementioned abiding in perpetual near riot
of wild behavior, indiscriminate coloring, and only
the Good Lord Himself can say what diverse soliciting
of promiscuous cross-fertilization

As I say, these roses, no matter what the apparent
background, training, tropistic tendencies, age,
or color, do not demonstrate the least inclination
toward categorization, specified allegiance, resolute
preference, consideration of the needs of others, or
any other minimal traits of decency

May I point out that I did not assiduously seek out
this colony, as it were, and that these certain
unidentified roses remain open to viewing even by
children, with or without suitable supervision

(My wife asks me to append a note as regards the
seasonal but nevertheless seriously licentious
phenomenon of honeysuckle under the moon that one may

apprehend at the corner of Nelson and Main

However, I have recommended that she undertake direct
correspondence with you, as regards this: yet
another civic disturbance in our midst)

I am confident that you will devise and pursue
appropriate legal response to the roses in question
If I may aid your efforts in this respect, please
do not hesitate to call me into consultation

Respectfully yours,

◆◆◆

POEM ABOUT POLICE VIOLENCE

Tell me something
what you think would happen if
everytime they kill a black boy
then we kill a cop
everytime they kill a black man
then we kill a cop

you think the accident rate would lower
subsequently?

sometimes the feeling like amaze me baby
comes back to my mouth and I am quiet
like Olympian pools from the running the
mountainous snows under the sun

sometimes thinking about the 12th House of the Cosmos
or the way your ear ensnares the tip
of my tongue or signs that I have never seen
like DANGER WOMEN WORKING

I lose consciousness of ugly bestial rabid
and repetitive affront as when they tell me
18 cops in order to subdue one man
18 strangled him to death in the ensuing scuffle (don't
you idolize the diction of the powerful: *subdue* and
scuffle my oh my) and that the murder
that the killing of Arthur Miller on a Brooklyn
street was just a "justifiable accident" again
(again)

People been having accidents all over the globe
so long like that I reckon that the only
suitable insurance is a gun
I'm saying war is not to understand or rerun
war is to be fought and won

sometimes the feeling like amaze me baby
blots it out/the bestial but
not too often

tell me something
what you think would happen if
everytime they kill a black boy
then we kill a cop
everytime they kill a black man
then we kill a cop

you think the accident rate would lower
subsequently?

◆◆◆

A POEM ABOUT INTELLIGENCE FOR MY BROTHERS AND SISTERS

A few years back and they told me Black
means a hole where other folks
got brain/it was like the cells in the heads
of Black children was out to every hour on the hour naps
Scientists called the phenomenon the Notorious
Jensen Lapse, remember?
Anyway I was thinking
about how to devise
a test for the wise
like a Stanford-Binet
for the C.I.A.
you know?
Take Einstein
being the most the unquestionable the outstanding
the maximal mind of the century
right?
And I'm struggling against this lapse leftover
from my Black childhood to fathom why
anybody should say so:
E=mc squared?
I try that on this old lady live on my block:
She sweeping away Saturday night from the stoop
and mad as can be because some absolute
jackass have left a kingsize mattress where
she have to sweep around it stains and all she
don't want to know nothing about in the first place
"Mrs. Johnson!" I say, leaning on the gate
between us: "What you think about somebody come up
with an *E* equals *M C 2*?"
"How you doin," she answer me, sideways, like she don't
want to let on she know I ain'
combed my hair yet and here it is
Sunday morning but still I have the nerve

to be bothering serious work with these crazy
questions about
"E equals what you say again, dear?"
Then I tell her, "Well
also this same guy? I think
he was undisputed Father of the Atom Bomb!"
"That right." She mumbles or grumbles, not too politely
"And dint remember to wear socks when he put on
his shoes!" I add on (getting desperate)
at which point Mrs. Johnson take herself and her broom
a very big step down the stoop away from me
"And never did nothing for nobody in particular
lessen it was a committee
and
used to say, 'What time is it?'
and
you'd say, 'Six o'clock.'
and
he'd say, 'Day or night?'
and
and he never made nobody a cup a tea
in his whole brilliant life!
and
[my voice rises slightly]
and
he dint never boogie neither: never!"

"Well," say Mrs. Johnson, "Well, honey,
I do guess
that's genius for you."

◆◆◆

1977: POEM FOR MRS. FANNIE LOU HAMER

You used to say, "June?
Honey when you come down here you
supposed to stay with me. Where
else?"
Meanin home
against the beer the shotguns and the
point of view of whitemen don'
never see Black anybodies without
some violent itch start up.
                              The ones who
said, "No Nigga's Votin in This Town...
lessen it be feet first to the booth"
Then jailed you
beat you brutal
bloody/battered/beat
you blue beyond the feeling
of the terrible
And failed to stop you.

Only God could but He
wouldn't stop
you
fortress from self-
pity

Humble as a woman anywhere
I remember finding you inside the laundromat
in Ruleville

                    lion spine relaxed/hell
                    what's the point to courage
                    when you washin' clothes?

But that took courage

just to sit there/target
to the killers lookin
for your singin face
perspirey through the rinse
and spin

and later
you stood mighty in the door on James Street
loud callin:

"BULLETS OR NO BULLETS!
THE FOOD IS COOKED
AN' GETTING COLD!"

We ate
A family tremulous but fortified
by turnips/okra/handpicked
like the lilies

filled to the very living
full

one solid gospel
                    (*sanctified*)

one gospel
                    (*peace*)

one full Black lily
luminescent
in a homemade field

of love

◆◆◆

POEM FOR SOUTH AFRICAN WOMEN

Commemoration of the 40,000 women and children who, August 9, 1956, presented themselves in bodily protest against the "dompass" in the capital of apartheid. Presented at The United Nations, August 9, 1978.

Our own shadows disappear as the feet of thousands
by the tens of thousands pound the fallow land
into new dust that
rising like a marvelous pollen will be
fertile
even as the first woman whispering
imagination to the trees around her made
for righteous fruit
from such deliberate defense of life
as no other still
will claim inferior to any other safety
in the world

The whispers too they
intimate to the inmost ear of every spirit
now aroused they
carousing in ferocious affirmation
of all peaceable and loving amplitude
sound a certainly unbounded heat
from a baptismal smoke where yes
there will be fire

And the babies cease alarm as mothers
raising arms
and heart high as the stars so far unseen
nevertheless hurl into the universe
a moving force
irreversible as light years
traveling to the open

eye

And who will join this standing up
and the ones who stood without sweet company
will sing and sing
back into the mountains and
if necessary
even under the sea

we are the ones we have been waiting for

◆◆◆

NOTES ON THE PEANUT

For the Poet David Henderson

Hi there. My name is George
Washington
Carver.
If you will bear with me
for a few minutes I
will share with you
a few
of the 30,117 uses to which
the lowly peanut has been put
by me
since yesterday afternoon.
If you will look at my feet you will notice
my sensible shoelaces made from unadulterated
peanut leaf composition that is biodegradable
in the extreme.
To your left you can observe the lovely Renoir
masterpiece reproduction that I have cleverly
pieced together from several million peanut
shell chips painted painstakingly so as to

accurately represent the colors of the original!
Overhead you will spot a squadron of Peanut B-52
Bombers flying due west.
I would extend my hands to greet you
at this time
except for the fact that I am holding a reserve
supply of high energy dry roasted peanuts
guaranteed to accelerate protein assimilation
precisely documented by my pocket peanut calculator;

May I ask when did you last contemplate the relationship
between the expanding peanut products industry
and the development of post-Marxian economic theory
which (Let me emphasize) need not exclude moral attrition
of prepuberty
polymorphic
prehensible skills within the population age sectors
of 8 to 15?
I hope you will excuse me if I appear to be staring at you
through these functional yet high fashion and prescriptive
peanut contact lenses providing for the most
minute observation of your physical response to all of this
ultimately nutritional information.
Peanut butter peanut soap peanut margarine peanut
brick houses and house and field peanut *per se* well
illustrate the diversified
potential of this lowly leguminous plant
to which you may correctly refer
also
as the goober the pindar the groundnut
and ground pea/let me
interrupt to take your name down on my
pocket peanut writing pad complete with matching
peanut pencil that only 3 or 4
chewing motions of the jaws will sharpen
into pyrotechnical utility

and no sweat.
Please:
Speak right into the peanut!

Your name?

◆◆◆

ALLA THA'S ALL RIGHT, BUT

Somebody come and carry me into a seven-day kiss
I can' use no historic no national no family bliss
I need an absolutely one to one a seven-day kiss

I can read the daily papers
I can even make a speech
But the news is stuff that tapers
down to salt poured in the breach

I been scheming about my people I been scheming about sex
I been dreaming about Africa and nightmaring Oedipus the Rex
But what I need is quite specific
terrifying rough stuff and terrific

I need an absolutely one to one a seven-day kiss
I can' use no more historic no national no bona fide family bliss
Somebody come and carry me into a seven-day kiss
Somebody come on
Somebody come on and carry me
over there!

◆◆◆

EVIDENTLY LOOKING AT THE MOON REQUIRES A CLEAN PLACE TO STAND

The forest dwindling narrow and irregular
to darken out the starlight on the ground
where needle shadows
signify the moon a harsh
a horizontal blank that lays the land
implicit to the movement of your body
is
the moon

You'd think I was lying to you
if I described precisely
how
implicit to the feeling of your lips
are luminous announcements
of more mystery than Arizona
more than just the imperturbable
convictions
of the cow

headfirst into a philosophy
and

so sexy
chewing up the grass

◆◆◆

A SHORT NOTE TO MY VERY CRITICAL AND WELL-BELOVED FRIENDS AND COMRADES

First they said I was too light
Then they said I was too dark

Then they said I was too different
Then they said I was too much the same
Then they said I was too young
Then they said I was too old
Then they said I was too interracial
Then they said I was too much a nationalist
Then they said I was too silly
Then they said I was too angry
Then they said I was too idealistic
Then they said I was too confusing altogether:
Make up your mind! They said. Are you militant
or sweet? Are you vegetarian or meat? Are you straight
or are you gay?

And I said, Hey! It's not about *my* mind.

◆◆◆

POEM ABOUT MY RIGHTS

Even tonight and I need to take a walk and clear
my head about this poem about why I can't
go out without changing my clothes my shoes
my body posture my gender identity my age
my status as a woman alone in the evening/
alone on the streets/alone not being the point/
the point being that I can't do what I want
to do with my own body because I am the wrong
sex the wrong age the wrong skin and
suppose it was not here in the city but down on the beach/
or far into the woods and I wanted to go
there by myself thinking about God/or thinking
about children or thinking about the world/all of it
disclosed by the stars and the silence:
I could not go and I could not think and I could not
stay there

alone
as I need to be
alone because I can't do what I want to do with my own
body and
who in the hell set things up
like this
and in France they say if the guy penetrates
but does not ejaculate then he did not rape me
and if after stabbing him if after screams if
after begging the bastard and if even after smashing
a hammer to his head if even after that if he
and his buddies fuck me after that
then I consented and there was
no rape because finally you understand finally
they fucked me over because I was wrong I was
wrong again to be me being me where I was/wrong
to be who I am
which is exactly like South Africa
penetrating into Namibia penetrating into
Angola and does that mean I mean how do you know if
Pretoria ejaculates what will the evidence look like the
proof of the monster jackboot ejaculation on Blackland
and if
after Namibia and if after Angola and if after Zimbabwe
and if after all of my kinsmen and women resist even to
self-immolation of the villages and if after that
we lose nevertheless what will the big boys say will they
claim my consent:
Do You Follow Me: We are the wrong people of
the wrong skin on the wrong continent and what
in the hell is everybody being reasonable about
and according to the *Times* this week
back in 1966 the C.I.A. decided that they had this problem
and the problem was this man named Nkrumah so they
killed him and before that it was Patrice Lumumba
and before that it was my father on the campus

of my Ivy League school and my father afraid
to walk into the cafeteria because he said he
was wrong the wrong age the wrong skin the wrong
gender identity and he was paying my tuition and
before that
it was my father saying I was wrong saying that
I should have been a boy because he wanted one/a
boy and that I should have been lighter skinned and
that I should have had straighter hair and that
I should not be so boy crazy but instead I should
just be one/a boy and before that
it was my mother pleading plastic surgery for
my nose and braces for my teeth and telling me
to let the books loose to let them loose in other
words
I am very familiar with the problems of the C.I.A.
and the problems of South Africa and the problems
of Exxon Corporation and the problems of white
America in general and the problems of the teachers
and the preachers and the F.B.I. and the social
workers and my particular Mom and Dad/I am very
familiar with the problems because the problems
turn out to be
me
I am the history of rape
I am the history of the rejection of who I am
I am the history of the terrorized incarceration of
my self
I am the history of battery assault and limitless
armies against whatever I want to do with my mind
and my body and my soul and
whether it's about walking out at night
or whether it's about the love that I feel or
whether it's about the sanctity of my vagina or
the sanctity of my national boundaries
or the sanctity of my leaders or the sanctity

of each and every desire
that I know from my personal and idiosyncratic
and indisputably single and singular heart
I have been raped
be-
cause I have been wrong the wrong sex the wrong age
the wrong skin the wrong nose the wrong hair the
wrong need the wrong dream the wrong geographic
the wrong sartorial I
I have been the meaning of rape
I have been the problem everyone seeks to
eliminate by forced
penetration with or without the evidence of slime and/
but let this be unmistakable this poem
is not consent I do not consent
to my mother to my father to the teachers to
the F.B.I. to South Africa to Bedford-Stuy
to Park Avenue to American Airlines to the hardon
idlers on the corners to the sneaky creeps in
cars
I am not wrong: Wrong is not my name
My name is my own my own my own
and I can't tell you who the hell set things up like this
but I can tell you that from now on my resistance
my simple and daily and nightly self-determination
may very well cost you your life

FROM *CIVIL WARS: OBSERVATIONS FROM THE FRONT LINES OF AMERICA*

(1981)

[From the start of her career, Jordan proved herself as powerful in prose as in poetry. *Civil Wars*, collecting texts written between 1964 and 1981, confirmed her as an insightful essayist and speaker, a provocative political analyst, adept critic, sly and delightful satirist of those in high places who make horrible decisions, and a one-of-a-kind unstoppable force for making sense out of nonsense. The essays—as elegant and prophetic as James Baldwin's, as sharp and wickedly funny as Gore Vidal's—range from the personal to the global; they take us from the Brooklyn of her childhood to the Angola of poet-president Agostinho Neto; from struggles for social justice in the public school system to those in the elite institutions of the Ivy League; from confrontations between fathers and daughters, corporations and workers, political allies, Blacks and Jews, Jews and Muslims, men and women, women and women, gays and straights and bisexuals. Jordan was on the forefront of pushing identity politics further into uncharted waters, dissecting also the conflicts between Blacks and Blacks, Black women and Black women, Black and white feminists.

Civil Wars is an ardent call for both individual action and collective resistance. Here are two crucial essays from *Civil Wars* that we have not already included in a thematic section.]

"WHERE IS THE LOVE?"

(1978)

[First given as a paper at a seminar entitled "Feminism and the Black Woman Writer" at the 1978 National Black Writers Conference at Howard University with Acklyn Lynch, Sonia Sanchez and Barbara Smith.]

As I think about anyone or any thing—whether history or literature or my father or political organizations or a poem or a film—as I seek to evaluate the potentiality, the life-supportive commitment/possibilities of anyone or any thing, the decisive question is, always, *where is the love?* The energies that flow from hatred, from negative and hateful habits and attitudes and dogma do not promise something good, something I would choose to cherish, to honor with my own life. It is always the love, whether we look to the spirit of Fannie Lou Hamer, or to the spirit of Agostinho Neto, it is always the love that will carry action into positive new places, that will carry your own nights and days beyond demoralization and away from suicide.

I am a feminist, and what that means to me is much the same as the meaning of the fact that I am Black: it means that I must undertake to love myself and to respect myself as though my very life depends upon self-love and self-respect. It means that I must everlastingly seek to cleanse myself of the hatred and the contempt that surrounds and permeates my identity, as a woman, and as a Black human being, in this particular world of ours. It means that the achievement of self-love and self-respect will require inordinate, hourly vigilance, and that I am entering my soul into a struggle that will most certainly transform the experience of all the peoples of the earth, as no other movement can, in fact, hope to claim: because the movement into self-love, self-respect, and self-determination is the movement now galvanizing the true, the unarguable majority of human beings everywhere. This movement explicitly demands the testing of the viability of a moral idea: that the health, the legitimacy of any status quo, any governing force, must be measured according to the experiences of those who are, comparatively, powerless. Virtue is not to be discovered in the conduct of the strong vis-à-vis the powerful, but rather it is to be found in our behavior and policies affecting those who are different, those who are weaker, or smaller than we. How do the strong, the powerful, treat children? How do we treat the aged among us? How do the strong and the powerful treat so-called minority members of the body politic? How do the powerful regard women? How do they treat us?

Easily you can see that, according to this criterion, the overwhelming reality of power and government and tradition is evil, is diseased, is illegitimate, and deserves nothing from us— no loyalty, no accommodation, no patience, no understanding—except a clear-minded resolve to utterly change this total situation and, thereby, to change our own destiny.

As a Black woman, as a Black feminist, I exist, simultaneously, as part of the powerless and as a part of the majority peoples of the world in two ways: I am powerless as compared to any man because women, per se, are kept powerless by men/by the powerful; I am powerless as compared to anyone white because Black and Third world peoples are kept powerless by whites/by the powerful. I am the majority because women constitute the majority gender. I am the majority because Black and Third World peoples constitute the majority of life on this planet.

And it is here, in this extreme, inviolable coincidence of my status as a Black feminist, my status as someone twice stigmatized, my status as a Black Woman who is twice kin to the despised majority of all the human life that there is, it is here, in that extremity, that I stand in a struggle against suicide. And it is here, in this extremity, that I ask, of myself, and of any one who would call me *sister, Where is the love?*

The love devolving from my quest for self-love and self-respect and self-determination must be, as I see it, something you can verify in the ways that I present myself to others, and in the ways that I approach people different from myself. How do I reach out to the people I would like to call my sisters and my brothers and my children and my lovers and my friends? If I am a Black feminist serious in the undertaking of self-love, then it seems to me that the legitimate, the morally defensible character of that self-love should be such that I gain and gain and gain in the socio-psychic strength needed so that I may, without fear, be able and willing to love and respect women, for example, who are not like me: women who are not feminists, women who are not professionals, women who are not as old or as young as I am, women who have neither job nor income, women who are not Black.

And it seems to me that the socio-psychic strength that should follow from a morally defensible Black feminism will mean that I become able and willing, without fear, to love and respect all men who are willing and able, without fear, to love and respect me. In short, if the acquirement of my self-determination is part of a worldwide, an inevitable, and a righteous movement, then I should become willing and able to embrace more and more of the whole world, without fear, and also without self-sacrifice.

This means that, as a Black feminist, I cannot be expected to respect what somebody else calls self-love if that concept of self-love requires my suicide to any degree. And this will hold true whether that somebody else is male, female, Black, or white. My Black feminism means that you cannot expect me to respect what somebody else identifies as the Good of The People, if that so-called Good (often translated into *manhood* or *family* or *nationalism*) requires the deferral or the diminution of my self-fulfillment. We are the people. And, as Black Women, we are most of the people, any people, you care to talk about. And, therefore, nothing that is Good for The People is good unless it is good for me, as I determine myself.

When I speak of Black feminism, then, I am speaking from an exacerbated consciousness of the truth that we, Black Women, huddle together, miserably, on the very lowest levels of the economic pyramid. We, Black women, subsist among the most tenuous and least likely economic conditions for survival.

When I speak of Black feminism, then, I am not speaking of sexuality. I am not speaking of heterosexuality or lesbianism or homosexuality or bisexuality; whatever sexuality anyone elects for his or her pursuit is not my business, nor the business of the state. And, furthermore, I cannot be persuaded that one kind of sexuality, as against another, will necessarily provide for the greater happiness of the two people involved. I am not talking about sexuality. I am talking about love, about a steady-state deep caring and respect for every other human being, a love that can only derive from a secure and positive self-love.

As a Black woman/feminist, I must look about me, with trembling, and with shocked anger, at the endless waste, the endless suffocation of my sisters: the bitter sufferings of hundreds of thousands of women who are the sole parents, the mothers of hundreds of thousands of children, the desolation and the futility of women trapped by demeaning, lowest-paying occupations, the unemployed, the bullied, the beaten, the battered, the ridiculed, the slandered, the trivialized, the raped, and the sterilized, the lost millions and multimillions of beautiful, creative, and momentous lives turned to ashes on the pyre of gender identity. I must look about me and, as a Black feminist, I must ask myself: *Where is the love?* How is my own lifework serving to end these tyrannies, these corrosions of sacred possibility?

As a Black feminist poet and writer I must look behind me with trembling, and with shocked anger, at the face of Black women writers until now. From the terrible graves of a traditional conspiracy against my sisters in art, I must exhume the works of women writers and poets such as Georgia Douglas Johnson (who?).

In the early flush of the Harlem Renaissance, Georgia Johnson accomplished an astonishing, illustrious life experience. Married to Henry Lincoln Johnson, U.S. Recorder of Deeds in Washington, D.C., the poet, in her own right, became no less than Commissioner of Conciliation for the U.S. Department of Labor (*who was that again? who?*). And she, this poet, furthermore enjoyed the intense, promotional attention of Dean Kelley Miller, here at Howard, and W.E.B. DuBois, and William Stanley Braithwaite, and Alain Locke. And she published three volumes of her own poetry and I found her work in Countee Cullen's anthology, *Caroling Dusk*, where, Countee Cullen reports, she, Georgia Douglas Johnson, thrived as a kind of Gwendolyn Brooks, holding regular Saturday night get-togethers with the young Black writers of the day.

And what did this poet of such acclaim, achievement, connection, and generosity, what did his poet have to say in her poetry, and who among us has ever heard of Georgia Douglas Johnson? And is there anybody in this room who can tell me the name of two or three other women poets from the Harlem Renaissance? And why did she die, and why does the work of all women die with no river carrying forward the record of such grace? How is the case that whether we have written novels or poetry or whether we have raised our children or cleaned and cooked and washed and ironed, it is all dismissed as "women's work"; it is all, finally, deposited as nothing important, and there is no trace, no echo of our days upon the earth?

Why is it not surprising that a Black woman as remarkably capable and gifted and proven as Georgia Douglas Johnson should be the poet of these pathetic, beggarly lines:

I'm folding up my little dreams
within my heart tonight
And praying I may soon forgot
the torture of their sight
    "My Little Dreams"

How long, how long will we let the dreams of women serve merely to torture and not to ignite, to enflame, and to ennoble the promise of the years of every lifetime? And here is Georgia Douglas Johnson's poem " The Heart of a Woman":

The heart of woman goes forth with the dawn,
As a lovebird, softwinging, so restlessly on,
Afar o'er life's turrets and vales does it roam
In the wake of those echoes the heart calls home.

The heart of a woman falls back with the night
And enters some alien cage in its plight,
And tries to forget it has dreamed of the stars,
While it breaks, breaks, breaks on the sheltering bars.

And it is against such sorrow, and it is against such suicide, and it is against such deliberated strangulation of the possible lives of women, of my sisters, and of powerless peoples—men and children—everywhere, that I work and live, now, as a feminist trusting that I will learn to love myself well enough to love you (whoever you are), well enough so that you will love me well enough so that we will know exactly where is the love: that it is here, between us, and growing stronger and growing stronger.

"CIVIL WARS"

(1980)

[The title essay of Jordan's collection, previously unpublished, was the last essay in the book.]

Sometimes it is sitting in the middle of a room with 200 other people. The name of the meeting or committee doesn't matter. You light a cigarette. That doesn't help. You take notes or raise your hand. That doesn't help. The problem is not a procedural point of order or the particular identity of the leader. Everybody's on best behavior: politely taking turns, preparing to vote or write letters. The problem is the yearning courtesies, the underlying patience, the honcho upfront and the followers who face him, or her.

Most likely the reason people came together was because something wrong, something rather extraordinary fell into their lives. Everybody in the room has been smashed by the same ax, and look at the gathering. Look at the meaning of the manners of the scene!

It reminds me of instant TV coverage when there's a disaster: A baby has been burned to death. The TV reporter approaches the surviving parents as they stand, dumbfounded by horror, on the street.

"How do you feel about the loss of your little girl?" the reporter asks, moving the microphone close to the mouth of the father. The young man, confronted by a microphone and cameras, struggles to recall what etiquette requires of him.

"Well," he manages to reply. "Of course we're in a state of shock. (Pause.) This is a terrible night in our lives. (Pause)."

But the reporter does not remove the microphone. Instead, there's a second question.

"What will you and your wife do now?"

The young man puts his arm around his wife and says, politely, "I don't know. We don't know."

In the context of tragedy, all polite behavior is a form of self-denial. I can remember being eight years old and there was my mother warning me to watch *the tone of my voice* in the middle of a violent fight between my father and myself. The purpose of polite behavior is never virtuous. Deceit, surrender, and concealment: these are not virtues. The goal of the mannerly is comfort, per se. I can remember my father leaving me alone, finally, when there was no longer space for consideration of my tone: When I pulled a knife from under my pillow and asked him, "What do you want?" it was then that he changed his mind: What he wanted, then, was somebody else to beat up.

Nevertheless, people lose their jobs or their lives and still the reaction is cooperative. We try to speak clearly and to spare the feelings of the listener. We shave and shower and put on a clean shirt for the meeting. We volunteer to make phone calls, or coffee, or submit to the outcome of a vote about what shall I do. I have been raped: Who will speak for me? What are the bylaws?

The courtesies of order, of ruly forms pursued from a heart of rage or terror or grief defame the truth of every human crisis. And that, indeed, is the plan: To defuse and to deform the motivating truth of critical human response to pain.

In his essay "The Pleasures of Hating," William Hazlitt earned himself the reputation of an irascible, outrageous crank by passionate lament for earlier and multiple occasions when he had permitted himself only a diluted/inadequate expression of his anger and hurt and thorough disgust. In my teens, I was shocked, awake, by that panegyric to the forbidden emotion. And I was haunted by the devious, the plaintive love so clearly protected by his reverence for the truth of things, especially the hateful truth of things.

But the lobby for polite behavior is fairly inescapable. Most often, the people who can least afford to further efface and deny the truth of what they experience, the people whose very existence is most endangered and, therefore, most in need of vigilantly truthful affirmation, these are the people—the poor and the children—who are punished most severely for departures from the civilities that grease oppression.

If you make and keep my life horrible then, when I can tell the truth, it will be a horrible truth; it will not sound good or look good or, God willing, feel good to you, either. There is nothing good about the evils of a life forced into useless and impotent drift and privation. There is very little that is attractive or soothing about being strangled to death, whether it is the literal death of the body or the actual death of the soul that lying, that the humiliation and the evil of self-denial, guarantees.

Extremity demands, and justifies, extreme response. Violation invites, and teaches, violence. Less than that, less than a scream or a fist, less than the absolute cessation of normal events in the lock of abnormal duress is a lie and, worse than that, it is blasphemous ridicule of the self.

Nonetheless, I am a liar. I am frequently polite. I go to meetings and sit, properly, in one chair. I write letters to Washington. It's been a long while since I actually hit anybody at all.

One of my friends is Frances Fox Piven. We became friends by fighting each other in the realm of tactics, during the early 60s. Frances was advocating rehabilitation of the ghetto. I was advocating that she, a white intellectual, mind her own damn business. And I was advocating a push for integration because I thought that, otherwise, you might achieve better housing for Black families but you would still lack supporting community services such as reliable garbage collection, police protection, and ambulance response. We did not change each other's minds but we did come to respect the sincerity of our differences. And then we became close friends.

At this time Frances was living in Harlem with her daughter, Sara, who was just a few years older and a few inches taller than my son, Christopher. Each of us was raising one child and also pursuing a complicated professional and political life.

You could accurately describe Frances as a brilliant and radical humanitarian; her commitment to poor people and to Black people cannot, anywhere, be easily matched.

But there are things that we never talk about, or never talk about, twice. Until a few months ago, as a matter of fact, the silent areas between us led me to let the friendship atrophy, for almost two years.

We'd met for lunch in the Village. She was very angry about my piece in *Seven Days*, the one about the Hassidim and Victor Rhodes. On the street, as we walked to the restaurant, I asked her about the impending referendum in California, the one that would mean, if it passed, that a teacher who expressed the opinion that sexual preference was not the business of the state could then be fired. "Oh, Gay rights," she said. "No," I said, "Civil Rights."

Well, about this we disagreed, and seriously. Of course, that had been one area of silence between us for many years: "Gay Rights," or my loving a woman, these were subjects excluded from the compass of her radical humanitarian concern. Compared to unemployment or shrunken Welfare moneys or hunger, Frances viewed such "deviant behavior" as frivolous distraction from these other, unarguably gut issues.

At lunch, our argument became a furious exchange. Frances felt that my identification of the Lubavitch Hassidim assailants of Victor Rhodes, and that my emphatic focus upon Victor and the Black community amounted to an act of anti-Semitism.

It would be hard to say which one of us was more outraged.

I remember thinking that the café table where we sat was really as large as the whole country and that now we had taken irreconcilable, opposite sides. It was the survival of her people, as we saw it, poised against the survival of my people.

What about all of our discussions and all of our trust and what about the truth, for God's sake? What about that? The truth, Frances retorted, was not merely that one "incident." The truth had to include the entire history of the Jews so that, for instance, a reader could appreciate the background for instinctive expectations of

persecution. I said I didn't think we really should get into a compar-
ison of histories; that seemed inherently otiose to me and no amount
of arguing would dissuade either of us from the conviction that our
people were suffering long and too long.

I said my concern, at the moment, was not the history of the Jews
or an understanding as to why Hassidic Jews might happen to murder
a Black child. My concern was that a Black child had been beaten
and that he lay, critical and in a coma, even as we sat in that restau-
rant, and that somebody Hassidic was responsible and that whoever
that might be should be duly prosecuted by the law, and that unless
somebody insisted on the facts, in mass media print, the odds against
such due process were pretty fucking high.

I said that, to my knowledge, the history of Black people in white
America was not a factor in regular press coverage of alleged Black
crime: That it was ridiculous to expect more generosity of me than I,
than my people, had ever received.

When we parted, Frances gave me a copy of *The Last of the Just*,
asking me to read it, in a rather somber voice. I took it home and was
bitterly dismayed to find that it is a novel tracing the relentlessly
vicious and evil persecution of the Jews through several centuries.
This did seem to mean that my friend seriously believed me to be an
anti-Semite. I was stunned.

We had finally had a fight beyond tactics. It seemed to me that
my silence on these issues and my continuing self-denial around the
"issue" of my bisexuality was what had kept the friendship alive.
Without my collaboration, without my self-censorship, the disagree-
ments between us seemed irreconcilable.

Whether it was about Zionism or Palestine or my own, evidently,
inadmissible feelings, I had chosen to keep silent and to politely slide
by, or omit, references to these explosive spaces between us. But now
that such silence was broken, and after our fight, I felt I had to make
a choice I had never expected to make. And so I did. I chose complete
silence. I could no longer participate in an exchange requiring acro-
batics of self-denial even for the sake of those real and enormous ar-
eas of mutual agreement where I respected Frances as my comrade.

And then the good news of Miami burst upon America. It was

such good news. A whole lot of silence had ended, at last! Misbegotten courtesies of behavior were put aside. There were no leaders. There was no organization and no spokesman. There was no agenda. There were no meetings, no negotiations. A violated people reacted with violence. An extremity of want, an extremity of neglect, and extremity of racist oppression had been met, at last, with an appropriate, extreme reaction: an outcry and a reaching for vengeance, a wreaking of havoc in return for wrecked lives, a mutilation of passers-by in return for generations mutilated by contempt and by the immutable mutilations of poverty. Miami was completely impolite.

There was no deceit, no surrender, no concealment.

And why should victims cover for their executioners? Why should the victims cooperate and agree to discuss or write letters about what is as blatant and as deadly as Nagasaki, as horrendous as Hiroshima?

But this has been the code, overwhelmingly, for the oppressed: That you keep cool and calm down and explore proper channels and above all, that you remain law-abiding and orderly precisely because it is the order of the day that you will beg and bleed, precisely because it is the power of the law of the terrorist state arrayed against you to force you to beg and bleed without acceptable recourse except for dumb endurance or mute perishing.

And while the terrorist State, the Bureaus of Welfare, of Unemployment and Education, the Police and the State Troopers and the Army immediately mass, respectively, to confuse or mollify or punish and extirpate the always short-lived incivility of the afflicted, who will punish the violent state?

And how else can you successfully act to punish the State (i.e., *the manner of standing* that is the general condition in which you find yourself) except to eliminate the aping of the manners that were devised to secure your own wretched status, and except by acting so that what stands must fall?

Miami is not without precedent. Past confrontations between striking workers and state violence deployed by management have several times risen to those levels of retaliation, for example. But within the history of Black and white confrontations in America, it has seldom if ever occurred before that the violent Black citizens reached beyond internalized rage and beyond self-destructive symbols to the enemy, himself: to his own courtroom beyond the boundaries of the black community, and to his own white body.

Various press-appointed and self-acclaimed Black leaders hastened to Miami, hoping "to keep the lid on" and "to coo things down." While a few mumbled one or two words about the justice of protest, all were quick to "condemn and deplore" the "violence and the brutality" of the protest. Not one of those leaders deplored "the violence and the brutality" of the obscenely engendering situation in which the Black people of Florida have been barely living. Not one of them condemned that act of State violence that took away the life of Arthur McDuffie.

In the massive Black peoples' uprising of Miami, 1980, however, there was no tolerance left for airplane leadership—the leaders who get a call from the White House and then free tickets to fly into and out of a revolution. Nobody listened to these models of professional leadership. In fact, the President himself could not utter a complete lie before he was shouted and pelted away.

Miami was a peoples' uprising, and not an organized demonstration. It was extraordinary; an authentic spontaneous combustion resulting from conflict between life and the degradation of life. It was on site. This was not about making Hong Kong or the Philippines safe for democracy. When this house caught on fire, everybody was home.

I waited and watched to see what would happen next. I looked for the emergence of spokesmen. I listened for news of negotiations urgently begun between city hall and the community. I asked around for the name of a group, a committee: some/any formal and comprehensible and orderly "Miami Rights Coalition" stepping forward with a list of logically enumerated demands, and an eloquent defense of these demands.

None of this happened; Miami was news.

It was anarchy in the best sense: it was pure. By the time the very mention of Miami could bring about shudderings and panic throughout America, the explosion of protest was over; it had not been instigated or conceived as a tactic toward 40 more jobs or five cents more an hour. It was an unadulterated, absolute response to the terrors of a merciless oppression. And it was more: It was an ending of self-hatred. The expression of hatred for your enemies is sometimes the only way to end self-hatred. Where there is conflict, conscious termination of self-hatred is the only means to rational possibilities for love. Miami was an act of love: love for Arthur Mc-Duffie and love for every jeopardized Black life.

When Miami happened, I had been thinking about leadership, per se. Again and again after the assassination of Martin Luther King, Jr., social commentators "deplored" the lack of Black leadership. But I had been thinking, maybe it's a good thing. Certainly, I couldn't see any white leadership around that left me envious. The concept of leadership itself seemed to me dangerous and tired.

How could you consciously commit yourself to the worldwide movement into self-determination, and then turn around and say where is my leader/who is speaking for me?

My immediate, personal reasons for reconsidering the value of leadership had been exacerbated some six months earlier. At the 1979 organized, nonviolent demonstration to protest the police murder of Luis Baez, and during the police riot that followed, my overwhelming sensation was that of suicidal rerun in the suicidal Black tradition of mass nonviolence:

- A multitude of followers faced a stage from which certain leaders presumed to tell us why we were there and what we felt and how we should march together out of the park. ("Peacefully," and "Four abreast, arms linked.")

- The multitude then followed the leaders into the night whereupon the leaders became invisible and inaudible to most of us, marching behind them. Certainly it was not possible to hear or ascertain what, if anything, the leaders had planned for our safety and for our effective, continuing protest. *Perforce*, we were following, blindly.

- When the police attacked, suddenly it was no longer about following the leadership or leadership responsibility: There were no leaders, only more than one thousand unarmed demonstrators, trapped.

A small group of black artists and writers who had been trapped by the police attack met at my house to brainstorm and to compile an eyewitness account. Between the night of the Baez demonstration and the night when our account, accompanied by recommendations for community response, was to be presented at an open People's Tribunal, a Black woman, Elizabeth Magnum, was murdered by the Brooklyn police.

At the People's Tribunal, the spokesperson for our group, Alexis DeVeaux, began her presentation. When she reached the section of the statement that addressed the police murder of Elizabeth Magnum, the honcho in charge of the proceedings came to the microphone and attempted to halt her testimony. Alexis was able to complete it, nonetheless, only because the hundred or so community people seated in the audience roared their approval and support.

After Alexis sat down, the honcho came to the mike and harangued the audience: this is not the place for speeches, he said. This is not the place for anything but the people, the community, and for the testimony about police violence!

We left the Tribunal, dazed. When our lives lay at risk on the Brooklyn streets, that particular turkey was nowhere in sight. Now he was playing the leader and presuming to choose who are and who are not "the people." He was presuming to decide, furthermore, what the people can and cannot say! It also occurred to me that I could not recall, North or South, an organized demonstration ever called to protest the death of any Black woman, let alone the murder of Elizabeth Magnum.

And so it came to me that I was sick of professional leaders and that I would never again agree to be cannon fodder for a nonviolent demonstration. I resolved that I was unwilling to be killed, unarmed, and physically allergic to meetings, in general.

It came to me that self-determination has to mean that the leader is your individual gut, and heart, and mind or we're talking about power, again, and its rather well-known impurities. Who is really going to care whether you live or die and who is going to know the most intimate motivation for your laughter and your tears is the only person to be trusted to speak for you and to decide what you will or will not do.

The only leadership I can respect is one that enables every man and woman to be his and her own leader: to abandon victim perspective and to faithfully rely upon the truth of the feeling that is his or hers and then to act on that, without apology.

Neither race nor gender provides the final definitions of jeopardy or refuge. The final risk or final safety lies within each one of us attuned to the messy and intricate and unending challenge of self-determination. I believe the ultimate power of all the people rests upon the individual ability to trust and to respect the authority of the truth of whatever it is that each of us feels, each of us means. On what basis should *what* authority exceed the authority of *this* truth?

And what should we fear? No movement, not the Republican, nor the Black nor the women's nor the environmental movement can exist without you and me. Likewise for leaders. And although Nestlé's corporation may circumnavigate the globe and fire its factory workers in Massachusetts and subjugate its workers in the Philippines into peonage and poison the babies in Africa, it is not, finally, impregnable. Nestlé's and every other multinational corporation, finally, needs that troublesome, maverick component: the people—you and me.

We are not powerless. We are indispensable despite all the atrocities of state and corporate policy to the contrary.

At a minimum we have the power to stop cooperating with our enemies. We have the power to stop the courtesies and to let the feelings be real. We have the power not to vote, and not to register for the draft, and not to applaud, and not to attend, and not to buy, and not to pay taxes or rent or utilities. At the very least, if we cannot control things we certainly can mess them up.

Arthur McDuffie died because three cops beat him to death because he went through a red light and he was Black. Where is the feeling about that, outside Miami?

Are the cops that murdered him still walking around? Still cops?

Still alive?

My son called me from Cambridge, the Sunday of the Miami uprising. I told him some of my ideas. He said, "Have you read Frances' book?" He meant *Poor People's Movements: Why They Succeed, How They Fail*, by Frances Piven and Richard Cloward. No, I hadn't. "Read it," he said. "You have to."

Actually, what I had to do first was to consider the silence between us. And I did. And I decided to let it stand: to let the failures of the friendship stand and to reach out, instead, to Frances in areas of mutual, urgent concern, to engage once again in talk about tactics of struggle.

I read *Poor Peoples' Movements*, sometimes without stopping to sleep. Here it was: Documented historical proof that we are not powerless, that no one is powerless. With meticulous research and the most scrupulous open analysis of four movements—the unemployed workers' movement, the workers' movement of the Depression, the Civil Rights movement, and then the Welfare Rights movement—Frances Piven and Richard Cloward present a working model for protest in America: for effective peoples' protest movements. Examining the factors of failure and of victory, they arrive at a paradigmatic construct for radical change in this country: change minus the distortions of leaders on a first-name basis with the enemy. You could look at this book and deeply take heart: That more than once those who have the least defenses against the violence of the powerful have dared to defy that power, dared to confront that violence, with their own. And, more than once, those with the most meager resources to resist oppression have won something important, as the result of that confrontation. And in every instance, it has never been *who is the leader* but rather *who are the people*. It has never been *what is the organization* but *what is the crisis*.

I had some questions to discuss with Frances: If the essence of a peoples' movement is its spontaneity, then how can you sustain it?

But I hesitated. I thought again about all the other things that we could not talk about and all the arguments that would persist between us, and my feeling was, "What the hell; friendship is not a tragedy; we can be polite."

And so I called her up, to talk.

"I NEED TO TALK ABOUT LIVING ROOM / BECAUSE I NEED TO TALK ABOUT HOME"

FROM *ON CALL: POLITICAL ESSAYS* (1985) & FROM *LIVING ROOM: NEW POEMS* (1985)

FROM *ON CALL: POLITICAL ESSAYS*

(1985)

["From Phillis Wheatley to Walt Whitman, from Stony Brook to Lebanon, these writings document my political efforts to coherently fathom all of my universe, and to arrive at a moral judgment that will determine my further political conduct." These essays were written during the first years of the Reagan administration, marked by the rise of the Religious Right, the huge increases in military and weapon spending and support of contras in Nicaragua, Israel's militarism and expansion, and the South African government's violent suppression of anti-Apartheid activists. At home, federal and state governments were enacting more laws and regulations to criminalize all Black, poor, gay men and lesbian women, and between 1979 and 1981, more than twenty Black children were murdered in Atlanta. Jordan's voice was indispensable.]

"REPORT FROM THE BAHAMAS"

(1982)

["My 'rights' and my 'freedom' and my 'desire' and a slew of other New world values; what would they sound like to this Black woman described on the card atop my hotel bureau as 'Olive the Maid'? 'Olive' is older than I am and I may smoke a cigarette while she changes the sheets on my bed. Whose rights? Whose freedom? Whose desire?" In "Report from the Bahamas," Jordan upends the conventional travel narrative with questions about race, class, privilege. Originally presented as a keynote address to the New England Women's Studies Association Conference, Salem, Massachusetts, 1982.]

I am staying in a hotel that calls itself The Sheraton British Colonial. One of the photographs advertising the place displays a middle-aged Black man in a waiter's tuxedo, smiling. What intrigues me most about the picture is just this: while the Black man bears a tray full of "colorful" drinks above his left shoulder, both of his feet, shoes and trouserlegs, up to ten inches above his ankles, stand in the also "colorful" Caribbean salt water. He is so delighted to serve you he will wade into the water to bring you Banana Daquiris while you float! More precisely, he will wade into the water, fully clothed, oblivious to the ruin of his shoes, his trousers, his health, and he will do it with a smile.

I am in the Bahamas. On the phone in my room, a spinning complement of plastic pages offers handy index clues such as CAR RENTAL and CASINOS, A message from the Ministry of Tourism appears among these travellers tips. Opening with a para-graph of "WELCOME," the message them proceeds to "A PAGE OF HISTORY," which reads as follows:

> New World History begins on the same day that modern Bahamian history begins—October 12, 1492. That's when Columbus stepped ashore—British influence came first with the Eleutherian Adventures of 1647—After the Revolutions. American Loyalists fled from the newly independent states and settled in the Bahamas. Confederate blockade-runners used the island as a haven during the War between the States, and after the War, a number of southerners moved to the Bahamas. ...

There it is again. Something proclaims itself a legitimate history and all it does is track white Mr. Columbus to the British Eleutherians through Confederate Southerners as they barge into New World surf, land on New World turf and nobody saying one word about the Bahamian people, the Black peoples, to whom the only thing new in their Island world was this world succession of crude intruders and its colonial consequences,

This is my consciousness of race as I unpack my bathing suit in the Sheraton British Colonial. Neither this hotel nor the British nor the long ago Italians nor the white Delta airline pilots belong here, of course. And every time I look at the photograph of that fool standing in the water with his shoes on I'm about to have a West Indian fit, even though I know he's no fool; he's a middle-aged Black man who needs a job and this is his job—pretending himself a service ancillary to the pleasures of the rich. (Compared to his options in life, I am a rich woman, Compared to most of the Black Americans arriving for this Easter weekend on a three nights four day's deal of bargain rates, the middle-aged waiter is a poor Black man.)

We will jostle along with the other (white) visitors and join them in the tee shirt shops or, launching together, learn ruthless rules of negotiation as we, Black Americans as well as white, argue down the price of handwoven goods at the nearby straw market while the merchants, frequently toothless Black women seated on the concrete in their only presentable dress, humble themselves in our careless games:

"Yes? You like it? Eight dollar,"

"Five."

"I give it to you Seven."

And so it continues, this weird succession of crude intruders that, now, includes me and my brothers and my sisters from the North.

This is my consciousness of class as I try to decide how much money I can spend on Bahamian gifts for my family back in Brooklyn. No matter that these other Black women incessantly weave words and flowers into the straw hats and bags piled beside them on the burning dusty street. No matter that these other Black women must work their sense of beauty into these things that we will take away as cheaply as we dare, or they will do without food.

We are not white, after all. The budget is limited. And we are harmlessly killing time between the poolside rum punch and "The Native show on the Patio" that will play tonight outside the hotel restaurant.

This is my consciousness of race and class and gender identity as I notice the fixed relations between these other Black women and myself, They sell and I buy or I don't. They risk not eating. I risk going broke on my first vacation afternoon.

We are not particularly women anymore; we are parties to a transaction designed to set as against each other.

"Olive" is the name of the Black woman who cleans my hotel room. On my way to the beach I am wondering what "Olive" would say if I told her why I chose The Sheraton British Colonial; If I told her I wanted to swim, I wanted to sleep, I did not want to be harassed by the middle-aged waiter, or his nephew. I did not want to be raped by anybody (white or Black) at all and I calculated that my safety as a Black woman alone would best be assured by a multinational hotel corporation. In my experience, the big guys take customer complaints more seriously than the little ones. I would suppose that's one reason why they're big, they don't like to lose money anymore than I like to be bothered when I'm trying to read a goddamned book underneath a palm tree I paid $264 to get next to. A Black woman seeking refuge in a multinational corporation may seem like a contradiction to some, but there you are. In this case it's a coincidence of entirely different self-interests Sheraton/cash = June Jordan's short run safety.

Anyway, I'm pretty sure "Olive" would look at me as though I came from someplace as far away as Brooklyn. Then she'd probably allow herself one indignant query before righteously removing her vacuum cleaner from my room; "and why in the first place you come down you without your husband?"

I cannot imagine how I would begin so answer her.

My "rights" and my "freedom" and my "desire" and a slew of other New World values; what would they sound like to this Black woman described on the card atop my hotel bureau as "Olive the Maid"? "Olive" is older than I am and I may smoke a cigarette while she changes the sheets on my bed. Whose rights? Whose freedom? Whose desire?

And why should she give a shit about mine unless I do something, for real, about hers?

It happens that the book that I finished reading under a palm tree further today was the novel, *The Bread Givers*, by Anzia Yezierska. Definitely autobiographical, Yezierska lays out the difficulties of being both female and "a person" inside a traditional Jewish family at the start of the 20th century. That any Jewish woman became anything more than the abused servant of her father or her husband is really an improbable piece of news. Yet Yezierska managed such an unlikely outcome for her own life. In *The Bread Givers*, the heroine also manages an important, although partial, escape from traditional Jewish female destiny. And in the unpardonable, despite father, the Talmudic scholar of that Jewish family, did I not see my own and hate him twice again? When the heroine, the young Jewish child, wanders the streets with a filthy pail she borrows to sell herring in order to raise the ghetto rent and when she cries, "Nothing was before me but the hunger in our house, and no bread for the next meal if I didn't sell the herring. No longer like a fire engine, but like a houseful of hungry mouths my heart cried, 'herring—herring! Two cents apiece!'" who would doubt the case, the sisterhood of conversation possible between that white girl and the Black women selling straw bags on the streets of paradise because they do not want to die? And is it not obvious that the wife of that Talmudic scholar and "Olive," who cleans my room here at the hotel, have more in common than I can claim with either one of them?

This is my consciousness of race and class and gender identity as I collect wet towels, sunglasses, wristwatch, and head towards a shower.

I am thinking about the boy who learned this novel to me. He's white and he's Jewish and he's pursuing an independent study projects with me, at the State University where I teach whether or not I feel like it, where I teach without stint because, like the waiter, I am no fool. It's my job and either I work or I do without everything you need money to buy. The boy loaned me the novel because he thought I'd be interested to know how a Jewish-American writer used English so that syntax, and therefore the cultural habits of mind expressed by the Yiddish language, could survive translation. He did this because he wanted to create another connection between us on the basis of language, between his knowledge/his love of Yiddish and my knowledge/my love of Black English.

He has been right about the forceful survival of the Yiddish. And I had become excited by this further evidence of the written voice of spoken language protected from the monodrone of "standard" English, and so we had grown closer on this account. But then our talk shifted to student affairs more generally, and I had learned that this student does not care one way or the other about currently jeopardized Federal Student Loan Programs because, as he explained it to me, they do not affect him. He does not need financial help outside his family. My own son, however, is Black. And I am the only family help available to him and that means, if Reagan succeeds in eliminating Federal Programs to aid minority students, he will have to forget about furthering his studies, or he or I or both of us will have to hit the numbers pretty big. For these reasons of difference, the student and I had moved away from each other, even while we continued to talk.

My consciousness turned to race, again, and class.

Sitting in the same chair as the boy, several weeks ago, a graduate student came to discuss her grade. I praised the excellence of her final paper; indeed it had seemed to me an extra-ordinary pulling together of recent left brain/right brain research with the themes of transcendental poetry.

She told me that, for her part, she'd completed her reading of my political essays. "You are so lucky." She exclaimed.

"What do you mean by that?"

"You have a cause. You have a purpose to your life."

I looked carefully at this white woman; what was she really saying to me?

"What do you mean? I repeated.

"Poverty. Police violence. Discrimination in general."

(Jesus Christ, I thought: Is that her idea of lucky?)

"And how about you?" I asked.

"Me?"

"Yeah, you. Don't you have a cause?"

"Me? I'm just a middle aged woman, a housewife and a mother, I'm nobody."

For a while, I made no response.

First of all, speaking of race and class and gender in one breath, what she said meant that these lucky preoccupations of mine, from police violence to nuclear wipe-out, were not shared. They were mine and not hers. But here she sat, friendly as an old stuffed animal, beaming good will or more "luck" in my direction.

In the second place, what this white woman said to me meant that she did not believe she was " a person" precisely because she had fulfilled the traditional female functions revered by the father of that Jewish immigrant, Anzia Yezierska. And the woman in front of one was not a Jew. That was not the connection. The link was strictly female. Nevertheless, how should that woman and I, another female, connect beyond this bizarre exchange?

If she believed me lucky to have regular hurdles of discrimination then why shouldn't I insist that she's lucky to be a middle class white Warp female who lives in such well-sanctioned and normative comfort that she even has the luxury to deny the power of the privileges that paralyze her life?

If she deserts me and "my cause" where we differ, if, for example, she abandons me to "my" problems of race, then why should I support her in "her" problems of housewifely oblivion?

Recollection of this peculiar moment brings me to the shower in the bathroom cleaned by "Olive." She reminds me of the usual Women's Studies curriculum because it has nothing to do with her or her jobs. You won't find "Olive" anywhere on the reading list. You will likewise seldom hear of Anzia Yezierska. But yes, you will find from Florence Nightingale to Adrienne Rich, a white procession of independently well-to-do woman writers. (Gertrude Stein/Virginia Woolf/Hilda Doolittle are standard names among the essential woman writers).

In other words, most of women of the world—Black and First World and white who work because we meet—most of the women of the world persist far from the heart of the usual Women's Studies syllabus.

Similarly, the typical Black History course will slide by the majority experience it pretends to represent. For example, Mary McLeod Bethune will scarcely receive as much attention as Nat Turner, even though Black women who bravely and efficiently provided for the education of Black people hugely outnumber these few Black men who led successful or deemed rebellions against slavery. In fact, Mary McLeod Bethune may not receive honorable mention because Black History often apes those ridiculous white history courses which produce such dangerous gibberish as The Sheraton British Colonial "history" of the Bahamas. Both Black and white history courses exclude from their central consideration those people who neither killed nor conquered anyone as the means to new identity, those people who took care of every one of the people who wanted to become "a person," those people who still take care of the life at issue: the others who wish and who feed and who teach and who diligently decorate straw hats and bags with all of their historically unrequired gentle love: the women.

Oh the old rugged cross
on a hill far away
Well I cherish the old rugged cross.

It's Good Friday in the Bahamas. Seventy-eight degrees in the shade. Except for Sheraton territory, everything's closed.

It so happens that for truly secular reasons I've been fasting for three days. My hunger has now reached nearly violent proportions. In the hotel sandwich shop, the Black woman handling the counter complaints about the tourists; why isn't the shop closed and why don't the tourists stop eating for once in their lives. I'm famished and I order chicken salad and cottage cheese and lettuce and tomato and a hard boiled egg and a hot cross bun and apple juice.

She eyes me with disgust.

To be sure, the timing of my stomach offends her serious religious practices. Neither one of us apologizes to the other. She seasons the chicken salad to the peppery max while I listen to the loud radio gospel she plays to console herself. It's a country Black version of "The Old Rugged Cross."

As I leave much chicken into my mouth tears start. It's not the pepper. I am, after all, a West Indian daughter. It's the Good Friday music that dominates the humid atmosphere.

Well I cherish the old rugged cross

And I am back, faster than a 747, in Brooklyn, in the home of my patents where we are wondering, as we do every year, if the sky will darken until Christ has been buried in the tomb. The sky should darken if God is in His heavens. And then, around 3 p.m., at the conclusions of our mournful church service at the neighborhood St. Phillips, and even while we dumbly stare at the black cloth covering the gold altar and the slender until candles, the sun should return through the high gothic windows and vindicate our waiting faith that the Lord will rise again, on Easter.

How I used to bow my head at the very name of Jesus: ecstatic to abuse myself in difference to His majesty.

My mouth is full of salad. I can't seem to eat quickly enough. I can't think how I should lessen the offence of my appetite. The other Black woman on the premises, the one who disapprovingly prepared this very tasty break from my fast, makes no remark. She is no fool. This is a job that she needs. I suppose she notices that at least I included a hot cross bun among my edibles. That's something in my favor. I decide that's enough.

I am suddenly eager to walk off the food. Up a fairly steep hill I walk without hurrying. Through the pasted desolation of the little town, the road brings me to a confectionary pink and white plantation house. At the gates, an unnecessarily large statue of Christopher Columbus face me down, or tries to. His hand is fisted to one hip. I look back at him, laugh without deference, and turn left.

It's time to pack it up. Catch my plane. I scan the hotel room for things not to forget. There's that white report card on the bureau.

"Dear Guests" it says, under the name "Olive." I am your maid for the day. Please rate me: Excellent. Good, Average, Poor. Thank you."

I track this moments from the Sheraton British Colonial into my notebook. How would "Olive" rate me? What would it mean for us to seem "good" to each other? What would that rating require?

But I am hastening to leave. Neither turtle soup nor kidney pie nor any coach shell delight shall delay my departure. I have rested here, in the Bahamas, and I'm ready to return to my usual job, my usual work. But the skin on my body has changed and so has my mind. On the Delta flight home. I realize I am burning up, indeed.

So far as I can see, the usual race and class concepts of connections, or gender assumptions of unity, do not apply very well. I doubt that they ever did. Otherwise why would Black folks forever bemoan our lack of solidarity when the deal turns real. And if unity on the basis of sexual oppression is something natural then why do we women, the majority people on the planet, still have a problem?

The plane's ready for takeoff. I fasten my seatbelt and let the tumult inside my head run free. Yes; race and class and gender remain as real as the weather. But what they must mean about the contact between two individuals is less obvious and, like the weather is not predictable.

And when these factors of race and class and gender absolutely collapse to whichever you try to see them as automatic concepts of connections. They may serve well as indicators of commonly felt conflict, but as elements of connection they seem about as reliable as precipitation probability for the day after the night before the day.

It occurs to me that much organizational grief could be avoided if people understood that partnership in misery does not necessarily provide for partnership for change: *When we get the monsters off our backs all of us may want to run in very different directions.*

And not only that even though both "Olive" and "I" live inside a conflict neither one of us created, and even though both of us therefore hurt inside that conflict, I may be one of the monsters she needs to eliminate from her universe and, in a sense, she may be one of the monsters in mine.

I am reaching for the words to describe the difference between a common identity that has been imposed and the individual identity any one of us will choose, once she gains that chance.

That difference is the one that keeps us stupid in the face of new, specific information about somebody else with whom we are supposed to have a connection because a third party, hostile to both of us, has worked it so that the two of us, like it or not, share a common enemy. *What happens beyond the idea of that enemy and beyond the consequences of that enemy?*

I am saying that the ultimate connection cannot be the enemy. The ultimate connections must be the need that we find between us. It is said only who you are, in other words, but what we can do for each other that will determine the connection.

I am flying back to my job. I have been teaching contemporary women's poetry this semester. One quandary I have set myself to explore with my students is the one of taking responsibility without power. We had been wrestling ideas of the floor for several sessions when a young Black woman, a South Africa, asked me for help, after class.

Sokutu told me she was "in a trance" and that she'd been unable to eat for two weeks.

"What's going on?" I asked her, even as my eyes startled at her trembling and emaciated appearance.

"My husband, He drinks all the time. He beats me up. I go to the hospital. I can't eat. I don't know what/anything."

In my office, she described her situation. I did not dare to let her sense my fear and horror. She was dragging about, hour by hour, in dread. Her husband, a young Black South African, was drinking himself into more and more deadly violence against her.

Sokutu told me how she could keep nothing down. She weighed 90lbs. at the outside, as she spoke to me, She'd already been hospitalized as a result of her husband's battering rage.

I knew both of them because I had organized a campus group to aid the liberation struggles of Southern Africa.

Nausea rose in my throat. What about this presumable connection this husband and this wife fled from that homeland of hatred against them, and now what? He was destroying himself. If not stopped, he would certainly murder his wife.

She needed a doctor, right away. It was a medical emergency. She needed protection. It was a security crisis. She needed refuge for battered wives and personal therapy and legal counsel. She needed a friend.

I get on the phone and called every number in the campus directory that I could imagine might prove helpful. Nothing worked. There were no Institutional resources designed to meet her enormous, multifaceted, and ordinary woman's need.

I called various students. I asked the Chairperson of the English Department for advice. I asked everyone for help.

Finally, another one of my students, Cathy, a young Irish woman active in campus IRA activities, responded. She asked for further details, I gave them to her.

"Her husband," Cathy told me, "is an alcoholic. You have to understand about alcoholics. It's not the same as anything else. And it's a disease you can't treat any old way.

I listened, fearfully. Did this mean there was nothing we could do?

"That's not what I'm saying." She said. "But you have to keep the alcoholic part of the thing central in everybody's mind, otherwise her husband will kill her. Or he'll kill himself."

She spoke calmly, I felt there was nothing to do but to assume she knew what she was talking about.

"Will you come with me?" I asked her, after a silence, "Will you come with me and help us figure out what to do next?"

Cathy said she would but that she felt shy; Sokutu comes from South Africa. What would she think about Cathy?

"I don't know," I said, "But let's go."

We left to find a dormitory room for the young battered wife.

It was late, now, and dark outside.

On Cathy's VW that I followed behind with my own car was the sticker that reads BOBBY SANDS FREE AT LAST. My eyes blurred as I read and reread the weeds. This was another connection: Bobby Sands and Martin Luther King, Jr. and who would believe it? I would not have believed it; I grew up terrorized by Irish kids who introduced me to the word "nigga."

And here I was following an Irish woman to the room of a Black South African. We were going to that room so try to save a life together.

When we reached the little room, we found ourselves awkward and large. Sokutu attempted to treat us with utmost courtesy, as though we were honored guests. She seemed surprised by Cathy, but mostly Sokutu was flushed with relief and joy because we were there, with her.

I did not know how we should ever terminate her heartfelt courtesies and address, directly, the reason for our visit her starvation and her extreme physical danger.

Finally, Cathy sat on the floor and reached out her hands to Sokutu.

"I'm here." she said quietly, "Because June has told me what has happened to you. And I know what it is. Your husband is an alcoholic. He has a disease. I know what it is. My father was an alcoholic. He killed himself. He almost killed my mother. I want to be your friend."

"Oh," was the only small sound that escaped from Sokutu's mouth. And then she embraced the other student And then everything changed and I watched all of this happen so I know that this happened: this connection.

And after we called the police and exchanged phone numbers and plans were made for the night and for the next morning, the young South African woman walked down the dormitory hallway, saying goodbye and saying thank you to us.

I walked behind them, the young Irish woman and the young South African and I saw them walking as sisters walk, hugging each other, and whispering and sure of each other and I felt how it was not who they were but what they both know and what they were both preparing to do about what they know that was going to make them both free at last.

And I look out the windows of the plane and I see clouds that will not kill me and I know that someday soon other clouds may erupt to kill us all.

And I tell the stewardess No thanks to the cocktails she offers me. But I look about the cabin at the hundred strangers drinking as they fly and I think even here and ever now. I must make the connection real between me and these strangers everywhere before those other clouds unify this ragged bunch of us, too late.

FROM *LIVING ROOM: NEW POEMS*

(1985)

["I need to talk about living room / Because I need to talk about home." In fact, Jordan had been talking about living room and home since the start of her writing career. "Where we are physically is enmeshed with our deepest consciousness of self," she wrote in 1965 in her collaboration with Buckminster Fuller,

In 1979, Audre Lorde delivered her controversial address, "The Master's Tools Will Never Dismantle the Master's House," sparking widespread discussion and dispute in the feminist community; Lorde had "outed" the movement for merely advocating "tolerance of difference between women" rather than celebrating difference as the "fund of necessary polarities between which our creativity can spark [...] true visions of our future." Lorde's famous speech (later published in

Sister Outsider) and its title line became the slogan reminding feminists that they should not settle for reform if what's needed is revolution.

Jordan's *Living Room* is its rhetorically brilliant sister in poetry. In this collection, she re-appropriates the true meaning of living room. (The Nazis had appropriated the German term "Lebensraum," which translates to "living space," to sugarcoat their agenda to annex other peoples and countries in order to further their own pursuit of power; Jordan literally takes the term back.) She makes sure we look at the lives of individuals and listen to the voices of those who have been deprived of their room to live—in Nicaragua, Chile, Lebanon, and here at home.

In *On Call* (1985), writing of the struggle against apartheid in South Africa, she declared, "I know my life depends on making this fight my own." In *Living Room*, she wrote the line that embodies an internationalist Black feminism, and breaks through the stranglehold of identity politics: "I was born a Black woman / and now / I am become a Palestinian."]

◆◆◆

THIRD POEM FROM NICARAGUA LIBRE: PHOTOGRAPH OF MANAGUA

The man is not cute.
The man is not ugly.
The man is teaching himself
to read.
He sits in a kitchen chair
under a banana tree.
He holds the newspaper.
He tracks each word with a finger
and opens his mouth to the sound.
Next to the chair the old V-Z rifle
leans at the ready.

His wife chases a baby pig with a homemade
broom and then she chases her daughter running
behind the baby pig.
His neighbor washes up with water from the barrel
after work.
The dirt floor of his house has been swept.
The dirt around the chair where he sits
has been swept.
He has swept the dirt twice.
The dirt is clean.
The dirt is his dirt.
The man is not cute.
The man is not ugly.
The man is teaching himself
to read.

◆◆◆

DIRECTIONS FOR CARRYING EXPLOSIVE NUCLEAR WASTES THROUGH METROPOLITAN NEW YORK

Enter the Long Island Expressway at Brookhaven.
Proceed West. Exit at Hoyt Street in Astoria.
Turn left onto Astoria Boulevard. Trundle
under the elevated tracks there. Turn
right to ramp for the 59th Street Bridge.
Cross the Bridge. Follow local streets traveling
West until Amsterdam Avenue. At Amsterdam
turn right. Proceed North.

SPECIAL NOTE TO DRIVERS OF TRUCKS CARRYING
EXPLOSIVE NUCLEAR WASTES THROUGH
METROPOLITAN NEW YORK:

Check oil levels every five miles.

Change fan belt every thousand.
Check tire pressure every morning.
Change tires.
Buy radials.
Check shocks every fifty miles.
Change shocks every hundred.
Check rearview mirror and sideview mirror
incessantly.
Keep eyes on road.
Grant all other vehicles and each pedestrian
the right of way.
Do not pass.
Do not drive in the rain.
Do not drive in the snow.
Do not drive in the dark.
Signal.
Use headlights on high beam.
Go slow.
Do not brake suddenly or
otherwise.
Think about your mother
and look out for the crazies.

◆◆◆

PROBLEMS OF TRANSLATION: PROBLEMS OF LANGUAGE

Dedicated to Myriam Díaz-Diocaretz

1

I turn to my Rand McNally Atlas.
Europe appears right after the Map of the World.
All of Italy can be seen page 9.
Half of Chile page 29.
I take out my ruler.
In global perspective Italy

amounts to less than half an inch.
Chile measures more than an inch and a quarter
of an inch.
Approximately
Chile is as long as China
is wide:
Back to the Atlas:
Chunk of China page 17.
All of France page 5: As we say in New York:
Who do France and Italy know
at Rand McNally?

2

I see the four mountains in Chile higher
than any mountain of North America.
I see Ojos del Salado the highest.
I see Chile unequivocal as crystal thread.
I see the Atacama Desert dry in Chile more than the rest
of the world is dry.
I see Chile dissolving into water.
I do not see what keeps the blue land of Chile
out of blue water.
I do not see the hand of Pablo Neruda on the blue land.

3

As the plane flies flat to the trees
below Brazil
below Bolivia
below five thousand miles below
my Brooklyn windows
and beside the shifted Pacific waters
welled away from the Atlantic at Cape Horn
La Isla Negra that is not an island La
Isla Negra
that is not black
is stone and stone of Chile

feeding clouds to color
scale and undertake terrestrial forms
of everything unspeakable

4

In your country how
do you say copper
for my country?

5

Blood rising under the Andes and above
the Andes blood
spilling down the rock
corrupted by the amorality
of so much space
that leaves such little trace of blood
rising to the irritated skin the face
of the confession far
from home:

I confess I did not resist interrogation.
I confess that by the next day I was no longer sure
of my identity.
I confess I knew the hunger.
I confess I saw the guns.
I confess I was afraid.
I confess I did not die.

6

What you Americans call a boycott
of the junta?
Who will that feed?

7

Not just the message but the sound.

8

Early morning now and I remember
corriendo a la madrugada from a different
English poem,
I remember from the difficulties of the talk
an argument
athwart the wine the dinner and the dancing
meant to welcome you
you did not understand the commonplace expression
of my heart:

the truth is in the life
la verdad de la vida

Early morning:
do you say *la mañanita?*
But then we lose
the idea of the sky uncurling to the light:

Early morning and I do not think we lose:
the rose we left behind
broken to a glass of water on the table
at the restaurant stands
even sweeter
por la mañanita

◆◆◆

MENU

We got crispy chicken
we got frisky chicken
we got digital chicken
we got Chicken Evergreen

We got chicken salad

we got chicken with rice
we got radar chicken
we got chicken in the first degree

but we ain't got no fried chicken.

We got Chicken Red Light
we got drive-in chicken
we got felony chicken
we got chicken gravy

but we ain't got no fried chicken.

We got half a chicken
we got 2 chickens
we got Chicken Tylenol
we got chicken on ice

but we ain't got no fried chicken.

We got King Chicken
we got chicken à la mode
we got no-lead chicken

We got chainsaw chicken
we got chicken in a chair
we got borderline chicken
we got Chicken for the Young at Heart

We got aerosol chicken
we got Chicken Guitar

but we ain't got no fried chicken.

We got Coast Guard Chicken
we got sixpack chicken

we got Chicken Las Vegas
we got chicken to burn

but we ain't got no fried chicken.

We got 10-speed chicken
we got atomic chicken
we got chicken on tape
We got day-care chicken
we got Chicken Mascara
we got second-hand chicken

but we ain't got no fried chicken.

We got dead chicken
we got chicken on the hoof
we got open admissions chicken
we got Chicken Motel

We got astronaut chicken
we got chicken to go

We got gospel chicken
we got four-wheel drive chicken
we got chain gang chicken
we got chicken transfusions

but we ain't got no fried chicken.

We got wrong turn chicken
we got rough draft chicken
we got chicken sodas
we got Chicken Deluxe

but we ain't
got

no

fried chicken.

◆◆◆

DELIZA SPEND THE DAY IN THE CITY

DeLiza drive the car to fetch Alexis
running from she building past the pickets
make she gap tooth laugh why don't
they think up something new they picket now
for three months soon it be too cold
to care

Opposite the Thrift Shop
Alexis ask to stop at the Botanica
St. Jacques Majeur find oil to heal she
sister lying in the hospital from lymphoma
and much western drug agenda

DeLiza stop. Alexis running back
with oil and myrrh and frankincense and coal
to burn these odors free the myrrh like rocks
a baby break to pieces fit inside the palm
of long or short lifelines

DeLiza driving and Alexis
point out Nyabinghi's African emporium
of gems and cloth and Kwanza cards and clay:
DeLiza look.

Alexis opening the envelope to give DeLiza
faint gray copies of she article on refugees
from Haiti and some other thing on one white
male one

David Mayer
sixty-six
a second world war veteran
who want America to stop atomic arms
who want America to live without the nuclear death
who want it bad enough to say he'll blow
the Washington
D.C. Monument into the southside of the White House
where the First White Lady counting up she
$209,000 china plates and cups and bowls
but cops blow him away
blow him/he David Mayer
man of peace
away
Alexis saying, "Shit.
He could be Jesus. Died to save you,
didn't he?"
DeLiza nod she head.
God do not seem entirely to be dead.

◆◆◆

APOLOGIES TO ALL THE PEOPLE IN LEBANON

Dedicated to the 60,000 Palestinian men,
women, and children
who lived in Lebanon from 1948-1983.

I didn't know and nobody told me and what
could I do or say, anyway?

They said you shot the London Ambassador
and when that wasn't true
they said so
what
They said you shelled their northern villages

and when U.N. forces reported that was not true
because your side of the cease-fire was holding
since more than a year before
they said so
what
They said they wanted simply to carve
a 25 mile buffer zone and then
they ravaged your
water supplies your electricity your
hospitals your schools your highways and byways all
the way north to Beirut because they said this
was their quest for peace
They blew up your homes and demolished the grocery
stores and blocked the Red Cross and took away doctors
to jail and they cluster-bombed girls and boys
whose bodies
swelled purple and black into twice the original size
and tore the buttocks from a four month old baby
and then
they said this was brilliant
military accomplishment and this was done
they said in the name of self-defense they said
that is the noblest concept
of mankind isn't that obvious?
They said something about never again and then
they made close to one million human beings homeless
in less than three weeks and they killed or maimed
40,000 of your men and your women and your children

But I didn't know and nobody told me and what
could I do or say, anyway?

They said they were victims. They said you were
Arabs.
They called   your apartments and gardens   guerrilla
strongholds.

They called   the screaming devastation
that they created   the rubble.
Then they told you to leave, didn't they?

Didn't you read the leaflets that they dropped
from their hotshot fighter jets?
They told you to go.
One hundred and thirty-five thousand
Palestinians in Beirut and why
didn't you take the hint?
Go!
There was the Mediterranean: You
could walk into the water and stay
there.
What was the problem?

I didn't know and nobody told me and what
could I do or say, anyway?

Yes, I did know it was the money I earned as a poet that
paid
for the bombs and the planes and the tanks
that they used to massacre your family

But I am not an evil person
The people of my country aren't so bad

You can expect but so much
from those of us who have to pay taxes and watch
American TV

You see my point;

I'm sorry.
I really am sorry.

◆◆◆

MOVING TOWARDS HOME

"Where is Abu Fadi," she wailed
"Who will bring me my loved one?"

The New York Times 9/20/82

I do not wish to speak about the bulldozer and the
red dirt
not quite covering all of the arms and legs
Nor do I wish to speak about the nightlong screams
that reached
the observation posts where soldiers lounged about
Nor do I wish to speak about the woman who shoved
her baby
into the stranger's hands before she was led away
Nor do I wish to speak about the father whose sons
were shot
through the head while they slit his own throat before
the eyes
of his wife
Nor do I wish to speak about the army that lit continuous
flares into the darkness so that the others could see
the backs of their victims lined against the wall
Nor do I wish to speak about the piled up bodies and
the stench
that will not float
Nor do I wish to speak about the nurse again and
again raped
before they murdered her on the hospital floor
Nor do I wish to speak about the rattling bullets that
did not
halt on that keening trajectory
Nor do I wish to speak about the pounding on the
doors and
the breaking of windows and the hauling of families into
the world of the dead

I do not wish to speak about the bulldozer and the
red dirt
not quite covering all of the arms and legs
because I do not wish to speak about unspeakable events
that must follow from those who dare
"to purify" a people
those who dare
"to exterminate" a people
those who dare
to describe human beings as "beasts with two legs"
those who dare
"to mop up"
"to tighten the noose"
"to step up the military pressure"
"to ring around" civilian streets with tanks
those who dare
to close the universities
to abolish the press
to kill the elected representatives
of the people who refuse to be purified
those are the ones from whom we must redeem
the words of our beginning

because I need to speak about home
I need to speak about living room
where the land is not bullied and beaten to
a tombstone
I need to speak about living room
where the talk will take place in my language
I need to speak about living room
where my children will grow without horror
I need to speak about living room where the men
of my family between the ages of six and sixty-five
are not
marched into a roundup that leads to the grave
I need to talk about living room

where I can sit without grief without wailing aloud
for my loved ones
where I must not ask where is Abu Fadi
because he will be there beside me
I need to talk about living room
because I need to talk about home

I was born a Black woman
and now
I am become a Palestinian
against the relentless laughter of evil
there is less and less living room
and where are my loved ones?

It is time to make our way home.

EVERY NIGHT THE WATERS OF THE WORLD

FROM *NAMING OUR DESTINY: NEW & SELECTED POEMS 1985-1989* (1989)

[In 1988, Jordan accepted a joint appointment as Professor of African-American Studies and Women's Studies at the University of California, Berkeley. She spent the academic year prior to her move at the University of Wisconsin in Madison, as Visiting Professor in African-American Studies. In 1989, after having lived her entire life in New York, she moved to Berkeley. She was fifty-three. She settled into a small house shaded by manzanita trees with a small garden and a shed she turned into a writing studio. She lived next to an elementary school, where the sound of children laughing and hollering in the playground delighted her, got a dog (she named him Buck) from the pound, and began bringing it to Berkeley. The change was thrilling: Jordan perceived California as the "forecast for the rest of America."

Soon after her arrival, Jordan's second *New and Selected Poems* was published, bringing together work from over thirty years predicated on the conviction that "poetry is about telling the truth." To the more than forty poems written since 1985, she assigned the section title "North Star" with this epigraph:

Stellar guide to freedom for African men and women making their escape from slavery

Signpost in the sky for sailors on the open sea
—The Abolitionist *newspaper founded by Frederick Douglas in 1847*

Fierce and exuberant, these poems travel far and wide, whether she's overturning presumptions about exactly who was threatened in the infamous Bernhard Goetz case of 1984; sending a consoling message across the miles to Winnie Mandela in South Africa; using a theorem from quantum physics to analyze a breakup with a lover; or introducing an insouciant new speaker in the DeLiza persona poems. (The poem "Something Like a Sonnet for Phillis Miracle Wheatley," which Jordan included in *Naming Our Destiny*, is included in this Reader in the essay about Phillis Wheatley on pp. 194-207.) Jordan's poems continue to talk back to the status quo.]

◆◆◆

POEM FROM TAPED TESTIMONY IN THE TRADITION OF BERNHARD GOETZ

1

This was not I repeat this was not a racial incident.

2

I was sitting down and it happened to me
before that I was sitting down or I was standing
up and I was by myself because of course

a lot of the time I am by myself because
I am not married or famous or super-im-
portant enough to have shadows or body-
guards so I was alone as it happens when
I was sitting down or let me retract that
I wasn't with anybody else regardless
who else was there
and I know I am not blind I could see
other people around me but the point
is that I wasn't with them I wasn't
with anybody else and like I said
it happened before two three
times it had happened that I was
sitting down or I was standing up
when one of them or one time it was
more than one I think it was two
of them anyway they just jumped
me I mean they jumped on me like
I was chump change and I know
I am not blind I could see they were
laughing at me they thought it was
funny to make me feel humiliated or I don't
know ugly or weak or really too small
to fight back so they were just laughing
at me in a way I mean you didn't
necessarily see some kind of a smile
or hear them laughing but I could feel
it like I could feel I could always
feel this shiver thing this fear take
me over when I would have to come into a room
full of them and I would be by myself
and they would just look at you you know what
I mean you can't know what I mean
you're not Black

3

How would you know
how that feels when mostly you move through
outnumbered and you are the one doesn't
fit in doesn't look right doesn't read
right because you're not white
but you live
in this place in this city where
again and again
there you are inside but outside or off
and you're different and I would never know when
it would happen again that the talking
would stop or the talking would start
or somebody would say something
stupid or nasty to me like nigga
or honey or bitch or not say
anything at all like the drugstore on Sunday
and I was standing in line but the girl
behind the counter couldn't get it
together to say, "Yes. Can I help
you?" or anything at all she was counting
on silence to make me
disappear or beg or I don't know
what and okay I'm visiting New Hampshire
but also
I live here I mean in this country
I live here and you should have seen
the look of her eyes they were shining
I know I am not blind and she wanted
to make believe me this irreducible this me
into a no-count what you gone do about
it/zip

4

So one of them a policeman a long
time ago but I remember it he kicked

in the teeth of Jeffrey Underwood who
lived on my block and who had been the best
looking boy in the neighborhood and he was tall
and skinny even and kind of shy and he/
Jeffrey went up on the roof with fire
crackers I mean it was the roof of the house
of a family that knew him and they knew
Jeffrey's parents too and
my cousin told me the next morning how
this policeman asked Jeffrey to come
down so Jeffrey left the roof and came
down to the street where we lived and
then the policeman beat Jeffrey
unconscious and he/the
policeman who was one of them he kicked
Jeffrey's teeth out and I never wanted to see
Jeffrey anymore but I kept seeing
these policemen and I remember how
my cousin who was older than I was I remember how
she whispered to me, "That's what they
do to you"

5

and the stinging of my face when some of
them my mother told me they were
Irish and when some of them shot at me
with zip guns and howled out "li'l nigga"
I was eight years old by myself walking
with my book bag to a public school
and I remember my mother
asking me to kneel down beside her to pray
for the Irish

6

So much later and of course this is not something
I keep on the front burner but then again

it's nothing you want to forget because
enough is enough and it has happened before
and it happens so often but when you turn around
for help or the punishment of these people
where can you go I mean I was raped six
years ago by one of them who was good he told me
with a rifle and he raped me and his
brother was the judge in town and so forth all
of them have brothers all over town there
are so many of them everywhere you go so
either you become the routine
setup
or you have to figure out
some self-defense

7

I was sitting down and it happened
before that I was sitting down and I was
by myself because not one of them was
with me not one of them was cognizant
(to use a better word) of me where I
was sitting down and they filled up
the room around me and one of them
sat down to my left and another one
of them sat down beside my right fist
on the table (next to the silverware) and
I was sitting there quiet and mild-
mannered which is how I am you can
ask my neighbors you can read about
it in the papers everyday the papers
tell you I am quiet and mild-mannered which is
how I sat there at this table in a room
full of them and then the one to the right
of my right fist she started up about this South
African novel she was reading and she said to the one
to my left by which I mean she ignored me in the middle

and it felt like I was
not there but I was I was sitting
in my chair at the table where
she the one to my right said to the one
to my left she said, "And the writer
expects the reader to be sympathetic
to that character!" And then the
one to my left said to the one to my
right she said, "Exactly! And it's
so cheap. It's so disgusting. She (the
writer) makes her (the character)
marry not one but two Black revolutionaries!" And something
   snapped
inside me I could see across the table
more of them just sitting there eyes
shining
and I know I am not blind
I could see them laughing at me and I went
cold because in a situation like that
you have to be cold a cold
killer or they will ridicule you
right there at the dining table and
I wanted to murder
I wanted them to hurt and bleed I wanted
them to leave me alone
and so I became cold I became a cold
killer and I took out my gun and
I shot the one to my right and then
I shot the one to my left and then I looked
across the table and I thought, "They
look all right," and so I shot them too
and it was self-defense I wanted
them to stop playing with me
I wanted them to know it's not cheap
or disgusting to love a Black
revolutionary and

as a matter of fact
I wanted them to know you'd
better love a Black revolutionary before she
gets the idea

that you don't

◆◆◆

TO FREE NELSON MANDELA

Every night Winnie Mandela
Every night the waters of the world
turn to the softly burning
light of the moon

Every night Winnie Mandela
Every night

Have they killed the twelve-year-old girl?
Have they hung the poet?
Have they shot down the students?
Have they splashed the clinic the house
and the faces of the children
with blood?

Every night Winnie Mandela
Every night the waters of the world
turn to the softly burning
light of the moon

They have murdered Victoria Mxenge
They have murdered her
victorious now
that the earth recoils from that crime
of her murder now

that the very dirt shudders from the falling blood
the thud of bodies fallen
into the sickening
into the thickening
crimes of apartheid

Every night
Every night Winnie Mandela

Every night Winnie Mandela
Every night the waters of the world
turn to the softly burning
light of the moon

At last the bullets boomerang
At last the artifice of exile explodes
At last no one obeys the bossman of atrocities

At last the carpenters the midwives
the miners the weavers the anonymous
housekeepers the anonymous
street sweepers
the diggers of the ditch
the sentries the scouts the ministers
the mob the pallbearers the practical
nurse
the diggers of the ditch
the banned
the tortured
the detained
the everlastingly insulted
the twelve-year-old girl and her brothers at last
the diggers of the ditch
despise the meal without grace
        the water without wine
        the trial without rights

the work without rest
at last the diggers of the ditch
begin the living funeral
for death

Every night Winnie Mandela
Every night

Every night Winnie Mandela
Every night the waters of the world
turn to the softly burning
light of the moon

Every night Winnie Mandela
Every night

◆◆◆

POEM NUMBER TWO ON BELL'S THEOREM, OR THE NEW PHYSICALITY OF LONG DISTANCE LOVE

There is no chance that we will fall apart
There is no chance
There are no parts.

◆◆◆

DELIZA COME TO LONDON TOWN

A birthday poem for Mark

DeLiza walk across the Waterloo
at night
She short but happy that she maybe have
one inch or two

on Bonaparte
who (anyway) look peculiar up against the backdrop
of Big Ben

She cogitate
on glory and the sword/she
smoke a cigarette among a hundred homeless
white men
them the Queen forget to decorate
with bed or blanket
softening the bottomline along the lamp-lit
dirty river

DeLiza race away from Waterloo
at night
She run she clutch she hotel key real tight:
DeLiza shaken from the speculation
on The Empire and The Crown:

> Them that will not kiss the family
> like as not to kill
> the strangers that they meet

◆◆◆

DELIZA AND THE TV NEWS

DeLiza watch one hostage then
she watch two hostage
then she think it must be
she descend
from something like that
only some may call it slavery and
a middle passage

DeLiza say you call it

what you want to
she think
the original hostage
holocaust kill some 22 million
African hostage
so they die

And somebody real popular
have high-jack that history
to this very day

◆◆◆

SOMETIMES DELIZA

Sometimes DeLiza
she forget about location
and she wondering what to do
to make she Black self
just a little more
conspicuous

(She thinking
maybe she wear pink
or smoke a pipe)

But when she realize
she altogether in New Hampshire
not
The Planet

Then
DeLiza laugh out loud

13

"MISBEGOTTEN AMERICAN DREAMS HAVE MAIMED US ALL"

FROM *TECHNICAL DIFFICULTIES: AFRICAN AMERICAN NOTES ON THE STATE OF THE UNION* (1992)

[With the war in Iraq just behind (but Saddam Hussein still in power) President Bush, in his 1992 State of the Union Address, declared that the world welcomed America's hegemony: "They trust us to be fair, and restrained. They trust us to be on the side of decency. They trust us to do what's right."

That same year, with the essays of *Technical Difficulties*, Jordan delivered her own State of the Union address. She was, of course, in great doubt about George Bush's claim and spoke instead for those who were suffering the consequences of American superpower. Jordan drew together the pieces for the collection from speeches she had delivered at colleges, university, rallies, and conferences; articles published in the *Village Voice* and *The New York Times*, and from her regular column, beginning in 1989, for *The Progressive*. The Wisconsin-based monthly, dedicated to astute liberal thought and action since 1909 (contributors have included Noam Chomsky, Lincoln Steffens, James Baldwin, Molly Ivins) gave her the opportunity to weigh in immediately on current events, from the ramifications of the fall of the Berlin Wall and the collapse of the Soviet Union, to the sexy and "scandalous" Madonna and Sandra Bernhard performance of "I've Got You Babe" at the Brooklyn Academy of Music. Two of Jordan's most audacious essays are reprinted here, each in its way exploring how American dreams, gone awry, lead to American nightmares.

Similar to the companionship of the essays of *On Call* and the poems of *Living Room* (both published in 1985), *Technical Difficulties*, in parallel reading with the new poems of *Naming Our Destiny*, shows Jordan to be both one of the most gifted poets of her time and one of the most unorthodox, yet practical, of political thinkers.]

"WAKING UP IN THE MIDDLE OF SOME AMERICAN DREAMS"

(1986)

[Jordan addressed the horror of rape on many occasions and in many forms. See particularly "Poem about My Rights" from *Passion* (1980; pp. 342-349). She first delivered the text presented here as the keynote address at the *Agenda for the 90s Conference* in Portland, Oregon, May 18, 1986.]

I have rejected propaganda teaching me about the beautiful the truly rare:

Supposedly the ocean at the hushpoint of the shore

supposedly

the ocean at the hushpoint of the shore

is beautiful

for instance

but the beautiful can stay out there

unless I see

a bird seize sandflies

or your self

approach me

laughing out a sound to spoil

the pretty picture ...

-June Jordan, from "Poem on a New
Year's Eve"

I remember living in a coastal wilderness, by myself. No once could
see the little house from the road. And all that I could see, looking
through the long glass walls that frequently confused the birds, was
wildlife sanctuary marsh, bay waters, and an always restless, unpre-
dictable sky. Occasionally, a hawk would shudder and soar, his huge
wings inches from my face. More often, one or another jackrabbit
would try to adopt me, daily hopping closer and closer to my car un-
til I had to teach it to beware of creatures like myself.

Day and night I pursued my lonely "constitutionals:" those
mile-and-a-half to two-mile compulsive treks leading to a complete-
ly uninhabited beach laden with crunchy shell-life, under foot. By
December or January, these unremarkable habits thrust me into
bitter, howling circumstances such that I easily imagined my body an
eroded, baffling skeleton flung next to the carcass, say, of a horse-
shoe crab. But whether it was December or April or July, whenever
the moon failed to appear, that unmitigated, that waiting darkness
outside aroused every one of my instincts for panic, and flight. And
yet, I did not run. Nor did I abandon any of my rather demanding out-
door routines. I think I was practicing to cross the Rocky Mountains.
Or I think I was trying to learn something intimate about the Long
March of the Chinese revolution. Or I think I was, rather obliquely, to

be sure, training myself for a different, a social kind of duress. Or I think I was immersing myself in privacy paradise. East Coast.

I did not have a dog. Or a cat. I almost had no phone, as I hardly ever bothered to answer it and not too many people bothered to call. Regularly I would finish a poem and then drive from my house, at two or three o'clock in the morning, to the post office in town. That was my notion of a pretty exciting Friday or Saturday night, in fact. And I also remember another artist, an American painter whose name has risen now, as illustrious as that of Pablo Picasso's. I remember that elder kinsman who also lived in that wilderness and who, more or less once a month, would drink a whole bottle of booze, mount his three-speed bicycle, and then attempt to ride it, straight down the white line dividing the main highway. I thought he was just a wee bit crazy; as for me, I thought I was lucky. I knew about him after all: somebody older and wiser who lived by himself, somebody who had surrounded himself with acres and acres of private property on which he could keep an enormous, silent house. As for me, I could walk to the beach in any season of the year and find nobody else, ever, on the sand. If I sat quite still in the evenings, I could hear the spiders weaving their webs. And I thought I was lucky.

One day a feature writer for a Long Island newspaper came to interview and photograph me "at home." My first doubts about my paradise of privacy arose when I saw the published story, complete with a photograph depicting me absolutely alone among a million tall marsh reeds. I looked and I looked at that strange picture: Was that really the idea? Was that really the world of my dreams? To my credit, however dim, I did suspect a lunatic skew to that photograph, that summary of my place, my role. Nevertheless, truly traditional/deranged/American images of the good life kept me in that wilderness, that willful loneliness, until somebody else came into the little house and raped me. I remember thinking that there was no point to scream, there was no point to struggling towards those enormous clear windows. There as nobody, anywhere around, to help. And afterwards, when I could make myself talk again, I crawled to the telephone and placed two long-distance calls: there was nobody local who would care.

That brilliant elder artist applied himself to a huge canvas taunt-
ing his vision and his craft, seven days a week. In fact, he never took
a day off, or a vacation. And, of course, I respected him, completely.
Once, when I asked him why he worked that way, without respite,
he shrugged his shoulders, "What else is there to do?" I remember
absorbing his response as ultimate proof of his wisdom and of his ge-
nius as a human being: He lived alone. He worked all of the time. He
was famous. He was rich. Nobody disturbed him. Nobody lived close
enough to try. By our American standards he had become indisput-
ably successful. Soon people in general would refer to him as A Great
Man. Already, international critics proclaimed him an exemplar, a
positive legend of our century. And I, twenty-five to thirty years his
junior, I turned away from the flickering question: What does it mean
to be a legend to all and a friend to none?

And I, a young Black woman poet, duly emulated the isolating
rigors of his artistic commitment. Didn't everyone approve, if not
admit, the ostracizing dedication of his art? Did he not have a child
whom he seldom saw? Did I not have a son whom I saw, seldom? What
besides race and sex and class could block me from being a clearly
successful American, A Great White Man? Now, in that wilderness
period of my life, no one ever disturbed the expensive isolation of the
famous painter. But someone raped me in the middle of my rented,
pseudo-Walden Pond. Someone had insinuated himself into that
awkward, tiny shelter of my thoughts and dreams. He had dealt with
me as egotistically as, in another way, I had postponed dealing with
anyone besides myself. He had overpowered the supposed protection
of my privacy, he had violated the boundaries of my single self. He
had acted as though nothing mattered so much as his certainly brute
impulse, the one that ruled my friends and my family and my neigh-
bors out of the usual universe?

That famous painter guarded himself against trespass while I
tried to protect myself from all violation. But dangers of trespass did
not push The Great Man out on a highway, drunk on his bike. Nor was
possible violation of my person the underlying threat to my isolated
life-style. On the contrary: what jeopardized his and my safety, and
our happiness, was the absence of connections between us and the

absence of a sharing, a dependency between the two of us and other people who would care about us because we cared about them.

American illusions of autonomy, American delusions of individuality, seduced the painter into monthly bouts of arrogance and potential suicide. These same American illusions held me, finally, a prisoner to the merciless whimsies of a rapist in my home.

Not only did that painter/that father and this poet/this mother believe ourselves eminently respectable in the conscientiously selfish design of our days, we considered ourselves virtuous and self-sacrificing. The very obvious, deep, social deficiencies of our lives merely convinced each of us that we must be profoundly inspired, if not exalted, in our ambitious, unremitting labors.

So it seems to me that I am not entirely different from the painter or the rapist. Misbegotten American dreams have maimed us all. And one of these, especially, continues to distort and paralyze our simplest capabilities for cooperation as a species. Beloved, national myths about you and me as gloriously rugged, independent individuals pervade our consciousness. Every one of us knows that, to whatever extent she is worthy of affection or praise or promotion or functional housing or a faithful husband or respect or diligent medical attention or honest car repair or satisfactory sex or civil civil servants (such as mannerly policemen or courteous desk clerks in the Office of Social Security) or sensitive legal counsel or accurate political representation or a safe and beautiful community or a 100 percent perfect day in the country—perfect weather perfect traffic conditions perfect timing—every one of us knows that, to whatever extent he or she secures any of the above, it happens not because he is a God-given human being, not because she is an American citizen, not because he has worked hard at a dumb job for fifteen years and never knowingly hurt or cheated anybody, not because she has done her best, always, to be good: a good girl, a good friend, a good date, a good lover a good wife a good mother: Ever American one of us knows that these fundamental and democratic amenities of existence will fall into your lap because, as our most popular greeting cards express it, again and again: You're different. I'm different. You're special. I'm special. Every single American grows up believing that,

in the happy ending ahead of us, we will just gleefully dust our class-
mates and our fellow workers and our compatriots and then, to really
mix up the metaphors, we will leave them grounded, like so many
ugly ducklings, while we wheel and speed and plummet and, steadily
glittering, rise: 235 million Jonathan Livingston Seagulls with nary
a thought for the welfare of the flock, or companionship, or a resting
or a nesting environment!

The flipside of this delusional disease, this infantile and appar-
ently implacable trust in mass individuality, is equally absurd, and
destructive. Because every American one of us is different and spe-
cial, it follows that every problem or crisis is exclusively our own, or,
conversely, your problem—not mine.

Anywhere U.S.A. and you may, easily, imagine a gigantic traf-
fic jam: somebody's radiator overheats and he turns off the engine,
thereby blocking several cars directly behind him. One of the oth-
er drivers approaches the disabled vehicle. "What's the matter?"
he asks. The man inside the car points to the smoke escaping from
under the hood. "You can see for yourself," he says. The other driver
snaps back, "That's your problem! Get it out of my way!" Or, look at
the Civil Rights Movement. I personally know of hundreds of Negro
mothers and fathers who failed forever, as it seemed to us, their chil-
dren, before they would admit:

a. That they survived desperate barriers to their pursuit of hap-
piness.
b. That these barriers issued from racist loathing of us, regard-
less whether we practiced the piano or shined our shoes.

As though the horror and the dread of lynching and jim crow
translated into something shameful about the victims, something the
victims must keep secret, terrible years passed before these parents,
mine among them, realized that they must publicly proclaim and
publicly protest all of the injustice that their worn hands, slumped
shoulders, and lowered eyes made clear. And even more time passed
before these victims recognized the need to act, collectively, against
that outside evil force of hatred.

The Women's Movement has suffered from comparably personal assumptions: I am inherently special and different from every other woman in my neighborhood. No one else feels stranded in her own living room. No one else has been raped by a friend. No other woman's husband beats her up. I am the only woman blithely threatened by her boss with sexual propositions or demands. I am the only female no one listens to. And so I do not speak about my terror or my boredom. I do not acknowledge the common nature of my female predicament. I do not join with other women to deliver myself from the consequences of sexist contempt and nationwide institutions of misogyny. And so it goes, as well, for each elderly American who can no longer take care of himself, and each family with teenager addicted to drugs, and each household of the suddenly unemployed, and each person married to an alcoholic.

Do we not live in the generous, pastoral land of the Marlboro Man? The land of healthy and good-looking and young people who ski and ail and laugh and smoke cigarettes, all at the same tome, gracefully? If we do not match up to those images, then we have personally failed, somehow. And, naturally, you keep personal failure a secret.

American delusions of individuality now disfigure our national landscape with multitudes of disconnected pained human beings who pull down the shades on prolonged and needless agony. But if we would speak the unspeakable, if we would name and say the source of our sorrow and scars, we would find a tender and a powerful company of others struggling as we do, and we would know we should show to the world, at last, that shame belongs with blame, not on the victim.

We would undertake collective political action founded on admitted similarities and grateful connections among us, otherwise needful citizens who now regard each other as burdensome or frightening or irrelevant. This would mean a great national coming out—a coming out of our cars, a coming out of our deadpan passage through the streets of America, a coming out of the suburbs, a coming out of our perverted enthusiasm for whatever keeps us apart: home computers, answering machines, VCRs, and the the proverbial two weeks in a faraway cabin in the woods.

But each American one of us feels so special and so different that none of us assumes the validity of his or her outrage or longing inside the mythical context of "the American Mainstream." We become persuaded that the people of our country must be somebody else, not you and me, even as we regard our government as some alien, half-deaf, and unaccountable monarch to whom we—sooner or later—must pay homage or, at least, taxes. We tolerate insulting, homicidal proposals for national security—such as an aircraft carrier or a helmet and a bulletproof vest—when what we know is that national security must mean, for example, respectful and adequate and guaranteed tender care for elderly Americans and for any American one of us who cannot, do things without help. And meanwhile our American worship of space, open road space, frontier space, astral space and, more particularly, as much space as possible between me and whoever you are—on the bus, on my block, on my job, in my field—our American dreams of "the first" and "the only" produce an invariably mistaken self-centered perspective that repeatedly proves to be self-defeating and, even, antidemocratic. *Demos*, as in democratic, as in a democratic state, means people, not person. A democratic nation of persons, of individuals, is an impossibility, and a fratricidal goal. Each American one of us must consciously choose to become a willing and outspoken part of the people who, together, will determine our individual chances for happiness, and justice.

By people I mean the white people the Black people the female people the lonely people the terrorized people the elderly people the young people the visionary people the unemployed people the regular ordinary omnipresent people who crave grace and variety and surprise and safety and one new day after another.

Democratic anything presupposes equal membership in the body politic. But we will never even approximate the equality a democratic state depends upon, we will never even understand the equality each American one of us requires for our rightful self-respect, as long as we will deny all that we feel and need in common.

But I'm special. I'm different, just like you. I worried about putting together these sentences I have written, here, from my heart: What was the point? To whom should I present myself? What can I know of the doubts and the aching and the bitterness that may prey upon a middle-class nuclear family living in, for instance, Portland, Oregon?

And then I understood that the question was, rather, do I care? And then I understood that the answer is yes, yes, yes: I care because I want you to care about me. I care because I have become aware of my absolute dependency upon you, whoever you are, for the quality and the outcome of my social, my democratic experience.

And even if the white or Black nuclear families of Portland wanted to reject my offering as oddball ruminations beyond the perimeters of relevant American national fact, I know, rationally, that I am as ordinary as the rest of that majority of American women who are full-time employed, I know that the fastest-growing segment of our total population who compose single-parent and single-adult households and I know that the United States already needs some twenty million new housing units to accommodate our single status, because we will not disappear. And whether elderly or middle-aged or young, most of us can neither afford the money nor the labor-intensive upkeep nor the costly isolation that currently dominant modes of American dreaming imply. But still I am worried: I am so special and I am so different, just like you. I am different from the American dreams of individuality and space that have tortured my strivings. I am special, apparently, because the sum of my considerable, so-called individual success means that I have just received a letter from my lover whom I have not seen in three weeks, I have just written a letter to my son whom I will not see until a month from now, my friends send me photographs so that I will not forget them, I cannot afford the long-distance phone calls I must make whenever I need anything urgent, my kitchen table is strewn with plane tickets and airport-to-airport itineraries, an I have scheduled an appointment to visit my aunt sometime during the summer. Even as I compose this essay, this offering to strangers on whom I must rely for the sake of my usefulness and living connection, what I can hear, most clearly, is the ticking of the kitchen clock, and the inanimate whirring of the refrigerator: I am living by myself, in America.

I am a Black woman poet who has organized her American life

not unlike the life of any successful, white orthopedic surgeon whose
secretary will leave you feeling embarrassed if you ask to speak with
him, directly, or if you suggest that eight weeks is too long to wait
for a fifteen-minute consultation. I am a Black woman poet living in
an American-dream white cottage with tulips and hyacinth and vio-
lets blooming yellow and red and purple and lovely next to the front
door and, ... inside that ideal, spotless, American house there us
no one besides me and my answering machine and my VCR. I do not
even get to say hello to the wife of my landlord who lives in the big
house, the only other house on this ideal American estate of eight-
and-a-half acres. The landlord's wife drives her Cherokee Chief down
to the mailbox, next to the stone gate with the elegantly lettered sign
that reads PRIVATE: NO ADMITTANCE (*sic*), and then backs the jeep
up the lengthy driveway, alone and oblivious, past the cottage where
I sit watching her as I watch the squirrels, the doves, and the crows
who dart about, also singly and oblivious.

I had thought that the city was inhospitable to average yearnings
for a happy life. But I have learned, firsthand, about the wilderness
of the suburbs. I had thought I wanted, and perhaps deserved, to live
in a house. But I have learned that a house is not a community.

When I was still a young woman, I asked my friend and mentor,
R. Buckminster Fuller, about the several wristwatches that he al-
ways wore, simultaneously. He described to me his incessant, global
peregrinations and explained his wish to ascertain, easily, what time
it might be anywhere on the planet. I listened to him, puzzled, and
without envy. But why, I wondered, would anybody travel like that;
didn't he have a home? Didn't home matter to him? "A man is not a
tree," he told me. And in the decades since that conversation I have
gradually, and the hard way, comprehended what he meant: The
whole world will become a home to all of us, or none of us can hope
to live on it, peacefully. But much of the American dream mistakenly
supposes that, like a tree, we will grow and flourish, standing in one
place where we murmur doomed declarations about our roots, about
finding our roots, or putting down roots. In fact, of course, if we
remain where we start from we will neither grow nor flourish. And
much of the American dream furthermore supposes that our children

are, as we like to say, seeds. But, again, that is a peculiar metaphor for human beings who must change and challenge the old order of things into which we are born or we must forfeit our value as new and innocent life in the world.

And if we will claim the whole world as our living room, then it seems to me that we must alter our strangely American concepts of family and home, and we must make these alterations quickly!

This is the moment when we might intelligently exhume earlier systems of extended kinship and then stretch those systems into something suitable for the twenty-first century. Beginning with the given—the physically familiar and comfortable family that we discover as our own—we will have to cultivate courage enough to reach for and then to embrace the unexpected, the uncontrollable, the completely unfamiliar kinsmen and women who must either become our comrades or our enemies, as we work to preserve the species. Television satellites, nuclear missiles, and grievously felt contrasts between a two-car garage and famine will not permit us to do less. And so I submit to you that, in a democratic state, the city is not a mistake: our cities are not optional elements of a democratic civilization! We cannot leave behind us our failures to gratify our individual needs in the context of a heterogeneous, millionfold population. That is, exactly, the task of a rational democracy. That is, precisely, the task of any American one of us hoping to grow and flourish among equals with whom we can make, and keep, life-saving connections. We must learn how to satisfy our individual needs in the context of a heterogeneous, equally entitled, millionfold population of our peers. I am waking up in the middle of some American dreams that have tormented most of us throughout most of our American history!

Several times while writing this paper, my phone has rung and I have sprung forward to pick up the receiver. I am vacating the premises of this idyllic cottage. I am moving back to the city and I hope that one of the incoming calls will let me hear good news: news of an apartment smack in the middle of an unruly mix of other Americans who manage, somehow, *not* to act on brute impulse and not to expect others to submit to our stupefying images of ourselves as more special and more different than anyone else.

I look forward to my return to this new American dream, this dream of the civilized metropolis that will validate the democratic state. There I will have less time for theory (and which American one of us is somebody theoretical?) and there I will have more and more direct contact, direct conflict, to which I will have to react, remembering that the only escape from such difficult groundwork is fantasy. There I may become less "successful" but there I may hope to recover more of the actual touch of tenderness. There, in our American city, I am less likely to stare, like a retarded barbarian, at somebody who is an Arab or someone who is Filipino, or someone who speaks Spanish. As I awaken from my misbegotten dreams, I am planning to stop my American habits of genteel make-believe: I will not pretend that I do not understand terror, or terrorism. I will not pretend that it is privacy and fame and quiet that I want when what I need is a sanitary, a safe and reliable subway or public bus system, an attractive apartment that I can afford to rent, a clean and welcoming community Laundromat, a local and an inexpensive, crowded restaurant, and other different hundreds and thousands of unknown but knowable Americans always around me. And then, as often as possible, at night, I want and I need an ostensible stranger who will lie beside me becoming someone I love at least as much as I love myself.

I do not believe that these new American dreams of mine mark me as special, or different. In these longings, and in this faith, I do not believe that I am living alone in America. But you will have to let me know: Am I?

"REQUIEM FOR THE CHAMP"

(1992)

[Jordan saw herself in the story of Mike Tyson, and in writing about it, changed entirely the discourse of the time about the discredited athlete. The essay was first published in *The Progressive* in February 1992.]

Mike Tyson comes from Brooklyn, and so do I. Where he grew up was about a twenty-minute bus ride from my house. I always thought his neighborhood looked like a war zone. It reminded me of Berlin— immediately after World War II. I had never seen Berlin except for black-and-white photos in *Life* magazine, but that was bad enough: Rubble. Barren. Blasted. Everywhere you turned your eyes recoiled from the jagged edges of an office building or a cathedral, shattered, or the tops of apartment houses torn off, and nothing alive even intimated, anywhere. I used to think, "This is what it means to fight and really win or really lose. War means you hurt somebody, or something, until there's nothing soft or sensible left."

For sure I never had a boyfriend who came out of Mike Tyson's territory. Yes, I enjoyed my share of tough guys and/or gang members who walked and talked and fought and loved in quintessential Brooklyn ways: cool, tough, and deadly serious. But there was a code as rigid as romantic as anything that ever made the pages of traditional English literature. A guy would beat up another guy or, if appropriate, he'd kill him. But a guy talked different to a girl. A guy made other guys clean up their language around "his girl." A guy brought ribbons and candies and earrings and tulips to a girl. He took care of her. He walked her home. And if he got serious about that girl, and even if she was only twelve years old, then she became his "lady." And woe betide any other guy stupid enough to disrespect that particular young black female.

But none of the boys—none of the young men—none of the young Black male inhabitants of my universe and my heart ever came from Mike Tyson's streets or avenues. We didn't live someplace fancy or middle-class, but at least there were ten-cent gardens, front and back, and coin Laundromats, and grocery stores, and soda parlors, and barber shops, and Holly Roller churchfronts, and chicken shacks, and dry cleaners, and bars-and-grills, and a takeout Chinese restaurant, and all of that usable detail that does not survive a war. That kind of seasonal green turf and daily-life supporting pattern of establishments to meet your needs did not exist inside the gelid urban cemetery where Mike Tyson learned what he thought he needed to know.

I remember when the City of New York decided to construct a senior housing project there, in the childhood world of former heavyweight boxing champion Mike Tyson. I remember wondering, "Where in the hell will those old people have to go in order to find food? And how will they get there?"

I'm talking godforsaken. And much of living in Brooklyn was like that. But then it might rain or it might snow and, for example, I could look at the rain forcing forsythia into bloom or watch how snowflakes can tease bare tree limbs into temporary blossoms of snow dissolving into diadems of sunlight. And what did Mike Tyson ever see besides brick walls and garbage in the gutter and disintegrating concrete steps and boarded-up windows and broken car parts blocking the sidewalk and men, bitter, with their hands in their pockets, and women, bitter, with their heads down and their eyes almost closed?

In his neighborhood, where could you buy ribbons for a girl, or tulips?

Mike Tyson comes from Brooklyn. And so do I. In the big picture of America, I never had much going for me. And he had less. I only learned, last year, that I can stop whatever violence starts with me. I only learned, last year, that love is infinitely more interesting, and more exciting, and more powerful, than really winning or really losing a fight. I only learned, last year, that all war leads to death and that all love leads you away from death. I am more than twice Mike Tyson's age. And I'm not stupid. Or slow. But I'm Black. And I come from Brooklyn. And I grew up fighting. And I grew up and I got out of Brooklyn because I got pretty good at fighting. And winning. Or else, intimidating my would-be adversaries with my fists, my feet, and my mouth. And I never wanted to fight. I never wanted anybody to hit me. And I never wanted to hit anybody. But the bell would ring at the end of another dumb day in school and I'd head out with dread and a nervous sweat because I knew some jackass more or less my age and more or less my height would be waiting for me because she or he had nothing better to do than to wait for me and hope to kick my butt or tear up my books or break my pencils or pull hair out of my head.

This is the meaning of poverty: when you have nothing better to do than to hate somebody who, just exactly like yourself, has nothing better to do than to pick on you instead of trying to figure out how come there's nothing better to do. How come there's no gym/ no swimming pool/no dirt track/no soccer field/no ice-skating rink/ no bike/no bike path/no tennis courts/no language arts workshop/ no computer science center/no band practice/no choir rehearsal/no music lessons/no basketball or baseball team? How come neither one of you has his or her own room in a house where you can hang out and dance and make out or get on the telephone or eat and drink up everything in the kitchen that can move? How come nobody on your block and nobody in your class has any of these things?

I'm Black. Mike Tyson is Black. And neither one of us was ever supposed to win anything more than a fight between the two of us. And if you check out the mass-media material on "us," and if you check out the emergency-room reports on "us," you might well believe we're losing the fight to be more than our enemies have decreed. Our enemies would deprive us of everything except each other: hungry and furious and drug-addicted and rejected and ever convinced we can never be beautiful or right or true or different from the beggarly monsters our enemies envision and insist upon, and how should we then stand, Black man and Black woman, face to face?

Way back when I was born, Richard Wright had just published *Native Son* and, thereby, introduced white America to the monstrous product of its racist hatred.

Poverty does not beautify. Poverty does not teach generosity or allow us for sucker attributes of tenderness and restraint. In white America, hatred of Blackfolks has imposed horrible poverty upon us.

And so, back in the thirties, Richard Wright's *Native Son*, Bigger Thomas, did what he thought he had to do: he hideously murdered a white woman and he viciously murdered his Black girlfriend in what he conceived as self-defense. He did not perceive any options to these psychopathic, horrifying deeds. I do not believe he, Bigger Thomas, had any other choices open to him. Not to him, he who was meant to die like the rat he, Bigger Thomas, cornered and smashed to death in his mother's beggarly clean space.

I never thought Bigger Thomas was okay. I never thought he should skate back into my, or anyone's community. But I did and I do think he is my brother. The choices available to us dehumanize. And any single one of us, Black in this white country, we may be defeated, we may become dehumanized, by the monstrous hatred arrayed against us and our needy dreams.

And so I write this requiem for Mike Tyson: international celebrity, millionaire, former heavyweight boxing champion of the world, a big-time winner, a big-time loser, an African-American male in his twenties, and, now, a convicted rapist.

Do I believe he is guilty of rape?

Yes I do.

And what would I propose as appropriate punishment?

Whatever will force him to fear the justice of exact retribution, and whatever will force him, for the rest of his damned life, to regret and to detest the fact that he defiled, he subjugated, and he wounded somebody helpless to his power.

And do I therefore rejoice in the jury's finding?

I do not.

Well, would I like to see Mike Tyson a free man again?

He was never free!

And I do not excuse or condone or forget or minimize or forgive the crime of his violation of the young Black woman he raped!

But did anybody ever tell Mike Tyson that you talk different to a girl? Where would he learn that? Would he learn that from U.S. Senator Ted Kennedy? Or from hotshot/scot-free movie director Roman Polanski? Or from rap recording star Ice Cube? Or from Ronald Reagan and the Grenada escapade? Or from George Bush in Panama? Or from George Bush and Colin Powell in the Persian Gulf? Or from the military hero flyboys who returned from bombing the shit out of civilian cities in Iraq and then said, laughing and proud, on international TV: "All I need, now, is a woman"? Or from the hundreds of thousands of American football fans? Or from the millions of Americans who would, if they could, pay surrealistic amounts of money just to witness, up close, somebody like Mike Tyson beat the brains out of somebody?

And what could which university teach Mike Tyson about the difference between violence and love? Is there any citadel of higher education in the country that does not pay its football coach at least three times as much as the chancellor and six times as much as its professors and ten times as much as its social and psychological counselors?

In this America where Mike Tyson and I live together and bitterly, bitterly, apart, I say he became what he felt. He felt the stigma of a priori hatred and intentional poverty. He was given the choice of violence or violence, the violence of defeat or the violence of victory. Who would pay him to rehabilitate inner-city housing or to refurbish a bridge? Who would pay him what to study the facts of our collective history? Who would pay him what to plant and nurture trees of a forest? And who will write and who will play the songs that tell a guy like Mike Tyson how to talk to a girl?

What was America willing to love about Mike Tyson? Or any Black man? Or any man's man?

Tyson's neighborhood and my own have become the same no-win battleground. And he has fallen there. And I do not rejoice. I do not.

"LET ME BE VERY / VERY / VERY / VERY / VERY / SPECIFIC"

FROM *HARUKO / LOVE POEMS: NEW AND SELECTED LOVE POEMS* (1993), FROM *KISSING GOD GOODBYE: POEMS 1991-1997* (1997) & FROM *AFFIRMATIVE ACTS: POLITICAL ESSAYS* (1998)

[In early 1992, Jordan was diagnosed with breast cancer. The doctors recommended a partial mastectomy. Jordan was informed that chances of survival after a mastectomy were usually 80%; in her case, however, they were deemed 40%. She fought the disease with her characteristic energy, as an enemy that had to be taken on, remarking that she now had less stamina—but still more than other people had available to them. She took better care of her health, profited from her devoted circle of friends, and was very productive, with several new books and projects. "The prognosis is very bad, but I'm very well," she said, "I'm exercising, I've never been as fit as I am in my life before." During the 1990s, after surgery and chemotherapy, the cancer went into remission.]

FROM *HARUKO / LOVE POEMS: NEW AND SELECTED LOVE POEMS*

(1993)

"Haruko:
Oh! It's like stringbean *in French?"*

"No:
It's like hurricane
in English!"

[How to be sexy and smart, how to be both tender *and* furious, was a talent Jordan never lost, even in the eye of a hurricane. A tempestuous love affair in Berkeley with an Asian-American woman resulted in the twenty-six rapturous and raging lyrics of the *Haruko* poems. Here's a selection that includes two that have never been published: "Poem for One Little Girl Blue" (dated 9/30/91) and "Poem About 10/8/91: for HARUKO" (dated 10/14/91).

The *Haruko* poems were accompanied by a section of the book devoted to Jordan's love poems from 1970-1991. "I feel very strongly that love poems constitute a political body of writing; to write them is a political act," she said. In this context, it seems only natural that she included "I Must Become a Menace to My Enemies" (p. 215-217), not everyone's idea of a love poem. And yet...]

◆◆◆

POEM FOR HARUKO

I never thought I'd keep a record of my pain
or happiness
like candles lighting the entire soft lace
of the air
around the full length of your hair/a shower

organized by God
in brown and auburn
undulations luminous like particles
of flame

But now I do
retrieve an afternoon of apricots
and water interspersed with cigarettes
and sand and rocks
we walked across:
How easily you held
my hand
beside the low tide
of the world

Now I do
relive an evening of retreat
a bridge I left behind
where all the solid heat
of lust and tender trembling
lay as cruel and as kind
as passion spins its infinite
tergiversations in between the bitter
and the sweet

Alone and longing for you
now I do

♦♦♦

POEM ABOUT PROCESS AND PROGRESS

for Haruko

Hey Baby you betta
hurry it up!

Because
since you went totally
off
I seen a full moon
I seen a half moon
I seen a quarter moon
I seen no moon whatsoever!

I seen a equinox
I seen a solstice
I seen Mars and Venus on a line
I seen a mess a fickle stars
and lately
I seen this new kind a luva
on an' off the telephone
who like to talk to me
all the time

real nice

◆◆◆

"ADMITTEDLY"

Admittedly
I do not forget
the beauty of one braid
black silk that fell
as loose as it fell long
and everlasting as the twilight
anywhere

◆◆◆

POEM ABOUT HEARTBREAK THAT GO ON AND ON

bad love last like a big
ugly lizard crawl around the house
forever
never die
and never change itself

into a butterfly

◆◆◆

POEM FOR ONE LITTLE GIRL BLUE

She hangs onto sadness
the way somebody else treads water
waiting for the world
to see how much she hurts from family
madness pierced her rib cage
twenty years ago

And she'll continue to compete as Victim
Absolute
until she finally receives a gold
medallion for her suffering
or a truly purple heart complete
with ribbons
so that she can hang that up

and then
move right along
perhaps/at last
to someplace

really new

◆◆◆

POEM ABOUT 10/8/91: FOR HARUKO

Soon after you put me on hold
my regular watch broke down
but then
this morning (at last) the call came:
It's okay again.

And in the hospital after pulling the plug
on agony
and resigned to a final 48 hours
of terminal cancer
Rod rallied
better than he's been
for several months
and conscious and smiling

And on my answering machine
I found your message:
"Hi.   It's Haruko.
It's Tuesday: 10:40 A.M."

And like my regular but broken
watch
I'm fixed
I'm running now
(at last)
And it's okay
And it's okay
again

FROM *KISSING GOD GOODBYE: POEMS 1991-1997*

(1997)

["Saddam Hussein does not share our sanctity for human life," declared the White House as American bombs rained down on Iraqi civilians in early 1991. Jordan's outraged response to the first Gulf War, especially her powerful "The Bombing of Baghdad," is one of the most powerful and poignant rejoinders to American wrongheadedness. (Sadly, "The Bombing of Baghdad" was no less relevant when the second Bush unleashed the second war on Iraq in January 2003; Jordan's poem, once again, was read at anti-war rallies and demonstrations, and re-printed around the globe.) More than ever, building on her work in *Ceiling/ Sky*, the musicality of her writing intensified, and the poems sang in forms old and new, western and eastern. Even as she kissed God goodbye at the end of the century, Jordan was embracing the possibilities for love, hope, beauty, truth. The cancer returned in 1995. In "First Poem after Serious Surgery," Jordan described herself as on the "meridian of failure or recovery" where "I move / or stop respectful / of each day / but silent now / and slow." Not quite true. She may have been slow(er), but she was not silent.]

◆◆◆

STUDY #1

Let me be
very
very
very
very
very
specific

Let me not forget about
or
Let me not forget about
anything like
anything like
an eyelash
lost above your lips

When the President says no to legislation
to make cocaine more criminal like crack
or crack less criminal like cocaine
so that white men as well as black
get nailed for jail

When the President says no
When the President says no
When the President says no to Fidel Castro
When the President talks about Human Rights
and moral guiding lights and then
The President says yes
to a total mess of multi-multi-
millionfold
marketplace
potentate
Toms and Dicks and Harrys and then
And then when the President
says no to Fidel Castro

Let me be
very
very
very
very
very
specific

The criminal inertia
The criminal morality of inertia
The criminal morality of inertia nothing
nothing
nothing
not even the junked baby tied to the chair
not even the smashed face woman
      dragged through the house by
         what's left of her hair

nothing
nothing
interdicts
the criminal inertia
of suit and tie/
or my
complacency

Nothing
Nothing
Not even the beautiful man
parking my car or
sweeping the airport terminal floor
only because so far no
robot can
absolutely replace a beautiful man
while unemployment and huge profits rise
amid official spokesmanly lies
about the no jobs future
we're definitely due for

Nothing
Nothing interdicts
the criminal inertia
of suit and tie
or my

complacency
Or let me not forget
Or let me not forget about 2 miles
below my house
a train moves
moaning through the night
(I said:) 2 miles below my house
a train moves
moaning through the night

Let me be
very
very
very
very
very
specific
Now that the U.S. Congress agrees
That nobody American
has a right to anything besides
acute emotional
         physical
         and economic
         anxieties

Let me be
very
very
very
very
very
specific

Let me not forget about
or
Let me not forget about

anything like
anything like
an eyelash
lost above your lips

(please baby please)

◆◆◆

THE ECLIPSE OF 1996

Everybody out of the house!
Everybody up on the roof!
Run to the top of the street!
Pull back the branches of the trees!
Abandon all cars!
Do you hear me?
Bring the children!
Carry your babies into the night!
THE LIGHT'S ABOUT TO GO OUT!
We've finally managed to shut down the shining of the moon!

And you wouldn't want
to miss that

wouldya?

◆◆◆

FIRST POEM AFTER SERIOUS SURGERY

The breath continues but the breathing
hurts
Is this the way death wins its way
against all longing
and redemptive thrust from grief?

Head falls
Hands crawl
and pain becomes the only keeper
of my time

I am not held
I do not hold
And touch degenerates into new
agony

I feel
the healing of cut muscle/
broken nerves
as I return to hot and cold
sensations
of a body tortured by the flight
of feeling/normal
registrations of repulsion
or delight

On this meridian of failure or recovery
I move
or stop respectful
of each day
but silent now
and slow

◆◆◆

THE BOMBING OF BAGHDAD

1

began and did not terminate for 42 days
and 42 nights relentless minute after minute
more than 110,000 times
we bombed Iraq we bombed Baghdad

we bombed Basra/we bombed military
installations we bombed the National Museum
we bombed schools we bombed air raid
shelters we bombed water we bombed
electricity we bombed hospitals we
bombed streets we bombed highways
we bombed everything that moved/we
bombed everything that did not move we
bombed Baghdad
a city of 5.5 million human beings
we bombed radio towers we bombed
telephone poles we bombed mosques
we bombed runways we bombed tanks
we bombed trucks we bombed cars we bombed bridges
we bombed the darkness we bombed
the sunlight we bombed them and we
bombed them and we cluster bombed the citizens
of Iraq and we sulfur bombed the citizens of Iraq
and we napalm bombed the citizens of Iraq and we
complemented these bombings/these "sorties" with
Tomahawk cruise missiles which we shot
repeatedly by the thousands upon thousands
into Iraq
(you understand an Iraqi Scud missile
is *quote* militarily insignificant *unquote* and we
do not mess around with insignificant)
so we used cruise missiles repeatedly
we fired them into Iraq
And I am not pleased
I am not very pleased
None of this fits into my notion of "things going very well"

2
The bombing of Baghdad
did not obliterate the distance or the time
between my body and the breath

of my beloved

3

This was Custer's Next-To-Last Stand
I hear Crazy Horse singing as he dies
I dedicate myself to learn that song
I hear that music in the moaning of the Arab world

4

Custer got accustomed to just doing his job
Pushing westward into glory
Making promises
Searching for the savages/their fragile
temporary settlements
for raising children/dancing down the rain/and praying
for the mercy of a herd of buffalo
Custer/he pursued these savages
He attacked at dawn
He murdered the men/murdered the boys
He captured the women and converted
them (I'm sure)
to his religion
Oh, how gently did he bid his darling fiancée
farewell!
How sweet the gaze her eyes bestowed upon her warrior!
Loaded with guns and gunpowder he embraced
the guts and gore of manifest white destiny
He pushed westward
to annihilate the savages
("Attack at dawn!")
and seize their territories
　　seize their women
　　seize their natural wealth

5

And I am cheering for the arrows

and the braves

6

And all who believed some must die
they were already dead
And all who believe only they possess
human being and therefore human rights
they no longer stood among the possibly humane
And all who believed that retaliation/revenge/defense
derive from God-given prerogatives of white men
And all who believed that waging war is anything
        besides terrorist activity in the first
        place and in the last
And all who believed that F-15s/F-16s/ "Apache"
        helicopters/
B-52 bombers/smart bombs/dumb bombs/napalm/artillery/
battleships/nuclear warheads amount to anything other
than terrorist tools of a terrorist undertaking
And all who believed that holocaust means something
        that only happens to white people
And all who believed that Desert Storm
        signified anything besides the delivery of an American
        holocaust against the peoples of the Middle East
All who believed these things
they were already dead
They no longer stood among the possibly humane

And this is for Crazy Horse singing as he dies
because I live inside his grave
And this is for the victims of the bombing of Baghdad
because the enemy traveled from my house
        to blast your homeland
        into pieces of children
        and pieces of sand

And in the aftermath of carnage

perpetrated in my name
how should I dare to offer you my hand
how shall I negotiate the implications
                    of my shame?

My heart cannot confront
this death without relief
My soul will not control
this leaking of my grief

And this is for Crazy Horse singing as he dies
And here is my song of the living
who must sing against the dying
sing to join the living
with the dead

◆◆◆

FOCUS IN REAL TIME

Poem for Margaret who passed the California bar!

A bowl of rice
        as food
        as politics
        or metaphor
        as something valuable and good
        or something common to consume/exploit/ignore

Who grew these grains
Who owned the land
Who harvested the crop
Who converted these soft particles to money
Who kept the cash
Who shipped the consequences of the cash
Who else was going to eat the rice

Who else was going to convert the rice to cash
Who would design the flowers for the outside of the bowl
Who would hold the bowl between her hands
Who would give the bowl away
Who could share the rice
Who could fill that bowl with rice how many times a day
        how many times a week
Who would adore the hands that held the bowl that held the rice
Who would adore the look the smell the steam of boiled rice
      in a bowl

Who will analyze the cash the rice becomes
Who will sit beside the bowl or fight for rice
Who will write about the hands that hold the bowl
Who will want to own the land
      A bowl of rice

◆◆◆

POEM #1 FOR B.B.L.

5 months
eighteen days
three dinners
three countries
two transatlantic
two trans-Mediterranean
flights
one hundred trans-continental
e-mail messages
seven or eight Fed Ex deliveries
four or five letters
2 bowls of granola
146 phone calls
2x playing tennis
one walk

one drive
one salt water
one fresh water
swim
2 hotels
4 or 5 tapes
3 or 4 photographs
one taxi
two books
one movie
and some bimbo
asking me
what's the plan?
one/two/three/four/five months
18 days
3 dinners
spinning into one winner word
like "DUCK!"
that heedless
downy
feathered
thing

that one word
heedless
downy
feathered
three countries
2 transatlantic
okay
okay
so maybe
that's the plan?

◆◆◆

KISSING GOD GOODBYE

Poem in the face of Operation Rescue
Dedicated to Jennie Portnoff

You mean to tell me on the 12th day or the 13th
that the Lord
which is to say some wiseass
got more muscle than he
reasonably
can control or figure out / some
accidental hard disk
thunderbolt / some
big mouth
woman-hating / super
heterosexist heterosexual
kind of a guy guy
he decided who could live and who would die?

And after he did what?
created alleyways of death
and acid rain
and infant mortality rates
and sons of the gun
and something called the kitchenette
and trailer trucks to kill and carry
beautiful trees out of their natural
habitat / Oh! Not that guy?

Was it that other guy
who invented a snake
an apple and a really
retarded scenario so that
down to this very day
it is not a lot of fun
to give birth to a son of a gun?
And wasn't no woman in the picture

of the Lord?
He done the whole thing by himself?
The oceans and the skies
and the fish that swim and the bird
that flies?

You sure he didn't have some serious problems
of perspective
for example
coming up with mountains/valleys/rivers/rainbows
and no companionship/no coach/no
midwife/boyfriend/girlfriend/
no help whatsoever for a swollen
overactive
brain
unable to spell
sex

You mean to tell me that the planet
is the brainchild
of a single
       male
       head of household?

And everything he said and done
the floods/famines/plagues
and pestilence
the invention of the slave and the invention of the gun
the worship of war (especially whichever war
he won)
And after everything he thought about and made 2 million
megapronouncements about
(Like)
"Give not your strength to women"
and
"You shall not lie with a male as with a woman"

and
"An outsider shall not eat of a holy thing"
and
"If a woman conceives and bears a male child
then she shall be unclean
seven days... But if she bears
a female child, then she shall be unclean
2 weeks..."
and
"The leper who has the disease
shall wear torn clothes and let the hair
of his head hang loose
and he shall cover his upper lip
and cry, 'Unclean,
unclean!'"
and
"Behold, I have 2 daughters
who have not known a man,
let me bring them out to you, and do
to them as you please"
and
"I will greatly multiply your pain
in childbearing:
in pain shall you bring forth children"
and
"Take your son, your only son Isaac,
whom you love,
and go to the land of Moriah, and offer
him there as a burnt offering"
and in the middle of this lunatic lottery
there was Ruth saying to Naomi:
"Entreat me not
to leave you or to return
from following you; for where you go
I will go
and where you lodge I will lodge, your people

shall be my people
And your God my God;
where you die I will die,
and there I will be buried. May the Lord do so to me
and more also
if even death parts me from you."
and
David wailing aloud at the death of Jonathan who loved
          him
"more than his own soul" and David
inconsolable in lamentation
saying
"...very pleasant have you been to me;
your love to me was wonderful,
passing the love of women"
and
"If I give away all I have, and if I deliver
my body to be burned,
but have not love,
I gain nothing..."
and this chaos/this chaos
exploded tyrannical in scattershot scripture
(Like)
"...those who belong in Christ
Jesus have crucified the flesh
with its passions and desire"
and
"Cast out the slave and her son"
and
"If in spite of this you will not hearken
to me, then...
You shall eat the flesh of your sons,
you shall eat the flesh
of your daughters. And I will
destroy your high places... I will
lay your cities waste... I will

devastate your land... And
as for those of you that are left,
I will send faintness
into their hearts in the lands of their enemies
the sound of a driven leaf
shall put them to flight..."
etcetera etcetera
That guy?
That guy?
the ruler of all earth
and heaven too
The maker of all laws
and all taboo
The absolute supremacist
of power
the origin of the destiny
of molecules and Mars
The father and the son
the king and the prince
The prophet and the prophecy
The singer and the song
The man from whom
in whom
of whom
by whom
comes everything
without the womb
without that unclean
feminine
connection/
that guy?

The emperor of poverty
The czar of suffering
The wizard of disease
The joker of morality

The pioneer of slavery
The priest of sexuality
The host of violence
The Almighty fount of fear and trembling
That's the guy?
You mean to tell me on the 12th day or the 13th
that the Lord
which is to say some wiseass
got more muscle than he
reasonably
can control or figure out/some
accidental hard disk
thunderbolt/some
big mouth
woman-hating/super
heterosexist heterosexual
kind of a guy guy
he decided who could live and who would die?

And so
the names become
the names of the dead and the living
who love
Peter
John
Tede
Phil
Larry
Bob
Alan
Richard
Tom
Wayne
David
Jonathan
Bruce

Mike
Steve
And so
our names become
the names of the dead
and the living who love
Suzanne
Amy
Elizabeth
Margaret
Trude
Linda
Sara
Alexis
Frances
Nancy
Ruth
Naomi
Julie
Kate
Patricia
And out of that scriptural scattershot
our names become
the names of the dead

our names become
the names of the iniquitous
the names of the accursed
the names of the tribes of the abomination
because
my name is not Abraham
my name is not Moses/Leviticus/Solomon/Cain or Abel
my name is not Matthew/Luke/Saul or Paul
My name is not Adam
My name is female
my name is freedom

my name is the one who lives outside the tent of the father
my name is the one who is dark
my name is the one who fights for the end of the kingdom
my name is the one at home
my name is the one who bleeds
my name is the one with the womb
my name is female
my name is freedom
my name is the one the bible despised
my name is the one astrology cannot predict
my name is the name the law cannot invalidate
my name is the one who loves

and that guy
and that guy
you never even seen upclose

He cannot eat at my table
He cannot sleep in my bed
He cannot push me aside
He cannot make me commit or contemplate
        suicide

He cannot say my name
without shame
He cannot say my name
My name
My name is the name of the one who loves

And he
has no dominion over me
his hate has no dominion over me
I am she who will be free

And that guy
better not try to tell anybody about who

should live
and who should die
or why

His name is not holy
He is not my Lord
He is not my people
His name is not sacred
His name is not my name
His name is not the name of those who love the living

His name is not the name of those who love the living
and the dead

His name is not our name
we
who survive the death
of men and women
whose beloved
breath
becomes (at last)
our own

FROM *AFFIRMATIVE ACTS: POLITICAL ESSAYS*

(1998)

[In 1998, Jordan received the Lifetime Achievement Award from the National Black Writers' Conference and the American Institute of Architecture's Award for Architectural Design for her proposal for the African Burial Grounds Memorial in Lower Manhattan. She collaborated on a CD recording of *Ceiling/Sky* and published a new collection of timely political essays, *Affirmative Acts*, which she offered to her readers "as a warrior prayer for renewed, righteous insistence upon the values of justice and equality." Many of the new pieces were first published in *The Progressive*. She observed Nelson Mandela, and how he changed the world; reflected on her early disappointment in the Clinton administration; spoke out again against police brutality, most recently demonstrated in the videotaped beating of Rodney King by LA police officers; wrote again, this time in prose, about Clarence Thomas, "a man as different from [Thurgood] Marshall as George Bush [who nominated him to the Supreme Court described him] [was] from Mahatma Ghandi"; delivered a tribute to Paul Robeson, and a praise poem for the sung and unsung heroines in the history of jazz; and indicted the administration for the audacity and insult of authorizing the heaviest air assault in history on Iraq to coincide with Martin Luther King, Jr.'s birthday.

Jordan's *Progressive* columns have been collected in a single volume entitled *Life as Activism*, edited by Stacy Russo and published in 2014.]

"WILLING AND ABLE"

(1992)

[This essay championing the rights of people with disabilities first appeared in *The Progressive*, August 1992.]

Last June, Charlie Lubin graduated from Berkeley High School. Three days a week you can catch him at work in the cafeteria of his alma mater. Other times he's busy at a local silkscreen shop, producing T-shirts to order. Or he's out playing softball, or he's studying to become a clown.

Charlie Lubin is twenty-two years old. He was born with Down's syndrome. Right after his birth, hospital doctors and nurses counseled his mother with the words: "Don't see it!"

But Barbara Lubin refused to surrender her child into those waiting, professional hands of death. "That crazy woman with a retarded son" fought to keep him alive, and she kept fighting all the way to *Lubin vs. Berkeley Board of Education*, a 1978 landmark legal battle that established the rights of disabled children to an appropriate, and fully conceived and fully delivered, public education.

> He says, "Excuse me, I don't mean to be rude
> But I do not know what to call you.
> Is it physically challenged, mobility impaired?
> wheelchair bound, wheelchair user?
> Handicapped, handicapper, handicappable?
> crip, crippled, confined?
> deformed, defective, disabled?
> Inconvenienced, invalid?
> sick, special, survivor?
> Please tell me, what's the word?
> What. ..."
> I say, "Wait! How about calling me by my name?"

His name is Johnson Cheu. Twenty-two and a half years ago, Johnson arrived, premature. He was placed inside an incubator for eighty days and, at some awful moment, a technical malfunction deprived Johnson's brain cells of oxygen.

"I've just been very fortunate," he tells me. "I have a very light case of spastic cerebral palsy. That means that a lot of my muscles never relax from varying states of permanent contraction."

I have never seen Johnson out of a wheelchair and I ask if spastic cerebral palsy dictates the use of such support. "Not exactly," he says. "I can, actually, stand and walk around. But I'm limited by the fact that one of my steps is the energy-expended equivalent of two hundred and sixty-five steps of yours. The chair increases my endurance, my mobility."

In his last semester as an undergraduate, Johnson served as a voluntary tutor for Berkeley High School students. Today he teaches four different English classes there and, once or twice a day, he breaks for a cup of coffee or a bottle of juice from the cafeteria where Charlie Lubin is gainfully employed.

Besides teaching, Johnson writes poetry and leads a University of California-Berkeley poetry workshop. He will enter Stanford University next September and pursue an accelerated graduate-studies program to receive secondary teaching credentials and a Master's in the Art of Education.

Charlie Lubin and Johnson Cheu are two of the forty-three million Americans who persist among us despite the burdens of mental or physical disability.

Day after day, Charlie and Johnson meet with ignorant/fearful/indifferent and cruel stupidities of response that most of us commit whenever we notice somebody markedly different from ourselves. Terms such as "retarded" or "crippled" plainly express our panic or our disdain.

Johnson Cheu has written a poem about the daily indignities he faces, describing the "hateful grimace" or the "sad pity eyes" that meet him when he goes shopping. He refuses to ask for assistance because he knows people will respond "in baby talk/pat my head." "I am not a dog," he writes.

On campus one afternoon, I stood chatting with Johnson Cheu. Suddenly a huge moving van began to back into us. We yelled as loud as we could, but the van wheezed and rolled closer and closer. Johnson had to execute some almost magical, swift maneuvering of his wheelchair in order to escape. We were both breathless and furious when, finally, we could stop scrambling for safety.

People don't give a damn. People do not think about the stamina demanded of anyone disabled. We hardly ever bother to imagine what it takes to get dressed, or to cook, or to eat, or to learn algebra, or to cross the street, if you are not 100 percent able-bodied. Disability means difficult and tedious and isolated and outcast.

But Charlie Lubin and Johnson Cheu have won for themselves

a way out of no way. In 1991, the Americans with Disabilities Act (ADA) became law. ADA easily compares to the most important civil-rights legislation of the 1960s. Most situations of employment and public facilities (from schoolrooms to hotels to airport telephones) must no longer discriminate against disabled persons. Legal concepts of discrimination now include physical design and redesign requirements as well as new consumer and/or employee and/or citizen-at-large policies. The intent of the law is to fully enable the disabled to function on a competitive, decently self-sufficient basis. This is the best anything to emerge from the U.S. Congress since I don't know when.

And so I hope we get on with the next task of enforcement, and make that happen fast. I hope we properly perceive this legislative precedent as solid ground for the shock of further goods news: further revolutionary legislation that, for example, will enable the homeless and the sick to acquire the help they need, without humiliation.

If we will pay attention to the achievements of Charlie Lubin and Johnson Cheu, and if we will embrace and build upon the ADA, then, maybe, we will become part of some national good news that will lessen our national reasons for shame.

"GETTING DOWN ON MY STREET"

(1995)

[First published in *Affirmative Acts*, 1998.]

This is one big country. And if people in North Dakota spoke one language, while folks in South Dakota or New Mexico, spoke another, a different, language, that would seem reasonable to me, even appropriate. And, so, I dispute all the various "nationwide" analyses and projections, each one colder than cold. "Nationwide" is too wide, too broad, to mean anything.

On the block where I live, there are Black families, white families, Southeast Asian-Americans, Chinese-Americans, "interracial" students, elderly folks, newlyweds, Jews, and Christians. This is a short little street of great good calm. And I defy anybody to identify more than two or three things that I may have in common with the household next door. They're Black. I'm Black. They live on this street. So do I. But what does race or residence in this city mean to them? I have no idea. And beyond that? Personally, I would not assume anything about them or anybody else on my block except that they're likely to be friendly in a California ("If you *ever* need anything ...") way.

So when I started to read and hear about "the great racial divide," a week ago, I thought, "Sure. Is that something like Continental Drift? Or what?" And when I started to read and hear about race as the only and the biggest deal on the table, I thought, "Sure. Is that something like regular Black man Rodney King and multimillionaire O. J. Simpson equally symbolize what, exactly? And the fact that, for example, I'm female, is suddenly and forever beside the point?"

And, so, when some newspaper guy called from L.A. for a comment about the Million Man March, I said, "First of all, I was not invited. Second, I have one thing to say to and about anything or anybody who wants to sunder me from the Black man who is my son 'You can go to hell!'"

And when a colleague (of sorts) of mine went off about domestic violence "versus" Mark Fuhrman and the LAPD, I said, "How come you can't see that Mark Fuhrman and the LAPD and racism, per se, suck Mack trucks, absolutely, yes, and, also, anybody who busts up his wife is totally reprehensible, and I don't forgive or forget anything or anybody who's just plain ugly and wrong: Mark Fuhrman *and* O.J. Simpson."

And when Minister Farrakhan proclaimed himself "God's Messenger" with not so much as a momentary twinkle of quasi-uneasiness, and when Minister Farrakhan went lyrical about the number nine symbolizing a pregnant woman with "a male child" inside her, and so on and so forth, I thought, "Well, there it is: CNN gives this guy two and a half hours of uninterrupted international television time—way more than the Pope, President Clinton, or Nelson Mandela—and then what?" More "nationwide" pseudoanalysis and projection about "the significance" of the importance that CNN, and most of the American mass media, invest Farrakhan with.

And then I read and I heard about who supported and who opposed the Million Man March, for a couple of days, but then, happily, happily, I realized that my local, real life preempts all of these national constructions and destructions.

On Thursday, October 12, 1995, five thousand Americans of every description rallied at U.C.-Berkeley. There were "Queers for Affirmative Action," "Jews for Affirmative Action," "Asians for Affirmative Action," and Native American dances for affirmative action. Everybody was invited to the rally, and everybody showed up. As a matter of fact, the leadership for this fantastic success was a new U.C.-Berkeley student organization called Diversity in Action. As the name suggests, the members of this incredibly effective task force include African-American young men with dreads or shaved heads and Irish-American young men with blond ponytails and Chicana young women and Vietnamese-American young men and women, and like that, on and on.

This ecstatic, mighty throng gathered together to demand restoration of affirmative action throughout the University of California system, and to assert our intelligent resistance to demagogic, racialized, un-American manipulations that would deny American history, deplore American diversity, and destroy our manifest, principled unity.

When I spoke, I pointed to the very recent (September 12) finding by the 1995 National Research Council report on the quality of Ph.D education in the United States: With the most heterogeneous student population in the world, U.C.-Berkeley is the leading, the top, university in America, or, as the *New York Times* reported, "No other university even comes close."

Our main speaker for this great day was the Reverend Jesse Jackson, and we greeted him with an endless tumult of genuine cheers and excitement. He came through with a rousing argument in favor of "real world" politics and policies and, therefore, affirmative action. He implored us to "turn to" each other and "not turn on" each other. He inveighed against the list of odious visions out there: racism, sexism, anti-Semitism, homophobia. And he implored us to get angry and vote Gingrich and company out of power in 1996.

On Tuesday, October 17, 1995, our U.C. faculty senate voted 124 to 2 to rescind the U.C. Regents' ruling against affirmative action. This vote does not mean the Regents will have to reverse themselves, but it does mean that the faculty stands with the students who stand with the chancellors, united in opposition to the Regents, and united in passionate support of affirmative action.

The "nationwide" assault on affirmative action began right here, in Northern California. And it looks to me like we may bury that particular outrage right here, where it was born. For sure, the fight is on, and it does seem far from hopeless.

So, yes, this is one big country. I happen to live on the Pacific Rim, which, for better or worse, harbors the demographic and economic forecast for all of the USA in the twenty-first century.

And I trust what I can see and what I can hear and what I can do on my block, and around the corner, and on the campus where I teach.

And, just now, I am awfully glad to live nowhere else but here: right here.

ON TIME TANKA[9]

I refuse to choose
between lynch rope and gang rape
the blues is the blues!
My skin and my sex: Deep dues
I have no wish to escape

---

9   A tanka is an ancient Japanese poetry form, consisting of a five-syllable line followed by a seven-syllable line, followed by a five-syllable line, followed by two seven-syllable lines [Jordan's footnote].

I refuse to lose
the flame of my single space
this safety I choose
between your fist and my face
between my gender and race

All Black and blue news
withers the heart of my hand
and leads to abuse
no one needs to understand:
suicide wipes out the clues

Big-Time-Juicy-Fruit!
Celebrity-Rich-Hero
Rollin out the Rolls!
Proud cheatin on your (Black) wife
Loud beatin on your (white) wife

Real slime open mouth
police officer-true-creep
evil-and-uncouth
fixin to burn Black people
killin the song of our sleep

Neither one of you
gets any play in my day
I know what you do
your money your guns your say
so against my pepper spray

Okay! laugh away!
I hear you and I accuse
you both: I refuse
to choose: All Black and blue news
means that I hurt and I lose.

October 25, 1995

"I GUESS IT WAS MY DESTINY TO LIVE SO LONG"

FROM HER LAST POEMS (1997-2001) IN *DIRECTED BY DESIRE: THE COLLECTED POEMS OF JUNE JORDAN* (2005) & FROM *SOME OF US DID NOT DIE: NEW AND SELECTED ESSAYS* (2002)

[Despite often excruciating pain from her recurred cancer, surgery and chemotherapy, Jordan kept up her busy schedule during the last years of her life, at least as much as she could. She kept teaching, giving readings, speaking. Nearing the end of her life, she determined to explore her young self and finished *Soldier: A Poet's Childhood* in 2000. She also had another "pair" of books in mind, one a new and selected essays, the other a new selected poems representing her life's work. There was not enough time. She did complete *Some of Us Did Not Die: New and Selected Essays* (2002). She died on June 14, 2002 at home, in Berkeley, surrounded by friends. The book of essays was published in September. In December of 2005, her collected poems, *Directed by Desire*, was published, edited by Jan Heller Levi and Sara Miles.]

FROM HER LAST POEMS

(1997-2001)

◆◆◆

POEM ON THE DEATH OF PRINCESS DIANA

At least she was riding
beside
somebody going somewhere
fast
about love

◆◆◆

FOR ALICE WALKER (A SUMMERTIME TANKA)

Redwood grove and war
You and me talking Congo
gender grief and ash

I say, "God! It's all so huge"
You say, "These sweet trees: This tree"

◆◆◆

T'ANG POEM #2

    Homage

Rain grow gold dim stay
Plum branch flame break gray
Ditch rinse dirt steam rise
Wind keep wing make way

◆◆◆

I GUESS IT WAS MY DESTINY TO LIVE SO LONG

Death chase me down
death's way
uproot a breast
infest the lymph nodes
crack a femur
rip morale
to shreds

Death chase me down
death's way
tilt me off-kilter
crutch me slow
nobody show me
how
you make a cup of coffee
with no hands

Death chase me down
death's way
awkward in sunlight
single in a double bed at night
and hurtling out of mind
and out of sight

Don't chase me down
down
down
death chasing me
death's way

And I'm not done
I'm not about to blues my dues or beg

I am about to teach myself

to fly slip slide flip run
fast as I need to
on one leg

◆◆◆

POEM TO TAKE BACK THE NIGHT

What about moonlight
What about watching for the moon above
the tops of trees and standing
still enough to hear the raucous crickets
chittering invisible among the soon lit stones
trick pinpoints of positions even poise
sustained in solitary loss

What about moonlight
What about moonlight

What about watching for the moon
through the windows low enough to let the screams
and curses of the street the gunshots
and the drunken driver screeching tires
and the boom box big beat and the tinkle
bell ice cream truck
inside

What about moonlight
What about moonlight

What about watching for the moon
behind the locked doors and bolted shut bedrooms
and the blind side of venetian blinds and
cowering under the kitchen table and struggling
from the car and wrestling head
down when the surprise when the

stranger when the surprise when the
coach when the surprise when the
priest when the surprise when the
doctor when the surprise when the
family when the surprise when the
lover when the surprise when the
friend when the surprise

lacerates your throat
constricted into no
no more sound

who will whisper
what about moonlight
what about moonlight

What about watching for the moon
so far from where you tremble
where you bleed where you sob
out loud for help or mercy for
a thunderbolt of shame and
retribution where you plead
with God and devils with
the creatures in-between
to push the power key
and set you free
from filth and blasphemy
from everything you never wanted to feel
or see
to set you free

so you could brush your teeth
and comb your hair and maybe
throw on a jacket
or maybe not

you running
curious and so excited and
running and running into the
night
asking only asking

What about the moonlight
What about the moonlight

◆◆◆

MY VICTIM POEM

The soldiers are stirring hot stones in the soup,
to force feed the hungry ones out on the street
My children need carrots and muffins and meat,
but I am not part of a tough enough group.
Woe is me, woe is me, woe is me.
My ancestors died from the whip and the lash
My mother was treated like pitiful trash
My father spoke softly, afraid of his voice,
and I say, I'm sorry, I don't have a choice.

Woe is me, woe is me, woe is me.

I know I'm a woman, my fate is the same
as the millions of females who live without name
The world takes me lightly, or makes me its mule,
and I feel I am meant to be somebody's fool.
Woe is me, woe is me, woe is me.

Insanity rules out the song of my soul
The people in power lift death as the goal
My brothers and sisters beg wretched with fear,
but all I can do is contend with despair.

Woe is me, woe is me, woe is me.

My friends see me raging and shaken by truth
I meditate daily, and eat only fruit
Inner peace and transcend have become my pursuit,
and struggle seems ugly and tired, uncouth.

Woe is me, woe is me, woe is me.

I am the victim, I am the dead.
I am the meaning of grace without pride.
I am the meaning of race suicide
I am the victim, I am the dead

Woe is me. I could start fighting instead.
But no, I am the victim. I am already dead.
Woe is me. Woe is me. Indeed.

◆◆◆

OWED TO EMINEM

I'm the Slim Lady the real Slim Lady
the real Slim Lady just a little ole lady
uh-huh
uh-huh
I'm Slim Lady the real Slim Lady
all them other age ladies
just tryin to page me
but I'm Slim Lady the real Slim Lady
and I will
stand up
I will stand up

I assume that you fume while the
        dollar bills bloom

and you magnify scum while the
        critics stay mum
and you anguish and languish runnin
        straight to the bank
and you scheme and you team with
        false balls so you rank
at the top and you pop like the jury the
        victim
the judge
but the ghetto don't trip to the light
        stuff you flip
or the chain saw you skip
with
the rope and the knives and that bunk
        about tying who up like a punk in the
back of the trunk
or that dope about mothers and wives
        give you worse than a funeral hearse
fulla
hickies and hives
you fudge
where you come from or whether you
        mean it
the shit you can't make without
        sycophants see'n it
but nobody's dumb
enough to believe that you grieve
        because folks
can't conceive that you more than a
        moron
or why would you whore on
the hole in your soul?

At this stage of my rage
I'm a sage so I know how you blow
to the left then the right and you maim

every Columbine game about "No!
          Cuz he's white!"

But I am that I am
and I don't give a damn
and you mess with my jam
and I'll kill you
I will!

And if you insist listen in close for a dis
then you missin more than the gist in
          this
because
I gotcha pose by the nose

I hear how you laugh and cut corners
          in half
And I see you wigglin a line that's not
          flat
while you screwin around with more
          than all that

But I am that I am
and I don't give a damn
and you mess with my jam
and I'll kill you
I will!

Don't tell me you pissed or who's
          slashin whose wrists
or pretend about risks
to a blond millionaire
with a bodyguard crew that prey
behind shades and that pay
to get laid — What?
What's that about fair?

I'm not through with you!

I'm the bitch in the bedroom the
		faggot
you chump I'm the nigga for real so get
		ready to deal
I'm tired of wiggas that whine as they
		squeal
about bitches and faggots and little
		girls too!
I'm a Arab I'm a Muslim I'm a
		Orthodox Jew!

I'm the bitch come to take you
I'm the faggot to fake you
outta the closet
outta the closet
fulla the slime you deposit
for fun

rhyme and run
you the number one
phony-ass gun

Oh! I am that I am
and I don't give a damn
and you mess with my jam
and I'll kill you
I will!

(Hey, Shady
you know what I'm sayin
I'm just playin!
You know I love you!)

Sincerely,

Slim Lady

◆◆◆

IT'S HARD TO KEEP A CLEAN SHIRT CLEAN

Poem for Sriram Shamasunder
And All of Poetry for the People

It's a sunlit morning
with jasmine blooming
easily
and a drove of robin redbreasts
diving into the ivy covering
what used to be
a backyard fence
or doves shoving aside
the birch tree leaves
when
a young man walks among
the flowers
to my doorway
where he knocks
then stands still
brilliant in a clean white shirt

He lifts a soft fist
to that door
and knocks again

He's come to say this
was or that
was
not

and what's
anyone of us to do
about what's done
what's past
but prickling salt to sting
our eyes

What's anyone of us to do
about what's done

And 7-month-old Bingo
puppy leaps
and hits
that clean white shirt
with muddy paw
prints here
and here and there

And what's anyone of us to do
about what's done
I say I'll wash the shirt
no problem
two times through
the delicate blue cycle
of an old machine
the shirt spins in the soapy
suds and spins in rinse
and spins
and spins out dry

not clean

still marked by accidents
by energy of whatever serious or trifling cause
the shirt stays dirty
from that puppy's paws

I take that fine white shirt
from India
the threads as soft as baby
fingers weaving them
together
and I wash that shirt
between
between the knuckles of my own
two hands
I scrub and rub that shirt
to take the dirty
markings
out

At the pocket
and around the shoulder seam
and on both sleeves
the dirt the paw
prints tantalize my soap
my water my sweat
equity
invested in the restoration
of a clean white shirt

And on the eleventh try
I see no more
no anything unfortunate
no dirt

I hold the limp fine
cloth
between the faucet stream
of water as transparent
as a wish the moon stayed out
all day

How small it has become!
That clean white shirt!
How delicate!
How slight!
How like a soft fist knocking on my door!
And now I hang the shirt
to dry
as slowly as it needs
the air
to work its way
with everything

It's clean.
A clean white shirt
nobody wanted to spoil
or soil
that shirt
much cleaner now but also
not the same
as the first before that shirt
got hit got hurt
not perfect
anymore
just beautiful

a clean white shirt

It's hard to keep a clean shirt clean.

◆◆◆

TO BE CONTINUED:

The partial mastectomy took a long time to execute
And left a huge raggedy scar

Healing from that partial mastectomy took even longer
And devolved into a psychological chasm 2 times the depth
And breadth of the physical scar from the mastectomy that was
      raggedy
And huge
Metastatic reactivation of the breast cancer requiring partial
      mastectomy
That left a huge raggedy scar in the first place now pounds
To pieces
A wound head-set fifty times more implacable and more intractable
Than the psychological chasm produced by the healing process
That was twice as enormously damaging as the surgery
Which left a huge raggedy scar

And so I go
on

◆◆◆

POEM FOR SIDDHĀRTHA GAUTAMA OF THE SHĀKYAS: THE ORIGINAL BUDDHA

You say, "Close your eye to the butterfly!"
I say, "Don't blink!"

TONIGHT IT IS MY PRIVILEGE TO STAND WITH YOU

(2001)

[Jordan wrote these lines on the day after the 9/11 atrocities. Unpublished.]

1

grieving for the victims of Tuesday's catastrophe and summoning compassion for each family and each loved one so suddenly bereaved

2

mourning for the murder of those 1,000s of women and men and that 1 baby

3

reaching towards the survivor citizens of NYC and wishing them recovery of
community and clean air

4

praying that we will pursue and honor all roads leading to peace with outmost speed

5

hoping that we Americans will begin to learn, finally, and with humility now
the horrific meaning of
-the allied fire-bombing of Dresden
-the USA bombing of Hiroshima
-the Israeli bombing of Beirut
-the USA bombing of Baghdad

-the USA bombing of Belgrade
-and the continuous illegal Israeli military assaults upon the Pales-
tinian peoples

6
trusting that all good people everywhere will abhor and resist the
further
violence of demonization and racial hatred of every kind

7
assuming that we the American people will never again allow an
illegitimate
or a legitimate President to boycott any World Conference on Racism
for
any reason whatsoever

8
Determined to condemn and intervene against anti-Arab and an-
ti-Muslim
attitudes, actions, and policies

9
resolving to work harder than I have ever worked for the sake of
justice
which is the only true path to peace

10
believing that violence only leads to violence

FROM *SOME OF US DID NOT DIE: NEW AND SELECTED ESSAYS*

(2002)

[Jordan's *Some of Us Did Not Die* is the summation of her fierce, radical and, as it turns out, enduring political thinking as expressed in prose. "All my life I've been studying revolution," Jordan wrote in her 1984 essay "Nicaragua: Why I Had to Go There." "I've been looking for it, pushing at the possibilities and waiting for that moment when there's no more room for rhetoric, for research or for reason: when there's only my life or my death left to act upon."]

"INTRODUCTION: SOME OF US DID NOT DIE"

(2001)

Once through the fires of September 11, it's not easy to remember or recognize any power we continue to possess.

Understandably we shrivel and retreat into stricken consequences of that catastrophe.

But we have choices, and capitulation is only one of them.

I am always hoping to do better than to collaborate with whatever or whomever it is that means me no good.

For me, it's a mind game with everything at stake.

For example, what has what kind of savagery blurred or blocked or buried alive?

This is an excerpt from my "Poem To Take Back the Night":

What about moonlight
What about watching for the moon above
the tops of trees and standing
still enough to hear the raucous crickets
chittering invisible beneath the soon lit stones

What about moonlight
What about moonlight
What about watching for the moon
through windows low enough to let the screams
and curses of the street of gunshots
and the drunken driver screeching tires
and the boombox big beat and the tinkle
bell ice cream truck
inside

What about moonlight
What about moonlight...

Luckily, there are limitless, new ways to engage our tender, and possible responsibilities, obligations that our actual continuing coexistence here, in these United States and here, in our world, require.

For example, as the great Afghan poet, Rumi, has written:

"Bird song brings relief
to my longing...

Please, universal soul, practice
Some song, or something, through me!"

Thank you so much, Barnard's Women Center, and thank you Barnard College, for your notice and your faith! Thanks for asking me to speak, out loud, about the rough-hewn trajectories of my poet's life.

I am rather late as I try to tell you tonight about my gratitude.

Back in 1975, I wrote:

"To be honest, I expect apocalypse, or I look for and I work for defeat of international evil, indifference, and suffering, only when I am not otherwise stunned by the odds, temporarily paralyzed the revulsion and grieving despair.

But life itself compels an optimism. It does not seem reasonable that the majority of the peoples of the world should finally, lose joy, and rational justice, as a global experiment to be pursued and fiercely protected. It seems unreasonable that more than 400 million people, right now, struggle against hunger and starvation, even while there is arable earth aplenty to feed and nourish every one of us. It does not seem reasonable that the color of your skin should curse and condemn all of your days and the days of your children. It seems preposterous that gender, that being a woman, anywhere in the world, should elicit contempt, or fear, or ridicule, and serious deprivation of rights to be, to become, to embrace whatever you choose...

At Barnard, there was one great teacher whom I was privileged to know, Barry Ulanov. And in freshman English I remember two assignments for which I will always feel gratitude. One was a paper that would pull together, I think he said 'somehow,' Alfred North Whitehead's *Aims of Education* and Edith Hamilton's *Mythology*. Many of my classmates became more or less suicidal as they reflected on this task. But I thought, damn, if you can synthesize Whitehead with Greek mythology, then maybe you can bring the Parthenon to Bedford Stuyvesant, and make it all real."[10]

Back then, I meant to say that Barnard College never gave me the connection between the apparently unrelated worlds of black and white. But that is not quite true: because there was no obvious given connection between Barnard and Bedford Stuyvesant, I had to discover and invent that connection for myself—which is worthy work for anyone, for sure.

And because this/Barnard was the Parthenon, I got to thinking about how some of us choose to remember, and why, and how: why we

---

10   from "Notes of A Barnard Dropout," 1975, from *Civil Wars*

do not forget.

And I got to thinking about the moral meaning of memory, per se. And what it means to forget, what it means to fail to find and preserve the connection with the dead whose lives you, or I, want or need to honor with our own.

Before Barnard, I didn't even know there was a Parthenon, or a Pantheon—these are ideas at least as much as they are standing, if mostly ruined, remains of human pride and hope and a reaching for impossible, and imperative, accomplishments. So, however belatedly, thank you for that! And thank you for the man who became my husband and the father of my son.

"In between classes and in the middle of campus, I met him on a very cold day. He stood, without shivering, behind a small table on which an anti-McCarthy petition and pages of signatures lay, blowing about. He wore no overcoat, no gloves, no scarf, and I noticed that his cheeks seemed almost bitterly red with the wind. Although that happened some half century ago, I remember that he wore a bright yellow Oxford cloth button-down shirt, open at the neck, and no tie. He explained the petition to me. But I wanted to do something else. I wanted to excuse myself and find him a cup of coffee so he'd keep warm enough to continue standing out there, brave against Senator Joe McCarthy and the witch-hunts that terrorized America. He looked like a hero to me. It really was cold. He really didn't care. He stood there, by himself, on purpose. I went away to bring him back a cup of coffee, and, as I recall, that same afternoon I told a couple of my friends I had met the man I would marry.

That was 1954. He was a twenty-year-old senior at Columbia College. I was eighteen and a sophomore at Barnard College, across the street. It would be hard to say which one of us was young or more ignorant of the world beyond our books, our NAACP meetings, school parties, ping-pong, running hikes through Van Cortlandt Park, or our exhaustively romantic letter-writing at the rate of two or three letters a day. But he was taller and stronger, and he was white. We were not the same."

And beginning then, inside that interracial, state criminalized relationship, I learned all the way to my knees, the sometimes terrible consequence of difference, the sometimes fatal response of religious, and of political, and social systems set against differences among us, differences characterized by those most powerful as deviant, or pathological, or blasphemous, or beneath contempt.

That confrontation with heavyweight intolerance carried me through our Civil Rights Revolution and into our resistance to the War against Vietnam and then into the realm of gender and sexuality politics. And those strivings, in aggregate, carried me from Brooklyn to Mississippi, to South Africa, to Nicaragua, to Israel, to Palestine, to Lebanon and to Northern Ireland, and every single one of those embattled baptisms clarified pivotal connections among otherwise apparently disparate victories, or among apparently disparate events of suffering, and loss.

Issues of community control in New York City's public schools plunged me into the complicated facets of self-determination. And, then again, my personal recovery from actual rape catapulted me into difficult questions about resistance as a reluctant attitude for anyone who believes he or she has been violated and debased.

In turn, several intricate problems of resistance have taken me into repeated attempts at overview constructions and analyses of the world-wide absurdity of endangered female existence: I mean, why is that our universal situation? And when will we revolt against our indispensable-to-the-species'-power—and I do mean power: our verifiable ability to change things inside our own lives and in the lives of other folks, as well.

For example, I attended one of the best prep schools for girls in this country. And then I came here to Barnard.

And I did not know, I did not understand, the fantastic privilege such an education implied.

I think I more or less mostly tolerated school because, to me, it was just that, "school." And yet, here, in this new millennium, we are struggling with the consequences of the abysmal fact that education, that basic literacy, in fact, is not god-given, or a sovereign state entitlement. As a matter of fact, education is denied to most female

human beings on the planet. And even if you disregard the signifi-
cance of that for girls and women, you just might, nevertheless, begin
to care about the documented correlations between illiterate female
populations and the impoverishments, the barbaric hardship of every
society maintaining and/or imposing such an unequal, such a literal
ly suffocating status quo.

Before the Taliban took over most of Afghanistan, 90% of girls
and women were illiterate. After the Taliban, it is virtually 100%.
Now some of us knew about these deplorable conditions quite a while
ago. In my 1993 essay, "I Am Seeking an Attitude," I wrote:

> "It took longer than inexcusable indifference for folks inside the
> United States to even raise an outcry against the documented, sys-
> tematic, genocidal rape of more than 20,000 mostly Muslin women,
> and girls, inside the former Yugoslavia.
>
> It is still all quiet on the documented, horrifying fate of women,
> and girls, inside Afghanistan."

And yet it was years later, and not because our official govern-
ment cared about the sisters of the Taliban, before USA policies
stopped supporting the Taliban.

Indeed, it was American feminists including Jay Leno's wife, who
agitated for censure of horrible Taliban practices. And, neverthe-
less, as recently as 4 months ago, George W. Bush gave the Taliban
43 million dollars. Why? To cajole Taliban cooperation with our War
Against Drugs—Clearly a war way more important than a war against
the maiming and annihilation of Afghan women.

I have evolved from an observer to a victim to an activist passion-
ately formulating methods of resistance against tyranny of any kind.

And most important, I think, is this: I have faced my own culpa-
bility, my own absolute dirty hands, so to speak, in the continuation
of injustice and powerful intolerance.

I am discovering my own shameful functions as part of the prob-
lem, at least. I no longer think "They" are this or that, but rather,
"We" or "I" am not doing enough, for instance, or "I" have not done
my homework, and so on.

Here is one poem from my Kosovo Suite:

April 10, 1999
The enemies proliferate
by air
by land
they bomb the cities
they burn the earth
they force the families into miles and miles of violent exile

30 or 40 or 81,000 refugees
just before this
check-point
or who knows where
they disappear

the woman cannot find her brother
the man cannot recall the point of all
   the papers somebody took
   away from him
the rains fail to purify the river
the darkness does not slow the trembling
   message of the tanks
Hundreds of houses on fire and still
   the enemies seek and find
    the enemies

only the ones without water
only the ones without bread
only the ones without guns

There is international TV
There is no news

The enemies proliferate
The homeless multiply

And I
I watch I wait.

I am already far
and away
too late

too late

And as I have wrestled with my own violence, my own instincts to strike back, to strike out and smash what hurts me, or my people, or my country, or my ideal aspirations for my beloved America I have written in part:

"the bombing
began and did not terminate for 42 days
and 42 nights relentless minute after minute
more than 110,000 times
we bombed Iraq we bombed Baghdad
we bombed Basra/ we bombed military
installations we bombed the National Museum
we bombed schools we bombed air raid
shelters we bombed water we bombed
electricity we bombed hospitals we
bombed everything that moved/ we
bombed everything that did not move we
bombed Baghdad
a city of 5.5 million human beings"

And then, getting strictly personal, and strictly political, at the same time, I wrote *Soldier*, the story of my childhood:

"Maybe I should have been a boy. I think I dumbfounded my father. Whatever his plans and his hopes for me, he must have noticed now and again that I, his only child, was in fact a little girl modeling pastel sunbonnets color-coordinated with puffy-sleeved dresses that had to accommodate just-in-case cotton handkerchiefs printed to them.

I'm not sure.

Regardless of any particulars about me, he was convinced that a "Negro" parent had to produce a child who could become a virtual white man and therefore possess dignity and power.

Probably it seemed easier to change me than to change the meaning and complexion of power.

At any rate, he determined he'd transform me, his daughter, into something better, something more likely to succeed.

He taught me everything from the perspective of a recruiting warrior. There was a war on against colored people, against poor people. I had to become a soldier who would rise through the ranks and emerge a commander of men rather than an infantry pawn.

I would become that sturdy, brilliant soldier, or he would, well, beat me to death."

And sometimes, I suspect, whenever any of us feel defeated we may think maybe everybody should have been born a boy. Maybe everybody should have been capable of the awesome and inspiring heroism of our firefighters, and our police, who sought only to retrieve and rescue the living and the wounded from the infamy of September 11.

Maybe we should all of us be that strong that way.

Maybe that would be easier, all around.

But there is also the humble love of Ruth and Naomi I will place right next to the derring-do of David's love for Jonathan.

There is the bravery of the Women In Black who for more than a decade hold public, silent vigils to end the illegal Israeli occupation of Palestinian territory.

There are the ridiculed pink-beribboned people against violence in the bedroom, the kitchen, the streets, and in our domestic and foreign priorities. There is the bravery of women against the valorization of violence and force rather than the valorization of a negotiating wish and commitment to make merciful and just our coexistence with really different people trying, always, to fully and freely live on this one earth.

So, actually, I am ok with being a girl, and becoming a woman.

I am fighting breast cancer, and it's not a readily visible contest but you know, it's mine, and it's also the fight that a stupendous number of other women have no choice about.

Ode #2 Written During Chemotherapy at UCSF
or
Ode to I'd Really Rather be Sailing
Or failing to dive fast enough so fish
Marvel at the rapidity of my descent into the sea
So deep even sperm whales move on sound
So dark even what's electrical will not ignite into a luminous event

Oh, I'd rather be flying
Or lying beside somebody lift
My lips to lips
Averse to words
Lips articulate as colorings of an eye
About to blink me just beyond just lust
I'd rather be no answer
Or no cancer always stuck inside gray company
Of frail and bald and sagging melodrama
Intro-venous drips and problematic pokings in my veins
And daily pills that kill acuity of consciousness
And stats that say, "That's it! That's that!"

Oh, no lie!
I'd really rather be somebody's
Sweet potato pie!

In 1999, I published an essay, "Are You Hunting For Jews?"

"'You're looking for me.'

With those four, casual words, Aryan Nation member Buford O. Furrow Jr. presented himself to the FBI in Las Vegas, August 11, 1999.

One day earlier, Furrow was hunting for Jews. He wanted to kill Jews. He wanted America to wake up. He thought that killing Jews would help to interrupt a dangerous national sleep during which 'the spawn of the devil'—Jews, blacks, homosexuals—have gained something or other powerful and good at the expense of Christian white people...

And then, a few weeks later , I heard an Auschwitz survivor, Elly Gross, in an interview with Laura Flanders on Pacifica Radio.

Elly Gross is part of a class action suit seeking compensation for the slave labor forced upon her, and thousands of other Jews, in 1944.

What struck me to my soul was her spontaneous, on-air declaration. She said: 'I guess it was my destiny to live.'

She meant that her life hopes to honor the memory of her mother and her five-year-old brother who were waved to the lift—to their death—by a white-gloved Nazi officer, June 2, 1944, while she was waved to the right, first to Auschwitz, and then to the slave labor at Fallersleben.

She meant that to live is not just a given: To live means you owe something big to those whose lives are taken away from them"

And two things happened for me: I realized that regardless of the tragedy, regardless of the grief, regardless of the monstrous challenge, Some of Us Have Not Died.

Some of us did NOT die, for example, on September 11th. This is what Elly Gross meant by "I guess it was my destiny to live."

And I come among you, here, humbled by that attack against the World Trade Center, September 11, that atrocity against so many thousands of men and women, from more than 50 countries around the world and as I listen to and as I watch various New York City survivors express their rage and their terrified, seared consciousness, and their inconsolable longing for loved ones lost, and their sense of safety lost—may I just repeat this idea that, as Elly Gross said, I guess it was your destiny to live.

Indeed some of us did not die.

Some of you, some of us remain, despite that hatred that violence that murder that suicide that affront to our notions of civilized days and nights.

And what shall we do, we who did not die?

What shall we do now? How shall we grieve, and cry out loud, and face down despair? Is there an honorable non-violent means towards mourning and remembering who and what we loved?

Is there an honorable means to pursue and capture the perpetrators of that atrocity without ourselves becoming terrorists?

I don't know the answer to that.

But I do believe that fundamentalist anything bodes ill for the irreducible diversity of our species.

I do believe that fundamentalist conflict burns at the core of our international fratricide.

I do believe we cannot even aspire towards safety without respectful reckoning with completely different, religious, world views, embraced by most of humanity.

This will take study, and time.

And even as I study and I respect and I beg others to continue to do likewise, it seems clear to me that only inside a *secular* political state can we harbor and cherish diverse religions, as well as other moral systems, and practices.

Religious belief must stay separated from political power because, otherwise, the *secular* human potential of democracy itself will be compromised, or snuffed out, entirely. The humane secular potential of democracy rests upon the conviction that just because you exist you—male/female/Jew/Gentile/Muslim/poor/rich/smart/beautiful/lazy/scientific/artistic/gay/straight/bisexual/Republican—you are equal under the law and it is the law which reigns as the supreme organizing governance of our experiment, our United States. That is the human secular basis for a democratic state.

And so I hope we can bestir ourselves not to "Rally Around Caesar," as the recent *Economist* recommends. I hope we will bestir ourselves to rally around an emergency/militant reconstruction of a secular democracy consecrated to the equality of each and every living one of us.

Some of Us Did Not Die
We're Still Here
I Guess It Was Our Destiny To Live
So Let's get on with it!

Scenario Revision #1

Or
suppose that gorgeous
wings spread
speckled
hawk
begins to glide
above my body lying
down
like dead meat
maybe start to rot
a little bit
not moving
see
just flat
just limp
but hot
not moving
see
him circle closer
closing closer
for the kill
until
he makes that dive
to savage
me
and inches
from the blood flood lusty
beak
I roll away

I speak
I laugh out loud

Not yet
big bird of prey
not yet

ABOUT THE EDITORS

Christoph Keller, born in 1963 and raised in Switzerland, and now living in New York, is the author of numerous prize-winning novels, plays and essays in German, including *Gulp* (1988); *I'd Like My Country Flat* (Ich hätte das Land gern flach, 1996), for which he won the International Lake Constance Prize; and the Swiss best-selling memoir *The Best Dancer* (Der Beste Tänzer, 2003), which won the Zurich Kantonalbank Schiller Prize and the Puchheim Readers' Prize. His work as a playwright has also been acclaimed, with productions mounted in Switzerland, Austria, and Germany. Since 2003, Keller's stories in English appeared in *The Paris Review*, *BOMB*, *The Means*, and *Quadrant*, among other literary journals.

Jan Heller Levi's first collection of poems, *Once I Gazed at You in Wonder*, won the Walt Whitman Award of the Academy of American Poets, and poems from her second collection, *Skyspeak*, won The Emily Dickinson Award of the Poetry Society of America. She is the editor of *A Muriel Rukeyser Reader*, served as consulting editor for the new edition of *The Collected Poems of Muriel Rukeyser*, and is currently writing the biography of Rukeyser. She is also coeditor, with Sara Miles, of *Directed by Desire: The Collected Poems of June Jordan*. She lives in New York City with her husband, the Swiss novelist and playwright Christoph Keller, and teaches at Hunter College.

ABOUT THE CONTRIBUTOR

Rachel Eliza Griffiths is a poet and visual artist. Griffiths is the author of four collections of poetry, most recently *Lighting the Shadow* (Four Way Books 2015), which was a finalist for the 2015 Balcones Poetry Prize and the 2016 Phillis Wheatley Book Award in Poetry. Her literary and visual work has appeared widely including *The New York Times, Los Angeles Review of Books, Poets & Writers, American Poetry Review*, and many others. Griffiths' visual work is also featured in the National Museum of African American Culture and History. Currently, Griffiths teaches at Sarah Lawrence College and the Institute of American Indian Arts. She is working on her first novel.

BOOK BENEFACTORS

Alice James Books wishes to thank the following individuals who generously contributed toward the publication of We're On: A June Jordan Reader:

Anonymous

Anonymous

David & Margarete Harvey

Alessandra Lynch

Jane Mead

Stephen Motika

Brian Turner

Leroy Wilson

For more information about AJB's book benefactor program, contact us via phone or email, or visit alicejamesbooks.org to see a list of forthcoming titles.

RECENT TITLES FROM ALICE JAMES BOOKS

Alice James Books has been publishing poetry since 1973. The press was founded in Boston, Massachusetts as a cooperative wherein authors performed the day-to-day undertakings of the press. This collaborative element remains viable even today, as authors who publish with the press are also invited to become members of the editorial board and participate in editorial decisions at the press. The editorial board selects manuscripts for publication via the press's annual, national competition, the Alice James Award. Alice James Books seeks to support women writers and was named for Alice James, sister to William and Henry, whose extraordinary gift for writing went unrecognized during her lifetime.

Designed by Anna Reich
Annareichdesign.com

Printed by McNaughton & Gunn

June Jordan, 1936-2002

Somebody come and carry me into a seven-day kiss.